Always Ret   ง

Rightly Dividing the Word of Truth

———•◦•———

Rightly Dividing the Word of Truth is a paperback series published by the Reformed Free Publishing Association. Titles in this series are also referred to as Protestant Reformed Biblical Studies. Titles to date include the following:

2003 *Common Grace Revisited: A Response to Richard J. Mouw's "He Shines in All That's Fair,"* by David J. Engelsma

2004 *Reformed Worship,* by David J. Engelsma, Barry Gritters, and Charles Terpstra

2007 *The Sixteenth-Century Reformation of the Church,* edited by David J. Engelsma

2009 *Always Reforming: Continuation of the Sixteenth-Century Reformation,* edited by David J. Engelsma

Always Reforming

Continuation of the Sixteenth-Century Reformation

Edited by
David J. Engelsma

Reformed Free Publishing Association
Jenison, Michigan

© 2009 Reformed Free Publishing Association
All rights reserved
Printed in the United States of America

No part of this book may be used or reprinted in any form without permission from the publisher, except in the case of a brief quotation used in connection with a critical article or review. Material of this book was originally published in the Reformed Free Publishing Association's *Standard Bearer,* October 1995–March 2008.

Scriptures cited by the author are taken from the Authorized (King James) Version of the Bible, also referred to as the AV.

For information, contact:
Reformed Free Publishing Association
1894 Georgetown Center Dr.
Jenison, MI 49428-7137
Phone: (616) 457-5970
Fax: (616) 457-5980
Website: www.rfpa.org
E-mail: mail@rfpa.org

ISBN 978-0-916206-99-4
LCCN 2009927113

Contents

Preface ix

Part 1: The Synod of Dordt, 1618–1619

1 The Events Leading up to the Great Synod,
  Russell J. Dykstra 3

2 The Poisonous Petals of the Arminian LILAC,
  Charles J. Terpstra 9

3 The Men at Dordt,
  Herman C. Hanko 17

4 Dordt—Set for the Defense of the Gospel,
  Kenneth Koole 25

5 Our Debt to Dordt,
  Ronald L. Cammenga 30

6 The Significance of Dordt for Today,
  David J. Engelsma 36

Part 2: The Secession of 1834

7 Act of Secession or Return,
  translated by Homer C. Hoeksema 45

8 A Brief History of the *Afscheiding*,
  Ronald H. Hanko 48

Contents

9   The Food of Jesus,
Simon Van Velzen, translated by David J. Engelsma   65

10   The *Afscheiding* and the Well-Meant Gospel Offer,
Herman C. Hanko   74

11   The *Afscheiding's* Commitment to Psalm Singing,
Barrett L. Gritters   79

12   The *Afscheiding* and Christian Education,
Steven R. Key   87

13   The Secession of 1834 and the Struggle for the Church Order of Dordt,
Ronald L. Cammenga   93

14   The Covenant Doctrine of the Fathers of the Secession,
David J. Engelsma   100

Part 3: The Reformation of 1886 in the Netherlands

15   Abraham Kuyper: A Short Biography,
Herman C. Hanko   139

16   The *Doleantie,*
Ronald L. Cammenga   146

17   Abraham Kuyper and the Union of 1892,
Russell J. Dykstra   153

18   Abraham Kuyper as Defender of Particular Grace,
Marvin Kamps   161

Contents

19 Abraham Kuyper, Developer and Promoter of Common Grace,
   Charles J. Terpstra — 170

20 Abraham Kuyper's View of Presupposed Regeneration,
   James A. Laning — 178

21 Dr. Abraham Kuyper, Politician—A Critique,
   Kenneth Koole — 183

22 "Father" Abraham, or The Indebtedness of the Protestant Reformed Churches to Abraham Kuyper,
   David J. Engelsma — 190

Part 4: The Reformation of 1924 in North America

23 The Reformer of 1924: "Doctor of the Covenant",
   David J. Engelsma — 199

24 To Win the Battle but Lose the War—Common Grace and the Janssen Controversy,
   Herman C. Hanko — 206

25 The Preaching of the Gospel: Promise and Command,
   Robert D. Decker — 212

26 1924 and the Antithesis—A Reaffirmation,
   Russell J. Dykstra — 217

27 The Development of the Covenant of Grace: A Rich, Consistent Reformed View,
   Charles J. Terpstra — 223

Contents

28 Reformation of Church Government,
   Barrett L. Gritters — 231

Part 5: The Reformation of 1953 in the Protestant Reformed Churches

29 1953: Continuing Reformation,
   David J. Engelsma — 241

30 Through Warfare to Victory,
   Herman C. Hanko — 246

31 The Declaration of Principles: What? When? Why?
   Dale H. Kuiper — 254

32 God's Unconditional Covenant,
   Robert D. Decker — 261

33 How We View the Children of the Covenant,
   Arie den Hartog — 266

34 Authority of Major Assemblies: Advice or Jurisdiction?
   Gise J. Van Baren — 274

35 The Split of 1953: Reflections,
   Cornelius Hanko — 280

Endnotes — 287

Contributors — 307

Editor's Preface

To a seventeenth-century Dutch theologian is attributed the well-known description of a Reformed church: "A church reformed and always reforming."

Such is the common misuse of this motto in our day that a church's appeal to it almost always indicates that church's latest departure from the Reformed faith and life. In defense of some corruption of sound doctrine, some innovation in worship or liturgy, some radical change of distinctively Reformed church government, some defilement of the antithetical Reformed life, and even some outrage perpetrated on the Reformed confessions, the church's propaganda office releases the statement, "a church reformed and always reforming." Then the aphorism hides the reality that a particular Reformed denomination is always deforming.

Nevertheless, the saying itself is a good one, and true.

In light of the fact, seldom noted, that the full saying is, "a church reformed and always reforming, *according to the word of God*," the meaning is that the truly Reformed church continues to live by the word of God from age to age, applies the word of God to every aspect of the life of the church and her members, maintains the sound doctrine of the Reformed creeds uncompromisingly from generation to generation; resists every threat to the Reformed faith and life from within as well as from without, and develops the truth of the Reformed faith.

Always Reforming demonstrates that the Spirit of Christ has carried on the reforming work of Christ in the sixteenth century in one particular branch of the church of the Reformation. A successor volume to *The Sixteenth-Century Reformation*

Editor's Preface

of the Church (RFPA, 2007), this book traces the continuing reformation in the Reformed churches in the Netherlands in the seventeenth and nineteenth centuries and in the Protestant Reformed Churches in North America in the twentieth century.

The five-fold division of the book recognizes the ongoing reformation of these Reformed churches as having taken place in five distinct and doctrinally significant controversies. In these controversies, the churches contended for, maintained, and developed the faith restored to the church of Christ in the sixteenth-century Reformation.

All of the essays that comprise the content of this book appeared first as articles in the Reformed periodical called the *Standard Bearer.*

Prof. David J. Engelsma
*Theological School of the
Protestant Reformed Churches*

Part 1

The Synod of Dordt, 1618–1619

SOLEMN OATH SWORN BY EACH MEMBER OF THE SYNOD of Dordt:

> I promise before God, in whom I believe, and whom I worship, as being present in this place, and as being the Searcher of all hearts, that during the course of the proceedings of this Synod, which will examine and decide, not only the five points, and all the differences resulting from them, but also any other doctrine, I will use no human writing, but only the word of God, which is an infallible rule of faith. And during all these discussions, I will only aim at the glory of God, the peace of the church, and especially the preservation of the purity of doctrine. So help me, my Saviour, Jesus Christ! I beseech him to assist me by His Holy Spirit![1]

1

The Events Leading up to the Great Synod

Russell J. Dykstra

The history of the events leading up to the Synod of Dordt in 1618–1619 is a record of deceit, intrigue, and endurance. By this we refer to the incredible deceit of the Arminians, the political intrigue played out largely by the supporters of the heretics, and the endurance of those committed to the Reformed faith in the face of arduous struggle and hardship.

The seeds of deception were sown already in the Reformation in the Netherlands in the mid-1500s. When the Protestant Reformation swept through the Netherlands, many who were not truly converted to the Reformed faith joined the Reformed churches. This development had a weakening effect on the church. It was especially disastrous when priests became ministers in the Reformed churches, but still clung to their Romish beliefs. (Significantly, Rome's doctrine was—and is—semi-Pelagian at best, and Pelagian at worst.) At various times in the fifty years before the Synod of Dordt, synods had disciplined ministers who manifested their antipathy to the Reformed faith in their preaching or in their godless walk. It was undoubtedly this element that fiercely contested the practice of ministers subscribing to the creeds (the Heidelberg Catechism and the Belgic Confession of Faith).

Jacob Arminius himself was a master of deception. He was

born in 1560 into the bosom of the Reformed churches. Any early reservations Arminius had about the Reformed faith he kept to himself. Two Reformed ministers sponsored his training at the Academy at Leiden, and the merchant guild of Amsterdam financed his further studies in Geneva under Beza. Arminius returned to the Netherlands and became a minister in the church in Amsterdam in 1588.

Arminius was a gifted preacher, though there were suspicions about his soundness in the Reformed faith early in his ministry. His consistory asked him to refute the works of Dirk Volkertszoon Coornhert (1552–1609), a Roman Catholic writer who published powerful attacks on the doctrines of the Reformation, particularly predestination. However, Arminius never did reply to Coornhert. He kept putting off a response with one excuse or another. The real reason was that Arminius found that he agreed with Coornhert! It is generally thought that Arminius' views on the doctrine of salvation crystallized through his reading of Coornhert. These views became apparent in his series of sermons on Romans. From election to the final perseverance, Arminius placed the real power of salvation in the hand of man.

Up to this point, Arminius was under the supervision of a sound, Reformed consistory and could do little to promote his views. Under the providential hand of God, this was about to change.

In 1602 the professor of sacred theology at Leiden, Dr. Franciscus Junius, died. Jan Uytenbogaert, a personal friend of Arminius with much influence in the political sphere, highly recommended Jacob Arminius for the position. However, deputies of the church objected to his appointment out of concern for his orthodoxy, and the consistory in Amsterdam refused to give Arminius a testimonial of dismissal to take the position. Under continued pressure, the consistory finally granted the testimonial upon two conditions. First, Arminius was required to have a conference with the staunch Dr. Franciscus Gomarus, a professor at Leiden who opposed Arminius. Second, he was obligated to express his views before a conference of theologians. This latter conference was held in

The Events Leading up to the Great Synod

1603 by the curator of the university and the deputies of the synod. At that time Arminius

> testified that he expressly rejected the chief points of doctrine of the Pelagians: concerning natural grace, concerning the powers of the free will, concerning original sin, concerning the perfection of man in this life, concerning predestination, and others. He testified also that he agreed with all that which Augustine and other Fathers had written against the Pelagians... Moreover, he promised at the same time that he would teach nothing which conflicted with the adopted doctrine of the churches.[1]

Arminius was appointed as professor to the seminary, but he had lied to get the appointment. He soon used his position to teach the opposite of what he had promised. Calling the Reformed doctrines of grace into question, "he recommended the writings of Castalio, Cornhert, Suarez and such like writers to his pupils, and spoke deprecatingly of the writings of Calvin, Beza, Martyr, Zanchius, Ursinus, and other outstanding teachers of the Reformed Churches."[2]

The result was predictable. "His students, when they came home from the Academy or departed to other Academies, brazenly took position against the Reformed Churches, disputing, contradicting, and criticizing the doctrine."[3]

Reformed men in the churches were alarmed. The deputies of the synods of both North and South Holland soon approached Arminius with questions about his views. He refused to discuss anything unless they agreed not to report it to their synods, a condition they rejected.

In 1604 the consistory of Leiden (where Arminius was a member) admonished him to come to a friendly conference of theologians in the presence of the consistory. He balked, making excuses for not coming.

Arminius and his followers used every trick imaginable to avoid being condemned. They resisted all attempts to have a hearing before a synod. They managed to add the condition that, if a national synod were called, part of the agenda would be the revision of the creeds. If they were called to account by a consistory, they claimed that they were answerable to the States, not the churches.

In 1608, when the High Council of the States-General (the legislature of the Netherlands) called Arminius to a conference with Gomarus, Arminius refused to set forth his views. When the synod of the South Holland churches demanded that he express any disagreements he had with the confessions, he promised to submit them in writing. He never did. Arminius died in 1609, having by means of deception and delay escaped official condemnation.

Arminius' death did not bring an end to the struggle. His followers were not only active, but also they were far more bold in advocating his positions. They continued the same pattern of protraction, refusing to submit their views to any church body with the power to condemn them.

By 1610, however, the followers of Arminius, called the Remonstrants, were confident enough of their power that they gathered together at Gouda and drew up a document summarizing their doctrines in five main points.

Another notable feature of this history is the political maneuvering for the cause of the Remonstrants. That political forces could play so prominent a role in this struggle was due to the unusual relation of the church to the state at this time. The church, being virtually the state church, was dominated by the state. At the 1586 synod at the Hague, the Reformed churches had adopted a church order that gave the church most of the power to govern herself. The States-General had rejected this change and steadfastly refused to allow another national synod for some thirty-two years!

This power of the state over the affairs of the church was pressed into the service of the Remonstrants. This was due primarily to the great influence of the elder statesman Johan van Oldenbarnevelt. An advisor first to Prince William and later to his son Maurice, Oldenbarnevelt figured largely in the political arena in the five decades that preceded the Synod of Dordt. Though officially he held office in just one of the eleven provinces of the Netherlands, Oldenbarnevelt

The Events Leading up to the Great Synod

exercised tremendous influence in all branches of the national government.

Sad to say, Oldenbarnevelt sided with the Remonstrants. He desired political stability and unity and therefore wanted the Reformed churches to tolerate a broad spectrum of views —essentially all who rejected the Roman Catholic Church. Therefore, he did all in his power to protect the Remonstrants and hinder any effort at church discipline of a minister with errant views.

The result was schism and chaos in the churches. Godless ministers could not be disciplined. When a minister was condemned, be it for even more radical heresies than the Remonstrants', government officials prevented any discipline from being executed, often reinstating the suspended minister. In other places the authorities deposed faithful ministers. Congregations split.

Anti-confessional views were dividing the churches. Faithful consistories were desperate for a national synod to settle the differences and to deal with the doctrinal issues. But Oldenbarnevelt, pressing for tolerance, was determined that the Arminians not be condemned, and his influence carried the day. No amount of pleading from the churches could gain the permission of the States-General to hold a national synod.

Meanwhile, the supposed tolerance of differences evaporated wherever the Remonstrants gained the upper hand. In such places, ministers who courageously defended the Reformed faith were suspended, and some were deposed. As a result the faithful took to the fields to hear Reformed preaching, even though they suffered persecution for attending these outlawed meetings.

In the face of such opposition, the faithful battled for the truth of sovereign grace. Professor Gomarus is a prime example. His commitment to the truth of sovereign grace was rock solid. Tirelessly he defended the truth at every opportunity. No matter that Arminius and his followers lied, covered up their true beliefs, and refused all demands for accountability. Gomarus and others continued to defend the faith.

However, the Remonstrants were gaining in numbers and influence. By 1617, the Reformed believers must have well nigh despaired of ever rooting out these errors.

Then something remarkable happened. For whatever motive, Prince Maurice publicly aligned himself with the Reformed by attending a worship service of the separated faithful in the Hague.

Oldenbarnevelt and company were alarmed. Within a month they rushed through the States of Holland a resolution that allowed municipalities to muster their own standing armies. The goal of Oldenbarnevelt was to enable these municipalities to defend the Remonstrants in the event that a national synod were called that condemned them!

Again, God moved the heart of Prince Maurice. At an opportune moment he discharged the regiments of soldiers commissioned by the municipalities and removed Oldenbarnevelt and others from office.

The way was now open for the provincial synods to purge the ranks of the ministers guilty of godless living or heresy. This was done, although those who were accused only of supporting the Remonstrants' doctrines were not tried. This was left for the national synod. Yes, finally the States-General agreed that a national synod was necessary to resolve the issues tearing apart the churches and the nation. The synod was set to meet in 1618, in the city of Dordrecht.

2

The Poisonous Petals of the Arminian LILAC

Charles J. Terpstra

In God's creation the lilac, like the tulip, has a beautiful place. It is not a poisonous plant but a splendid flower of sweet perfume and purple hue. Its color symbolizes royalty and dominion. As such, the lilac would be a fit emblem of the Reformed faith and its key doctrine—the absolute sovereignty of God. But the lilac may be viewed as the emblem of the Arminian heresy, and then it takes on quite a different character. It becomes an ugly, stinking flower. Its color is the pale gray of disease and death. Its petals are poisonous.

The late Dr. John Gerstner, a Presbyterian minister, invented the acronym LILAC to summarize the five points of the Arminians. He did this because the tulip flower has been the symbol of the five points of Calvinism. The two "flowers" look like this:

T - Total Depravity
U - Unconditional Election
L - Limited Atonement
I - Irresistible Grace
P - Perseverance of the Saints

L - Limited Depravity
I - I Choose Christ
L - Limitless Atonement
A - Arrestible Grace
C - Carnal Security

In this chapter we examine briefly these poisonous petals of the Arminian LILAC. The reader will understand that we cannot launch into a detailed critique of the Arminian heresy here. For that consider the Canons of Dordt themselves, particularly the second part of each head of doctrine, where the Arminian errors are explicitly mentioned and refuted. We can only point out the main errors. Nevertheless, with the sweet smell of TULIP in our souls we will come to know the stench of the Arminian LILAC.

It was the Arminian party in the Dutch Reformed churches who first summarized their teachings into five points of doctrine. This they did following the death of Jacob Arminius, the man who initially advanced the erroneous doctrines and after whom the Arminian party was named. Arminius had been teaching the errors associated with his name for many years following his ordination into the ministry in 1588. Especially in his preaching on the book of Romans, he parted with the historic Reformed teaching concerning the state of the natural man and concerning the way in which the sinner is saved. But it was after Arminius' death in 1609 that his followers put his views together in summary form. In 1610 they set forth in five articles their Remonstrance (petition) as a defense of their position, which is why the Canons of Dordt consist of five heads of doctrine and why we speak of the five points of Calvinism. The first point of the Remonstrants expressed the Arminian view of predestination:

> That God, by an eternal, unchangeable purpose in Jesus Christ his Son, before the foundation of the world, hath determined, out of the fallen, sinful race of men, to save in Christ, for Christ's sake, and through Christ, those who, through the grace of the

The Poisonous Petals of the Arminian LILAC

> Holy Ghost, shall believe on this his Son Jesus, and shall persevere in this faith and obedience of faith, through this grace, even to the end; and, on the other hand, to leave the incorrigible and unbelieving in sin and under wrath, and to condemn them as alienate from Christ, according to the word of the gospel in John 3:36: "He that believeth on the Son hath everlasting life: and he that believeth not the Son shall not see life; but the wrath of God abideth on him," and according to other passages of Scripture also.[1]

At first glance it may seem as if the Arminians were stating an orthodox doctrine of predestination. The language appears sound and straight. But in reality their view of divine election and reprobation is that they are conditional decrees. Notice that the article says that God chooses those who will believe and passes over those who will not believe. That is, God's choice of some persons to be saved is based on (conditioned by) their faith and their perseverance in faith; and his rejection of others for damnation is based on (conditioned by) their unbelief and disobedience. For the Arminians, God's decree of predestination is not sovereign and unconditional; it is not freely made without any regard to man's acts in time. Rather it is conditioned by what man does. In eternity God looks ahead and sees who will believe and who will not believe and predestinates accordingly. In this opening statement the Arminians revealed the heart of their heresy: God is not sovereign in salvation; man is. God's will does not rule in the redemption of mankind; man's does. God's grace does not account for salvation; man's faith does. The poisonous, putrid petal of the Arminian LILAC is: I choose God (Christ), and therefore he chooses me.

How pervasive that poison is in the churches today! Oh, that the smell of the beautiful, biblical TULIP would prevail as it did in the time of Dordt: God chose me to believe, sovereignly, unconditionally, entirely of grace!

This point, however, was just the beginning of the Arminian poison. In their second point the Arminians continued their vile errors:

That, agreeably thereto, Jesus Christ, the Savior of the world, died for all men and for every man, so that he has obtained for them all, by his death on the cross, redemption and the forgiveness of sins; yet that no one actually enjoys this forgiveness of sins except the believer, according to the word of the gospel of John 3:16, "God so loved the world that he gave his only-begotten Son, that whosoever believeth in him should not perish, but have everlasting life." And in the First Epistle of John 2:2: "And he is the propitiation for our sins; and not for ours only, but also for the sins of the whole world."[2]

In this statement the Arminians boldly set forth universal atonement: Christ has died for all men, head for head. His death on the cross covered the sins of all people that ever live. His sacrifice obtained forgiveness and freedom for every person in all of time and history. Christ's death, then, is not just for the elect of God; it is not limited to that select people determined by God. It is for all men without exception.

Yet at the same time the Arminians had to reckon with the fact that all men do not enjoy this salvation in the death of Christ. Some men perish in their unbelief and never receive the benefits Christ obtained for them. This assertion implies that Christ has died in vain for some; his death is not sufficient to secure some people's salvation. What is this but a denial of the efficacy and all-sufficiency of Christ's atonement? This poisonous petal of the Arminian LILAC insists that Christ's limitless atonement fails!

This is not the sweet fragrance of the gospel, as Arminians claimed; this is the stench of the lie. Besides, in this article the Arminians again grounded salvation in the faith of the sinner, not the sovereign work of God in Christ at the cross. At best Christ's death only makes salvation possible for the sinner. The determining factor in salvation is not what Christ did in dying but what the sinner does in believing. Christ has died in vain unless the sinner believes! This poisonous petal is also prominent in the churches of our day. Oh, that the sweet savor of the biblical, Reformed TULIP might prevail today as it did at Dordt: Christ died only for those elect given Him by the

Father—sufficiently, efficaciously, with everlasting security of their salvation.

In their third point the Arminians returned to their devilish deceptions and subtle subterfuges. They hid the truth of their position behind solid language:

> That man has not saving grace of himself, nor of the energy of his free will, inasmuch as he, in the state of apostasy and sin, can of and by himself neither think, will, nor do any thing that is truly good (such as saving Faith eminently is); but that it is needful that he be born again of God in Christ, through his Holy Spirit, and renewed in understanding, inclination, or will, and all his powers, in order that he may rightly understand, think, will, and effect what is truly good, according to the Word of Christ, John 15:5: "Without me ye can do nothing."[3]

It appears from this statement that the Arminians were upholding the Reformed doctrine of total depravity, that man is thoroughly corrupt in himself and incapable of doing any good apart from the grace of God. It appears that they were defending sovereign grace in the salvation of the sinner, so that only God by his regenerating Spirit causes man to repent and believe. It even seems that they condemn free will.

But this was a grievous deception. In reality, the Arminians taught just the opposite. A close reading of the Rejection of Errors section in Heads 3 and 4 of the Canons of Dordt reveals their true position on the nature of man's depravity and on the nature of God's saving grace.[4] From the Rejection of Errors we learn that the Arminians taught that man is only partially depraved and that he has retained his power of free will after the fall. Therefore, the unregenerate sinner is not totally dependent on the grace and Spirit of God for salvation. He is able to prepare himself for salvation and cooperate with God in salvation. According to the Arminians, fallen man can hunger and thirst after righteousness and life by himself; he can offer the sacrifice of a contrite and broken spirit apart from the Spirit. He can use his natural powers to meet God halfway on the road of salvation. God gives the sinner a common grace to show him Christ and encourage him to conversion, but it is up to man to exercise his free will and decide whether or not he will be saved. In the Arminian scheme, faith is not God's sovereign gift worked in man's heart by the power of the regenerating Spirit but an act of man that actually precedes regeneration.

So again, the Arminians denied the sovereignty of God's saving grace, this time by promoting the poisonous petal of "limited depravity." The fathers of Dordt saw this for what it was: nothing but a resurrection of the old Pelagian heresy which denied man's total depravity and advanced man's power of free will. Oh, that once more this poisonous perfume of the Arminian LILAC might be snuffed out in the churches and the precious scent of the Reformed TULIP be powerfully smelled and savored!

The fourth article of the Arminians must be viewed in the light of what we have just seen:

> That this grace of God is the beginning, continuance, and accomplishment of all good, even to this extent, that the regenerate man himself, without prevenient or assisting, awakening, following and cooperative grace, can neither think, will, nor do good, nor withstand any temptations to evil; so that all good deeds or movements, that can be conceived, must be ascribed to the grace of God in Christ. But as respects the mode of the operation of this grace, it is not irresistible, in as much as it is written concerning many, that they have resisted the Holy Ghost. Acts 7, and elsewhere in many places.[5]

Again, it seems as if the Arminians are defending sovereign grace, at least in the first part of the article. God's grace, they appear to say, accounts for all the good that man does.

But notice the words that are used to describe God's grace as it comes to the sinner. The article speaks of "assisting" grace and "cooperative" grace, implying that God simply needs to help man along in the attainment of salvation and that man works along with God to achieve this. The fourth point exposes the Arminians in their real position—that of Pelagianism. In addition, the Arminians plainly stated their

The Poisonous Petals of the Arminian LILAC

rejection of sovereign, irresistible grace. The grace of God as it comes to the sinner is able to be resisted by the sinner. God tries to save the sinner when he comes to him in the gospel. The Spirit approaches man with the grace of salvation, but God can be turned away by man's sovereign will. The Spirit comes with regenerating grace but cannot give it until man first believes by an act of his free will. And if a man does not want to believe, the Spirit is stopped in his tracks! Such is the stinking flower of the Arminians: arrestible grace.

How powerful is this poisonous petal in the churches! Oh, that the precious odor of the biblical TULIP might waft through the churches as it did at Dordt: God's sovereign grace is irresistible and conquers the wicked heart and will of the elect sinner, so that he is infallibly brought to faith and conversion by the Spirit alone!

In their last article the Arminians expressed their belief concerning the perseverance of the saints:

> That those who are incorporated into Christ by a true faith, and have thereby become partakers of his life-giving Spirit, have thereby full power to strive against Satan, sin, the world, and their own flesh, and to win the victory; it being well understood that it is ever through the assisting grace of the Holy Ghost; and that Jesus Christ assists them through his Spirit in all temptations, extends to them his hand, and if only they are ready for the conflict, and desire his help, and are not inactive, keeps them from falling, so that they, by no craft or power of Satan, can be misled nor plucked out of Christ's hands, according to the Word of Christ, John 10:28: "Neither shall any man pluck them out of my hand." But whether they are capable, through negligence, of forsaking again the first beginnings of their life in Christ, of again returning to this present evil world, of turning away from the holy doctrine which was delivered them, of losing a good conscience, of becoming devoid of grace, that must be more particularly determined out of the Holy Scripture, before we ourselves can teach it with the full persuasion of our minds.[6]

It should be evident that once more the Arminians revealed their true colors, this time by rejecting the absolute perseverance of believers. They are willing to say that God makes it possible for the saved to persevere. He gives them sufficient grace. He assists them in the battle of faith so that they can possibly overcome and reach the goal of eternal salvation. But notice two things concerning the Arminian position set forth in this article. First, they make perseverance dependent on the activity of the believer. Christ extends his hand to help the believer and will keep him, but only if he wants the help, makes himself ready for the battle, and works hard on his own. Once more, the position of human sovereignty in salvation is proclaimed. God cannot make the believer persevere unless the believer wills and works first. Second, the Arminians state in so many words that they do not believe the total preservation of believers and therefore the absolute security of the saved. In other words, they posit that a believer can lose his salvation. He can be saved today and perish tomorrow. He can be saved all his life, but in the very end he can be lost and join the wicked in hell. This last petal in the Arminian LILAC is another poisonous one: carnal security. It leaves the believer with no real assurance of being saved to the end. It leaves him trusting in himself for final deliverance. That is carnal security.

Of course, this final article follows from all that the Arminians teach. If at every point salvation is dependent on the will of man, then salvation is ever on shaky ground; it can never be safe and secure. Salvation can only be certain if it is dependent on God's will and God's work from start to finish and at every point in between. Such is the pure flower of biblical Calvinism: God keeps his own unto the end so that none are lost. He gives them grace to persevere so that they all arrive in glory. This is the sweet perfume of the Reformed TULIP. The petals of the Arminian LILAC emit a deadly poison. Which flower are you savoring?

3

The Men at Dordt

Herman C. Hanko

THE SYNOD OF DORDRECHT WAS THE GREATEST assembly of Reformed churches that ever met. Though some may argue that Dordt was exceeded in greatness by the Westminster Assembly, which met less than thirty years later, Westminster was not—as Dordt was—a gathering of the Reformed churches from all Europe. Nor were the theologians at Dordt in any respect inferior in learning, debating skill, or genuine orthodoxy than the best of Westminster.

The synod was necessary because of heretics present in the church, who were bent on destroying the Reformed faith because they hated the doctrines of sovereign grace. The wonder is that both faithful and unfaithful were used by God to give us our treasured Canons of Dordt. The truth of God is never developed in an ivory tower, far from the battlefield on which the great issues of God's truth are decided. The weapons of our spiritual warfare are forged in doctrinal controversy. So it has always been. So it was at Dordt.

Here are a few of the men of Dordt, some bad, many good.

Jacob Arminius

Although Arminius lived and died before the Synod of Dordt met, he was the most important character in the drama. The controversy and heresy that occasioned Dordt are known by his name, and the synod would not have been called if he had not spread his poison through the churches.

Born in 1560, he was left an orphan when his parents were killed by the Spaniards. A guild in Amsterdam took on the responsibility to support him in his studies, and this enabled him to acquire a good and solidly Reformed education in Leiden, Geneva, and Basel.

It is impossible to tell when Arminius began to entertain thoughts of heresy. It may have been during his studies under Theodore Beza, Calvin's successor in Geneva, even though Beza was a no-nonsense teacher of all the truths of sovereign grace. But whenever it was, his sentiments were not revealed until he became a minister in the Reformed Church in Amsterdam.

A characteristic of heretics is dishonesty. Arminius was never honest with the church. When he was asked to refute Dirk Coornhert, a theologian who denied the doctrine of sovereign predestination, Arminius never prepared the answer and never revealed that the reason for his refusal was his own disagreement with this crucial doctrine.

His duplicity also appeared in his preaching. While preaching on the book of Romans, and particularly on Romans 7, he denied that Paul's description of himself in verses 14–25 was a description of the apostle after his regeneration. Paul was, so Arminius claimed, describing himself as unregenerated—an interpretation that opens the door to a denial of total depravity ("The good that I would..."). And when he came to Romans 9, he flatly denied sovereign reprobation.

This was duplicity. The creeds (the Heidelberg Catechism and the Confession of Faith) binding the Reformed churches clearly taught these doctrines. Arminius knew it, and he always claimed to agree with and be faithful to the creeds, though in practice he denied them.

Surprisingly, Arminius was appointed professor of theology at the University of Leiden and became a colleague of Gomarus, the man who became his implacable foe. In Leiden too, when called to give an account of his teachings, Arminius was less than frank, devious in the extreme, and guilty of hiding his true sentiments as much as possible, all the while continuing to teach his students his erroneous views.

By the time Arminius died in 1609 (one year before the Five Articles of the Remonstrants were drawn up), the poison of his teachings had spread throughout the churches, especially through the preaching of those who had studied under him and had been led astray by his heresies.

Arminius was an extremely intelligent man, very learned, a brilliant thinker, and gifted preacher. He was friendly, a person whom people found easy to like. Although Arminius used all his extraordinary gifts to bring damnable heresies into the church, God turned the almost certain defeat of the Reformed faith into victory and used the heresy of Arminianism to give us our Canons.

Jan Uytenbogaert

Other than Arminius himself, no one had more influence in the Arminian cause than Jan Uytenbogaert. Born in 1557, three years before Arminius, he was converted from Roman Catholicism when Roman Catholic authorities forbade him to attend the services of a Protestant-inclined pastor. Uytenbogaert had intended to pursue a career in law, but, upon joining the Reformed churches, he decided to enter the ministry. Under the strange ways of God's providence, he studied in Geneva under Beza at the same time as Arminius. Arminius, not Beza, was the one who influenced Uytenbogaert, and he returned to the Netherlands a firm believer in the heresies of his fellow student.

Nevertheless, he became a preacher in the Reformed churches, and, perhaps because of his reputation for piety, was invited by Prince Maurice to become minister in the Hague. Many government dignitaries attended his church, and he became a close friend of Oldenbarnevelt, the effective ruler of the Netherlands.

Always a close friend of Arminius, Uytenbogaert assumed the leadership of the Arminian party when Arminius died and was chiefly responsible for composing the Five Articles of the Remonstrants, which outline the doctrinal position of the Arminians and against which the five articles of the Canons were written.

Just prior to the Synod of Dordt, when Oldenbarnevelt was arrested and tried for treason, Uytenbogaert thought it best to flee the country. The synod deposed him *in absentia,* banished him, and ordered his goods confiscated.

It was only after a change of government that he secretly returned from exile and became a pastor of a church where he continued till his death, promoting the cause of Arminianism in the Netherlands.

Simon Episcopius

Episcopius was born in 1583 and studied theology under both Gomarus and Arminius at the University of Leiden. The teachings of Arminius appealed to him rather than those of Gomarus, and he became a follower of his mentor and an eloquent defender of his views.

In 1610, the year the Five Articles of the Remonstrants were drawn up, he began his work as a pastor but soon took the place of Gomarus as professor in Leiden when Gomarus resigned. He was so widely known as Arminian in his thinking that he was cited along with twelve other pastors to appear at the Synod of Dordt to give account before the synod of his views.

Episcopius was the spokesman for the Arminians at the synod and the strategist of their campaign to delay the synod and prevent it from discussing the real problems. When in fury Johannes Bogerman, president of the synod, dismissed the Arminians from the synod, Episcopius left piously shouting, "With Christ I shall keep silence about all this. God shall judge between me and this synod."[1]

Episcopius was banished, but he returned in 1626 when the antipathy towards Arminianism had waned. He established an Arminian congregation and an Arminian seminary in which he taught, and he wrote an Arminian dogmatics. Of particular interest is the fact that Episcopius was living proof that Arminianism is incipient modernism, for his Arminianism led him in the direction of Socinianism, which denies the Trinity and the divinity of Christ. Would that present-day Arminians would learn this lesson from history!

Pieter Plancius

Pieter Plancius knew persecution. He was born in what is now Belgium, but fled when the Roman Catholic Church persecuted the Reformed.

He received his education in strongly Calvinistic schools in Germany and England, and he became a defender of the Reformed faith until the day of his death. His early ministry was spent in Brabant, Flanders, and Brussels, all of which came under Spanish domination.

Plancius occupies a notable place among the great men of Dordt because, in addition to being elected a delegate to the synod, he was one of the first to warn the churches against the horrors of the Arminian heresy.

Occasion for Plancius' warning came about because he was called to be a minister of the church of Amsterdam, where Arminius also became a minister. It was in the pulpit of the church in Amsterdam that Arminius first began to militate in his preaching against Reformed doctrine. Plancius was alarmed, and when Arminius' explanations proved unsatisfactory, he alerted the churches to the dangerous doctrines being proclaimed by Arminius. Sadly, the authorities would not listen, and Arminius and those he influenced were permitted to propound their views for many years before the Synod of Dordt finally condemned them. Plancius' role was a major one, for many were not aware of the grievous dangers hidden behind the subtle and devious teachings of those who would deny the great truth of God's sovereignty.

Plancius also worked on revising the Dutch translation of the Old Testament part of the Staten-Bijbel, which is to the Dutch what the Authorized Version of the Bible is to us. Equally as interesting, the church in Amsterdam was the calling church in sending missionaries along with the Dutch traders to all parts of the world. Plancius was responsible for the development of nautical and geographical knowledge and skills that were given to Dutch sea captains as they made the Netherlands for a short time "Queen of the Oceans."

Franciscus Gomarus

As suave and friendly as Arminius was, so gruff and blunt was his chief opponent, Franciscus Gomarus.

Born in Germany in 1563, he was a refugee from the Palatinate. His extensive education was the best available; he studied in Strasbourg, Oxford, Cambridge, and Heidelberg, enjoying instruction from Zacharias Ursinus (one of the authors of the Heidelberg Catechism) and Jerome Zanchius (who wrote a book on predestination, still popular with Calvinists).

Gomarus was first a pastor at Frankfurt, but his abilities and learning soon brought him a professorship at Frankfurt and later at Leiden. In Leiden, Gomarus was a colleague of Arminius, and he fought him as Plancius had done in Amsterdam. When Arminius died and Konrad Vorstius, a greater heretic than Arminius, was appointed to take Arminius' place, Gomarus resigned in utter disgust and took a pastorate in Middelburg, although at the demand of various schools he continued his career in teaching.

He was a professorial delegate to the Synod of Dordt and made his own deep love for the Reformed faith and his implacable opposition to Arminianism a factor in all the discussions.

Gomarus was a supralapsarian, a profound theologian, and a gifted and influential preacher. His name has almost become synonymous with consistent Calvinism, and he emerged from the conflict at Dordt with the justifiable reputation of one who loved the Lord and the Lord's truth more than anything or anyone else. The Arminians often wished him dead. The Lord used him, with all his bluntness and gruffness, to preserve the glorious truths of sovereign grace.

Johannes Bogerman

Though Johannes Bogerman is one of the lesser known men at Dordt, his name will be remembered by all who love the Reformed faith as the fiery president of the synod who became totally exasperated and dismissed the Arminians with such fierce words that they were literally driven out of the synod.

Bogerman was born in East Friesland in 1576 and served as a pastor in the Dutch Reformed churches. He was an ardent defender of the biblical truths of sovereign grace, and he fought from his pulpit the deadly heresies of Arminius that were strangling the churches.

Delegated to the Synod of Dordt, he was chosen as the president because of his commitment to the Reformed faith and his great ability. He was a short man, and he possessed a beard which reached his waist. He was an imposing figure, due chiefly to the fire that flashed from his eyes when he was angry.

And angry he did become—at the Arminians. Patiently and with as much understanding as he could muster, he led the synod during the many days when the Arminians used every delaying tactic they could think of to keep the synod from its work, when they vented their hatred and spite against the doctrines of the confessions, and when they attempted with subtlety and guile to win influence and approval among the foreign delegates and the representatives of the state.

But finally he had had enough. He rose in righteous indignation, and, after a short speech, ended with these words: "You have...begun and ended with lies. *Dimittimini, exite!* (You are dismissed, get out!)"[2]

So powerful was his voice and so fiery were his flashing eyes that the Arminians almost stumbled over each other in exiting the hall. It was the end of their presence at the synod, and without them the synod could now get on with its work.

The greatest part of that work is the Canons, an incomparable creed in the defense of the doctrines of sovereign and particular grace.

4

Dordt—Set for the Defense of the Gospel

Kenneth Koole

WHEN THE ENEMY LAUNCHED A FULL FRONTAL ASSAULT against the doctrinal walls of the church, the church responded with a "Canons" blast of confessional truth to ward off the assault, to show that those "set for the defence of the gospel" never intend to yield one precious inch of the heritage of truth "once delivered to the saints" (Phil. 1:17; Jude 3). This had been the response of the church in the fourth and fifth centuries when the doctrine of the person and natures of Christ suffered direct assault. She responded with the Christological creeds. This was the response of the church in the sixteenth and seventeenth centuries as well. When Arminianism launched a full frontal assault (see Gal. 1:6) against the apostolic gospel, aiming at the heart of the gospel, namely the grace so recently restored by the reformers to the preaching, what came from Dordt was a "Canons" blast in confessional form.

A study of the Canons of Dordt gives instruction about the strategy the general synod used in its battle against Arminianism.

Significant, first, is the heavy reliance of the Canons of Dordt on the Scriptures, quoting the word of God again and again in its counterblasts against the Arminian heresy. This is especially true of the first head of doctrine. The four sections that follow also make regular reference to Scripture, but especially the first is loaded with biblical quotations and proof texts. Its first two articles use five passages (one of which is

John 3:16 of all things, reminding us that there are no "Arminian passages"), and Article 3 basically is a quotation of Romans 10:14, 15. Biblical passages multiply from there. Clearly, the Canons are not interested in abstract doctrinal debate, in matching wits, or in an exercise of logic as has been charged, but in expounding the word of God. They demonstrate that Calvinism (the Reformed faith) really is an explanation of the Bible according to its own words.

A confession loaded with God's word is devastating to heresy. Of course, defenders of the truth ought to believe that the Bible is the infallible word of God, or they have no ammunition for the guns—in fact, no weapons at all. Today the Canons (with the other creeds) are museum pieces in most churches. Nominally Reformed churches may show them off a few Sunday mornings a year, but the pulpiteering tour guides themselves are Arminians. Such a state of affairs makes one weep. Rejecting the Scriptures as the very word of God amounts to spiking the Canons. They roar no longer.

Dordt was a better day.

Second, the Reformed faith associates the Canons with its five points of Calvinism, as well it should. There are five main heads of doctrine. Significantly, they are called the "doctrines of grace." Precisely correct! The general synod saw clearly what was at stake, where the main thrust of Arminianism and the Enemy was, namely at the purity and the power of grace.

Salvation all of grace—this is Calvinism. This is the Reformed faith, heart and soul. Grace is God's favor and saving power contrary to all deserving. Anything that diminishes or tarnishes or is inconsistent with that truth—salvation all of God's free grace—is to be refuted and rejected. This understanding of grace was Paul's blast against the Judaizers and their law-works in his day (Rom. 11:6), and so it has ever been for Christ's true and faithful church. This grace was what the synod was intent on defending and setting forth in clear, unmistakable language. So early on, the Canons quote Ephesians 2:8: "For by grace are ye saved through faith; and that not of yourselves..."

Significantly, in the Canons, the synod began with the doctrine "Of Divine Predestination." We learn the five points by beginning with "T" for TULIP and "Total Depravity." The Canons, however, as do the articles of the Remonstrants, begin with God's sovereign election. Why? In the interests of grace. There is no doctrine that demonstrates so clearly and powerfully that salvation is all of God, not of man's ability or worth, than does eternal election: "...in love: having predestinated us unto the adoption of children...to the praise of the glory of his grace" (Eph. 1:4–6). Why is one man saved, and not another? Why is one able to believe and love the Lord, but another, perhaps one's twin brother, cannot and will not? Shall God's people boast in their superior wisdom or worth? Of course not. It is election, the distinguishing grace of a merciful God.[1]

Third, notice that though the Canons begin with the doctrine of predestination, yet they begin their treatment of predestination by referring to the sin of Adam and its universal consequences, bringing all under the wrath of God.

The synod was not interested simply in out-arguing and outflanking the Arminians by showing all the logical errors and fallacies in Arminian thinking. The synod had preeminently a pastoral concern. The gospel, with its comfort, was at stake. We hold to divine predestination not simply because it is the only theology that is logically consistent, but also because predestinating grace is so absolutely necessary. Without it, what sinner, dead in trespasses and sins, could possibly be saved? The sinner's lost condition is what makes God's electing will and grace essential. From the outset the Canons are pastoral in their approach. That pastoral approach is woven throughout the Canons, bringing comfort even to grieving parents who have just lost a little one to the grave.[2]

A fourth element worth noting is the Canons' extensive treatment of the wonder of regeneration. Articles 11–16 of Heads 3 and 4 stand among the most beautiful sections of any of the great Christian creeds. The phrase that the grace of regeneration "...spiritually quickens, heals, corrects, and at the same time sweetly and powerfully bends [the will]" is one of the most exquisite phrases found anywhere in any creed.[3]

Crucial to being a Calvinist in distinction from an Arminian is one's position on the relationship of regeneration to faith, and that of regeneration to conversion. Which comes first? The Arminian puts one's faith and conversion first. One shows spiritual activity (of a major sort) before one is even born again. The Canons sweetly and powerfully refute such error. First one is born again (whereby the Spirit of God "pervades the inmost recesses of the man... [and] infuses new qualities into the will"), and then follows faith and conversion.[4] By this spiritual life bestowed, God renders the will "good, obedient, and pliable."[5] "And this is the regeneration so highly celebrated in Scripture."[6] This is truly Reformed. God must graciously bestow spiritual life before dead man can be spiritually active.

In connection with its treatment of regeneration, the synod also answered the Arminians' recurring accusation that the upshot of promoting a sovereign, electing, efficacious grace is practical antinomianism, a Christianity with little emphasis on godliness and spiritual activity in life. After all, it is God who has taken care of everything anyway. The recurring allegation was that high Calvinists "treat men as senseless stocks and blocks."[7] Many a Reformed man today has backed off from full-fledged Calvinism, evidently persuaded by this allegation.

Nothing is more contrary to the truth. As the Canons make clear, the work of efficacious grace does not ignore the will of man, but powerfully affects it and then uses it. As Article 12 states, "Whereupon the will thus renewed is not only actuated and influenced by God, but, in consequence of this influence, becomes itself active. Wherefore, also, man is himself rightly said to believe and repent, by virtue of that grace received."[8] Any zealot who in the name of his own Calvinism would minimize the call to a godly life and good works, excusing himself on the basis of his own weakness and corruption, must contend with the Canons, which declare that God, when he "...infuses new qualities into the will...actuates and strengthens it, that, like a good tree, it may bring forth the fruits of good actions."[9] Either godliness is found, or one's will has not yet been set free nor one's heart renewed.

Does Calvinism minimize the preaching of the gospel and its urgent call to faith and repentance? Quite the contrary. "And as it hath pleased God, by the preaching of the gospel, to begin this work of grace in us, so he preserves, continues, and perfects it by the hearing and reading of his Word, by meditation thereon, and by the exhortations, threatenings, and promises thereof, as well as by the use of the Sacraments."[10]

Finally, note that each head has a rejection of errors in addition to its positive development of truth. The synod shut the gates of the city to a variety of errors and to those who teach such things as well. Teachings that threaten the gospel and are contrary to it are identified in turn. The fathers of Dordt were not interested in ecumenical fellowship with churchmen who promoted errors contrary to the sovereign, free grace of the gospel. They were willing to discuss these things with others to show them the errors involved, but were not willing to invite them into the city to join in some common defense. Defense of what? If one does this with Rome or the Arminians, step-children of the fearful error of Pelagianism, he will find the guns turned against his own walls and foundations in short order. Either that or the powder will become so watered down that it will discharge nothing.

Dordt reminds us not only that we must stand for the right, but also that we must speak against error. We are all for unity, but unity in love for the gospel of sovereign, free grace. Those who would embrace those whom the synod rejected must hear again the Canons' roar. It is the roar of Jerusalem's King.

5

Our Debt to Dordt

Ronald L. Cammenga

———◆•◆•◆———

When one thinks of the Synod of Dordrecht, 1618–1619, what comes to mind first of all are the doctrinal pronouncements made by the Great Synod against the Arminians. Undoubtedly the Canons of Dordt are the great work for which this historic Dutch Reformed synod is known. The Canons repudiated the Arminian heresy that threatened the Dutch Reformed churches, and they defended the faith of the Reformation, in particular the sovereignty of God's grace in the salvation of sinners.

But our debt to Dordt goes beyond its Canons. The work of the synod was far broader than dealing only with the Arminian controversy. Many other matters were treated by the synod. The lasting significance of the Synod of Dordrecht also concerns decisions taken and work done in other areas vital to the life of Reformed churches. As the fruits of these other labors of Dordt were enjoyed by the Dutch Reformed churches of the early seventeenth century, so also are those fruits enjoyed today by churches whose ecclesiastical roots derive from Dordt.

Bible Translation

Discussion of the need for a new translation of the Bible in the Dutch language took place early in Dordt's deliberations.[1] The matter was raised by the president of the synod himself, Johannes Bogerman. Bogerman was convinced of the need for a new and improved Dutch Bible translation and pressed the synod to undertake such a worthwhile project.

Other Dutch Bible versions were in use among the people at this time. There was the Liesveldt Bible, published in 1526 and named after its publisher, Jacob VanLiesveldt of Antwerp. The Liesveldt Bible was a Dutch translation of Luther's German Bible. This was the popular version of the day. There was also the translation prepared by Jan Utenhove and published in 1556, as well as the Deux Aes Bible, published in 1562.

All of these versions had their shortcomings. Either they were translations of translations, or, although translated from the original languages, they were stilted and in need of improvement.

Earlier synods had faced the question of a new Bible translation. Synods at Emden (1571) and Dordrecht (1574 and again in 1578) had been persuaded of the need for a new translation but had postponed action on such a huge undertaking. Bogerman, however, was able to convince the Synod of Dordt to take up this worthwhile project.

The synod adopted the following guidelines for the new translation:

1) The original Hebrew and Greek would be the basis for the new translation.

2) The new translation would be a literal translation.

3) The translators would consult the existing versions, both in the Dutch language and other languages.

4) Any additional words or phrases deemed necessary for smooth translation would be included in brackets.

5) The Apocrypha would be included, but in different type and pagination, and with a preface explaining that they were not to be considered a part of the canon of Holy Scripture.

For various reasons, the translation project was delayed. It was not until September of 1637 that the new translation first appeared in print. Since the translation received the formal approval of the States General of the Netherlands, the new version became known as the Staten-Bijbel.

The Staten-Bijbel remains to this day a monument of Reformed biblical scholarship. Although more recent versions have to a great extent supplanted the Staten-Bijbel, still today there are many Dutch Reformed Christians who continue to use and cherish it. The principle upon which the Staten-Bijbel was based—a Bible in the language of the people based on the original biblical languages—is a principle esteemed by faithful Reformed churches down to the present.

On the basis of that same principle, many English-speaking churches continue to make use of the King James Version of the Bible.

Church Order

One of the most significant contributions of the Synod of Dordt was the church order drafted by the synod for the regulation of the affairs of the Dutch Reformed churches.

More often than not, in church controversies, the church is forced to deal not only with doctrinal issues but also with church political issues. Such was also the case in the Arminian controversy.

The Arminians opposed the principles of Reformed church government. They favored the regulation of the affairs of the church by the civil magistrate, and they were disinclined to give to the broader assemblies of the church real authority in decision-making.

The Church Order produced by the Synod of Dordt was not an altogether new venture. The synod relied heavily on the work that had been done in this area by former synods. Church orders had been produced by synods at Emden (1571), Dordrecht (1574 and 1578), The Hague (1586), and Middelburg (1591). The Synod of Dordt, 1618–1619, compiled and refined the church orders of the past, producing a new church order that for centuries to come would serve the

Dutch Reformed churches, as well as their daughters in other lands, in good stead.

The Church Order of Dordt enunciated clearly the biblical principles of sound church government. It insisted on the right of the church to govern her own affairs, especially in the calling of officebearers and in the exercise of Christian discipline. While it defended jealously the autonomy of the local congregation, the synod also firmly maintained the rightful authority of the broader assemblies. The decisions of the broader assemblies were to be considered settled and binding in the churches.

Many Reformed churches, including the Protestant Reformed Churches, are still governed by the Church Order of Dordt. Nearly four hundred years after Dordt, its church order still regulates the life and labor of Reformed churches. What a testimony to the enduring debt that these churches owe to Dordt!

Liturgy

There is yet another area in which Reformed churches are indebted to Dordt. That is the area of liturgy. The Synod of Dordt produced a whole body of liturgical forms that are still in use in many Reformed churches.

Over and over again, the Church Order of Dordt requires the congregations to make use of the adopted liturgical forms: Article 4, "Form of Ordination of the Ministers of God's Word"; Articles 22 and 24, "Form of Ordination of Elders and Deacons"; Article 58, "Form for the Administration of Baptism"; Article 62, "Form for the Administration of the Lord's Supper"; Article 70, "Form for the Confirmation of Marriage Before the Church"; Article 76, "Form of Excommunication"; and Article 78, "Form of Readmitting Excommunicated Persons."

Also in the area of liturgy the Synod of Dordt relied extensively on the work that had been done by past synods.

Liturgical forms had been produced and were in use in many of the churches. Dordt compiled and revised these forms and made the use of them mandatory. Whereas in the past not all the churches used the liturgical forms and not all who did used the same ones, Dordt ensured the unity of the churches by prescribing the use of the adopted forms.

> The Netherlands Liturgy in which are included the public prayers, and the forms for administering the sacraments, the exercise of ecclesiastical discipline, the ordination of ministers, elders, and deacons, and the solemnization of marriage shall be reviewed by the revisers of the condensed minutes or by the clerk of this synod, and having been reviewed shall be added to the public editions.[2]

This body of liturgy forms an important part of the "minor confessions" of our churches. These forms are "minor confessions" inasmuch as they contain important instruction regarding church offices, the sacraments, and discipline. The neglect and replacement of these forms in some Reformed churches today is one indication of the drift from Dordt.

Sabbath Observance

One last contribution of Dordt worth noting is its pronouncements with respect to the sabbath day.

These pronouncements were occasioned not only by the increasing incidence of sabbath desecration, but also by the growing influence of those who took the position that observance of the sabbath day was unnecessary in the New Testament. In the "Post-acta" of the synod, Session 163 observes that

> When the formulation concerning the removal of the dishonoring of the Sabbath [was discussed], a question is aired concerning the necessity of observing the Sabbath, which was beginning to be agitated in the churches of Zeeland.[3]

The result was the adoption by the Synod of Dordt of six pronouncements regarding the Sabbath:

> There is both a ceremonial and moral element in the fourth commandment of the divine law.
>
> The ceremonial [element] is the rest of the seventh day after creation, and the strict observance of the same day was especially enjoined upon the Jewish people.
>
> The moral [element] is that a certain and definite day be set aside for worship, and for the purpose that as much rest as is necessary for worship and for pious reflection upon it [be provided].
>
> The Jewish Sabbath having been abolished, Christians must solemnly keep Sunday holy.
>
> This day has always been observed from the time of the apostles in the ancient Catholic Church.
>
> This day must be so set aside for worship that on it people may rest from all ordinary labors (excluding those which love and present necessity demand) together with all such recreations that hinder worship.[4]

Dordt defended the enduring principle of the fourth commandment. Sunday is the New Testament sabbath and is to be sanctified by the New Testament Christian. Many Reformed churches in our day disdain this view of the sabbath. There is a sad neglect of the sabbath and a disturbing desecration of it. In recalling its Reformed heritage, the Reformed churches of our day need to return to Dordt's pronouncements concerning the sabbath day.

From all this it is plain how far-reaching was the work of the great Synod of Dordt. The contributions of the Great Synod endure to the present day. Clearly, the debt that Reformed churches owe to Dordt is far greater than only its doctrinal pronouncements that settled the Arminian controversy.

Thank God for Dordt!

6

The Significance of Dordt for Today

David J. Engelsma

THE STORY IS TOLD OF THE DELEGATE TO THE SYNOD of Dordt who, ever afterwards, when the synod was mentioned, doffed his hat and exclaimed, "Oh, most holy synod!" This is not the attitude toward the synod that prevails in Reformed churches today.

But it should be.

It is ours.

The Synod of Dordt (1618–1619) defended the gospel of salvation by sovereign grace alone in an hour when the gospel was under attack by the subtlest form of the lie that had ever assailed it. That lie was the teaching that the salvation of the sinner depends upon the sinner's own will. But that false gospel was forced to adopt a deceptive form, for the Reformation that had begun some one hundred years earlier had clearly exposed the doctrine of free will as the diseased heart of Roman Catholic heresy. In addition, the Belgic Confession in the fourteenth article explicitly rejects "all that is taught repugnant to this [doctrine of total depravity] concerning the free will of man."[1] And the false gospelers were bound by the Belgic Confession.

They cast their heresy, therefore, in the form of the teaching that only the grace of God can enable the will of the sinner to believe. This grace, however, is universal, at least to all who hear the gospel preached. Also, although it imparts the ability to believe in Christ, it does not infallibly bring about

The Significance of Dordt for Today

this believing. Grace, taught the Arminians, is resistible. "Grace, grace," they cried, to the deceiving of the undiscerning. But their grace was universal and ineffectual. It did not save. It merely enabled the sinner to save himself—by his own will. For all their talk of grace, salvation in the end was still "of him that willeth," to use the words by which Romans 9:16 repudiates this corruption of the gospel.

Basic to the subtle lie exposed and condemned at Dordt were the twin notions of universal grace and resistible grace.

Dordt's defense of the gospel—the one, true gospel—necessarily took the form of confessing that grace is particular and effectual, or irresistible. Like Jesus himself, whose saving favor and power it is, grace saves his people from their sins (Matt. 1:21). It does not merely enable all to save themselves, if they will. For Dordt, the source and foundation of particular, effectual grace, that is, real grace—God's grace—is eternal predestination: election of some and reprobation of the others. Upon the rock of the decreeing God, and only on this rock, the subtle, deadly lie of Arminian self-salvation was dashed to pieces. Not man's will is decisive for salvation, but God's will.

In setting forth the truth of gracious salvation against this subtle error of the Arminians, the Synod of Dordt not only maintained the Reformation's teachings but also developed them. The Canons' treatment of predestination, depravity, conversion, and preservation is full and systematic, as was no prior treatment. The unambiguous declaration that Jesus Christ died for the elect church alone was a real advance. Before Dordt, limited atonement was often more implied than expressed by the theologians. Even the earlier Reformed creeds did not spell out the truth of the extent of the atonement in words that stopped the mouths of the heretics in the churches.

The Synod of Dordt confessed the gospel of salvation by particular, sovereign grace alone, and it confessed this gospel fully, clearly, and systematically. At the same time, it explicitly condemned the subtlest form of the false gospel of salvation by man himself.

The document in which this is done is a creed of the Reformed churches. It has standing. It has authority. It is binding upon Reformed churches and people. It decides what is truly Reformed. Because of the presence and participation of the foreign delegates, Dordt had an ecumenical character. The *Christelijke Encyclopaedie voor het Nederlandsche Volk* is right when it says, "In a certain sense, one had in Dordt a Reformed ecumenical council."[2] This means that Dordt has authority regarding the Reformed faith worldwide.

Herein lies the significance of the Synod of Dordt for today.

Dordt preserved the Reformation. It was wonderfully used by God the Holy Spirit to pass on to the coming generations, including us, the gospel of grace. It gave us the testimony to the gospel of grace in fully developed form, making plain exactly what the good news of grace in the Bible consists of: double predestination; particular, limited atonement; depravity that is total, not partial; grace that is particular—to and in the elect alone; and the preservation of the elect, regenerated saints. Merely to have said, "Salvation is by grace," would not have helped. The Arminian party gladly said this as they worked at leading the Reformed churches in the Netherlands back to Rome.

Dordt dared to establish the message of the gospel by confessing reprobation—God's appointment of some specific humans to everlasting damnation—as one decree with eternal election. It confessed reprobation in the face of the deliberate, crafty policy of the heretics to destroy the gospel of grace by concentrating their assault on the doctrine of reprobation. The Arminians knew and appealed to man's natural aversion to reprobation.

Dordt never wavered. Denial of or silence about reprobation means the end of biblical election. And biblical election is the foundation and source of the message of grace. Dordt boldly confessed reprobation and wisely demanded that it be preached, if always in connection with election.

The impossibility of maintaining election apart from reprobation is evident today. Those in the Reformed churches who

The Significance of Dordt for Today

clamor for election without reprobation either proclaim an election that is universal or an election that is temporal. Both are the death of the gospel of grace.

The Synod of Dordt identified as the gospel the doctrines that were assailed by the Arminians. It exposed the lie of salvation by the will of man as the false gospel condemned by Paul in Romans 9:16 and in the book of Galatians. Calvinism is not a mere refinement of the gospel that Rome, Arminians, and Reformed have basically in common. Arminian freewillism is not a minor or even major defect in a message that is otherwise the gospel. The doctrines of the Canons are the gospel by which the Holy Spirit of the risen Christ saves elect sinners. They are the power of God unto salvation to every believer. The system of doctrine controlled by free will is another gospel, which is no gospel. The preachers of this gospel are cursed by the apostle in Galatians 1:6–9. Those who believe and practice this false gospel perish.

If the fathers at Dordt did not have this conviction, they never would have contended for the faith. The result would have been the apostasy of the Dutch churches. If we do not have this conviction, we will not contend for the faith today, as we Reformed office-bearers are sworn to do, positively and negatively, by our subscription to the Canons. Then God will take the faith away from us in his just judgment.

By its full, clear exposition of the gospel, accompanied by full exposure and ringing denunciation of the opposite errors, Dordt put Reformed churches in position to withstand the attacks, open and insidious, by the false gospel of salvation by human worth, works, and will. The churches can ward off the pressures and seductions from Rome and from the Arminian, freewillist, so-called evangelical churches. The Reformed churches can detect and banish the deadly errors threatening grace that appear within the Reformed churches themselves in the present day.

These errors are especially three. One is universalism: God loves, elects, redeems, and somehow in the end saves every human. A second is the doctrine that God is gracious to every person who hears the gospel. This is the popular theory of the "well-meant offer of the gospel." The third is the teaching that God's grace in Christ is directed in baptism to all children of believing parents, so that God desires their salvation and even makes their salvation possible if they will only fulfill the condition of believing.

All these doctrines deny the truth that God elects some in love and reprobates others in hatred. All three doctrines deny—obviously, explicitly, and indisputably deny—that the grace of God in Jesus Christ, the grace of the gospel, is particular and irresistible. All three doctrines oppose Dordt, and Dordt condemns all three doctrines.

It is important that Dordt presented the truth of the gospel as logical. All who read the Canons must recognize this, although many criticize Dordt for this. This is the meaning of the criticism of Dordt as "scholastic." Dordt showed its conviction that biblical truth is logical in its confession of reprobation. At a conference with the Arminians at the Hague in 1611, the orthodox Reformed party declared publicly that

> indeed when they state the eternal decree concerning the election of individual persons, they at the same time state the eternal decree concerning the reprobation or rejection of certain individual persons; because it could not be, that there should be election, but moreover there must be, at the same time, a certain reprobation or dereliction.[3]

One powerful engine to destroy the fortress of Dordt in our day is the insistence that the gospel is illogical, paradoxical (that is, contradictory), and irrational. In this case, Reformed people may believe that God loves only some and loves all; that Christ died only for the elect and for all; that grace is irresistible and resistible; and that salvation is 100% by grace and 100% by man's will. A simpleton can see that the result is the teaching that salvation is by man's will, indeed 100% by man's will. Further, the effect of such a view of truth is that we can know nothing. Christianity is absurdity. There can be neither certainty nor comfort. To this nonsense, Dordt said no, as all the ecumenical and Reformation creeds said—

and say!—no. God's yes is yes, not yes and no. His no is no, not no and yes. So are also the yes and the no of the true church.

Thus, through Dordt the Holy Spirit of Jesus Christ guides us to know, preach, and believe the truth that alone comforts sinners and glorifies the triune God.

I sometimes regret that we no longer wear hats. We can no longer doff them when Dordt is mentioned and say, from the heart, "Oh, most holy synod!"

Part 2

The Secession of 1834

7

Act of Secession or Return[1]

translated by Homer C. Hoeksema

We the undersigned, Overseers and members of the Reformed Congregation of Jesus Christ at Ulrum, having observed for a considerable time the corruption in the Netherlands Reformed Church (*Nederduitsch Hervormde Kerk*), as well in the mutilation or denial of the doctrine of our fathers, based on God's Word, as in the degeneration of the administration of the Holy Sacraments, according to the regulation of Christ in His Word, and in the almost complete neglect of ecclesiastical discipline; all of which matters are, according to our Reformed Confession, Article 29, distinguishing marks of the true Church; having received through God's grace a Pastor and Teacher who set forth to us according to the Word of God the pure doctrine of our fathers and who applied the same both in particular and in general; the congregation was thereby more and more awakened to direct its steps in confession and walk according to the rule of faith and of God's holy Word: Galatians 6:16, Philippians 3:16; and also to renounce the service of God according to human commandments, because God's Word tells us this is in vain, Matthew 15:9; and at the same time to make us watchful for the profaning of the signs and seals of God's eternal covenant of grace; through this the congregation lived in rest and peace; but that rest and peace was disturbed by the highly unjust and ungodly suspension of our commonly loved and esteemed Pastor as a consequence of his public testimony against false doctrine and against defiled public religious services; quietly and calmly has the congregation with their Pastor and Teacher conducted itself to this point; various very fair proposals were made, both by our Pastor and Teacher and by the rest of the Overseers of the congregation; repeatedly investigation and judgment on the ground of and according to God's Word was requested, but all in vain. Classical, Provincial, and Synodical Ecclesiastical Boards have refused this most just request, and on the contrary have demanded repentance and regret without pointing out any offense from God's holy Word, as well as unlimited subjection to Synodical regulations and prescriptions, without demonstrating that those are in all things based on God's Word; thereby this Netherlands Ecclesiastical Board has now made itself equivalent to the Popish Church rejected by our fathers; because not only is the previously mentioned corruption observed, but in addition God's Word is rejected or invalidated by ecclesiastical laws and decisions, Matthew 15:4–9, 23:4; Mark 7:7, 8, and they are persecuted who will live godly in Christ Jesus, according to His own prescriptions, recorded in His Word, and the consciences of men are bound; finally on the authority of the Provincial Ecclesiastical Board the preaching of the Word of God by a publicly acknowledged minister in our midst, the Rev. H. P. Scholte, Reformed Pastor at Doveren and Genderen, in the land of Heusden and Altena, Province of North Brabant, was forbidden, and the mutual assemblies of the believers, which were held with open doors, were punished by fines;—taking all of this together, it has now become more than plain that the Netherlands Reformed Church is not the true, but the false Church, according to God's Word and Article 29 of our Confession; for which reason the undersigned hereby declare: that they in accordance with the office of all believers, Article 28, separate themselves from those who are not of the Church, and therefore will have no more fellowship with the Netherlands Reformed Church, until it returns to the true service of the Lord; and declare at the same time their willingness to exercise fellowship with all true Reformed members, and to unite themselves with every gathering founded on God's infallible Word, in whatever place God has also united the same, testifying hereby that in all things we hold to God's holy Word and to our old forms of unity, in all things founded on that Word, namely, the Confession of Faith, the Heidelberg Catechism, and the Canons of the Synod of Dordrecht, held in the years 1618 and 1619; to order our public religious services according to the ancient ecclesiastical liturgy; and with respect to divine service and church government, for the present to hold to the Church Order instituted by the aforementioned Synod of Dordrecht.

Finally, we hereby declare that we continue to acknowledge our unjustly suspended Pastor.

Ulrum, the 13th of October, 1834.
(signed) J. J. Beukema, Elder; K. J. Barkema, Elder; K. A. van der Laan, Deacon; D. P. Ritsema, Deacon; Geert K. Bos, Deacon. [On Oct. 14 signed by 67 members in behalf of some 268.]

Translator's note: At the meeting of the congregation on October 14, 1834, at the home of the Widow Hulshoff, almost the entire congregation agreed with this position of the Consistory and also signed the Act of Secession or Return.

8

A Brief History of the *Afscheiding*

Ronald H. Hanko

THE *AFSCHEIDING* (SECESSION) WAS, AFTER THE REFORmation itself, the most important event in the history of the Reformed churches in the Netherlands. It took place in 1834 when a large group of dissenters separated from the only Reformed church in that country, a church that traced its history back to the Reformation. It was a movement that had a profound impact on the history of Reformed churches, not only in the Netherlands, but also around the world. The historical roots of many Reformed denominations, including the Protestant Reformed Churches, are in that Secession. The Dutch immigrants who first formed the Christian Reformed Church and then the Protestant Reformed Churches were almost all from the Secession.[1] Herman Hoeksema and George Ophoff, the founders of the Protestant Reformed Churches, were both from a Secession background. The history of the Secession, therefore, is a part of our history. It is history that has many lessons. It is history that we ought to know. It is history to which the words of Psalm 78 apply:

> Let children thus learn from history's light
> To hope in our God and walk in His sight,
> The God of their fathers to fear and obey,
> And ne'er, like their fathers, to turn from His way.[2]

A Brief History of the *Afscheiding*

The Causes

There were numerous causes for the Secession, but they all had to do with apostasy in the Dutch Reformed Church (Nederlandse Hervormde Kerk). This apostasy was protected by the reorganization of the Dutch Reformed Church into a full-fledged state church in 1816 by King William I. As a result of reorganization, the church was ruled from the top down by a national synod, and protest and reformation from within became impossible. Thus, the apostasy continued and grew until it became intolerable to those who loved God and his word.

The protests against this continuing apostasy focused on five matters: the replacement of Christ's headship and the word of God by synodical authority in the churches; the rejection of the old Church Order of Dordt, which was replaced by William I's new rules for the church; the rejection of the creeds and their binding authority, especially of the Canons of Dordt; the teaching of heretical doctrines by liberal, unbelieving ministers in the state church who no longer considered themselves bound by the creeds; and the introduction of a new hymnbook and rules making the use of these hymns obligatory.

In their "Appeal to the Faithful in America," Antonie Brummelkamp and Albertus C. Van Raalte, two leaders of the Secession, said of the state church, "We soon found ourselves standing in opposition to our national, or world-church, which in many instances is nothing but a mere State machine, dependent upon worldly government, and supported by the State fund, with a minister of public worship at its head."[3] In their various "Acts of Secession" the dissident ministers and their congregations called the state church the false church.

The old Church Order of Dordt was superseded by the rules William I and his government established for the church in 1816. Among other things, these rules gave the king the power to appoint the members of each synod, as well as its president and clerk; made the rulings of the synods subject to the approval of the king; and gave nearly unlimited power over the church to a political Minister of Public Worship appointed by the king.[4] The attitude of the seceders toward these changes is beautifully illustrated by a story of Rev. Cornelius Vander Meulen, ordained shortly after the Secession. When Vander Meulen was preaching near Axel, the service was interrupted by two armed officers who said, "In the name of the king we come to tell you that you may not preach before this group; we order you all to leave this place." Vander Meulen told them,

> You have indeed brought the message in the name of the king. But now I must say to you in the name of the King of kings that I am charged to proclaim the Gospel to the people gathered here... You have sinned, but those who sent you have sinned more grievously.[5]

The binding authority of the creeds was opened to question, and subscription became meaningless when in 1816 a new formula of subscription was adopted that no longer required candidates for the ministry and office bearers to subscribe to the creeds *because* they agreed with the word of God, but only *insofar as* the creeds agreed with Scripture. The attitude of the national church toward the creeds was seen when the national synod of the Reformed Church in the Netherlands, having commemorated in 1817 the three-hundredth anniversary of the Reformation, refused to commemorate the bicentennial of the Synod of Dordt in 1819.[6]

It was no wonder, then, that the spirit of unbelief already present flourished and grew in the churches. One writer says

> that Christ was simply an ethical teacher and that religion was essentially a matter of inculcating good morals. The ancient Reformed teaching of man's inability to do any good that would merit salvation in God's sight was misunderstood and ignored. Sermons often were simple moral discourses. Discipline was lax and doctrinal standards were neglected. Catechetical instruction was abandoned, at least in some places.[7]

Those who insisted on a return to the creeds and to the doctrines of Scripture were regarded as sectarian trouble-

A Brief History of the *Afscheiding*

makers. One modern writer calls them "believing, theologizing, psalm singing, quarreling, snarling, mutually slandering pilgrims" and calls the Secession a "schism," though he adds: "They were men and women who had the courage of their convictions, no matter how narrow-minded these may appear to us."[8]

The new hymnbook was disliked by the people and many of the ministers, not only because of a long tradition of psalm singing in the Dutch churches, but also because the hymns introduced unbiblical teachings into the church, as hymns so often do. The opposition to the hymns was so great that many members would hurry out of the services when one of these hymns was announced or cover their heads during the singing of them. Opposition to the hymns was a factor in the discipline of some leaders of the Secession: Hendrik de Cock, Antonie Brummelkamp, Gezelle Meerburg, and Simon Van Velzen.

The Secession was a true reformation of the church, of her doctrine, worship, government, and practice, and it came about through the power of the word of God as it worked first in individual hearts and then—through the preaching of the gospel of grace—in congregations. It was a return to the creeds and Church Order of Dordt and through them to the word of God itself.

The Leading Figures

Some of the leading figures of the Secession have already been named, but the history of the Secession cannot adequately be told without mentioning some details from the lives of several of them. The principal figures were:

Hendrik C. de Cock (1801–42). De Cock was the first light of the Secession, the oldest of its leaders, the first to suffer for his opposition to the practices and doctrines of the state church, and one whose biography is a summary of the history of the Secession. Later we will look at his history separately and in more detail.

Hendrik Pieter Scholte (1805–68). Next to de Cock, Scholte was the leading figure in the Secession. It was at the University of Leiden, in a club named after himself, the Scholte Club, that many of the other leaders of the Secession were prepared for their places in the Secession and in the churches born out of the Secession. From a Lutheran background, Scholte was ordained a minister in North Brabant in the state church in 1833, only a year before the Secession. Suspended from the ministry for preaching in de Cock's church, he and his congregation seceded in October 1834. A proud and outspoken man, he was deposed in 1840 by the churches of the Secession and in 1847 sailed with a large part of his congregation to the United States, settling in Pella, Iowa. There he and his congregation remained independent until his death in 1868, when what was left of the congregation disbanded. In the meantime many who had disagreed with Scholte formed a new congregation that in 1866 became the First Christian Reformed Church of Pella.

Antonie Brummelkamp (1811–88). Brummelkamp was ordained the year of the Secession, 1834, in Hattem, Gelderland. He was deposed from office in the state church in 1835, without having first been suspended from office, for refusing to baptize the children of non-members and for refusing to use the new hymns. He had been a member of the Scholte Club, but later fell out with Scholte and was accused by him of Pelagianism and Arminianism.[9] Though he encouraged emigration to America, he himself remained in Holland. He was later appointed professor of theology at the University of Kampen when it was established in 1854.

Simon Van Velzen (1809–96). Van Velzen was also a member of the Scholte Club and was ordained around the same time as Brummelkamp, though his installation was delayed. He was very quickly thereafter suspended for allowing Brummelkamp and Van Raalte to preach for him (though they were still in good standing at the time) and for refusing to pledge unconditional submission to the church regulations of 1816. He and his congregation seceded in 1835. He, like

A Brief History of the *Afscheiding*

Brummelkamp, remained in the Netherlands. He was the strongest of all the Secession leaders doctrinally, holding an unconditional covenant and a particular gospel promise.

Albertus Christiaan Van Raalte (1811–76). Van Raalte, along with Scholte, is among the best known of the leaders of the Secession. He too was a member of the Scholte Club and was never ordained in the state church, because he would not promise unconditional obedience to the synodical laws. He was ordained in 1836 as pastor of the Secession congregations in Genemuiden and Mastenbroek, and thereafter served congregations in Ommen and Arnhem. With a large group he emigrated to the United States in 1846, settling in the area of Holland, Michigan, thereafter joining the Reformed Church in America (RCA). Van Raalte was in many ways more liberal than some of the other Secession leaders and for that reason did not leave the RCA when many of the other seceders left to form the Christian Reformed Church (CRC). He was much vilified for his domineering ways, but it is doubtful that the new colony in Michigan would have succeeded without his strong leadership. It is to be regretted, however, that he remained in the RCA, a denomination that already then was losing its Reformed character.[10]

Others, such as Gisbertus Haan, the elder who led the seceders out of the RCA in the United States and founded the CRC; G. F. Gezelle Meerburg and Louis Baehler, the other members of the Scholte Club; N. Schotsman of Leiden, who waged an unending battle for the creeds in the years before the Secession; and Cornelius Vander Meulen, an important Secession preacher, could also have their histories given, but it must be acknowledged that all of the Secession leaders were but men, and were therefore instruments in the hands of the Almighty for the preservation and rebuilding of his church. To him alone must be the glory for the reformation of the church in 1834 and the years following.

Hendrik de Cock

De Cock was the oldest of the Secession leaders, the first to take an active stand against unbiblical doctrines and practices in the state church; the first to be disciplined; the first, with his congregation, to secede from the Dutch Reformed Church; and also the first of the leaders to die, for he saw only the beginnings of the Secession, dying already in 1842, just eight years after its beginning and at the young age of 41. His history is the history of the early years of the Secession.

As is often the case with church reformation, the Secession began with a reformation in the life and soul of de Cock. So desperate were conditions in the state church that de Cock learned virtually nothing of sin and grace and of salvation through Jesus Christ, in spite of his upbringing in a nominally Christian home, his attendance at Christian schools, and his graduation from the University of Groningen as a candidate for the ministry of the gospel.

During the early years of his ministry he preached a modernist gospel and later judged himself to have been at that time an unconverted man. To bring him to a knowledge of himself, of the truth, and of the Savior, God used the testimony of an elderly farm worker, Klaas Kuipenga, who told de Cock, "If I must add even one sigh to my own salvation, then I would be eternally lost."[11] This happened at a time when Kuipenga was receiving instruction from de Cock in a private catechism class in preparation for church membership. So, by God's grace, the teacher became the student.

God also used two pamphlets by Count Van Zuylen Van Nijevelt, "The Only Deliverance" and "Reformed Doctrine," as well as Calvin's *Institutes of the Christian Religion*, to teach him the Reformed faith. Until he discovered the *Institutes* in the study of a fellow minister, de Cock had not even known of them. Through Calvin he became acquainted with other earlier Reformed writers. He discovered the Reformed creeds as well when an elderly widow in his congregation gave him a copy of the Canons, which, to his dismay, taught doctrines that he had never learned, even as a seminary student.[12]

He had been in the ministry ten years and was serving a rural congregation in Ulrum in Groningen at the time of the Secession. In Ulrum his preaching of the gospel attracted crowds who were not hearing the gospel elsewhere. Some of the visitors asked him to baptize their children, since they could not in good conscience have them baptized in the liberal congregations to which they belonged.[13] This, as well as his preaching of the gospel, his writings, in which he referred to several liberal ministers as "wolves in the sheepfold of Christ," and his opposition to hymns, led to his suspension from the ministry in 1833.

In spite of many injustices, he submitted to his suspension for a year. When the authorities refused to allow the Rev. H. P. Scholte to preach for him at the time of the death of his infant daughter, de Cock and his consistory saw that their only hope lay in secession. So it was that on October 13, 1834, an "Act of Secession," signed by two elders and three deacons, was presented to the congregation in Ulrum and signed by 140 members and heads of families representing 247 souls (only eight members did not sign). This act was quickly followed by the secessions of Scholte, Brummelkamp, Meerburg, Van Velzen, and others, all of whom were also deposed.

De Cock continued to suffer for his convictions and actions, as did the other leaders and their congregations, enduring harassment, fines, imprisonment, and slander. He had twelve soldiers billeted in his home in Ulrum, was subsequently forbidden to preach in his congregation there, was expelled from his home, had his worship services interrupted, was attacked and thrown into a thorn hedge by a mob while returning from a meeting, and spent three months in prison. He died before the persecution eased.

Persecution

What de Cock suffered was the lot of all the seceders. One minister, a Rev. H. J. Budding, was fined 40,000 florins. When

Always Reforming

the seceders were unable to pay their fines, which most of them were unable to do, their possessions were seized and sold, often on the Lord's day, so that their possessions could not be repurchased. So severe was the persecution that it was noticed in other countries. A French periodical carried the following notice in 1839:

> Holland, which owes its praise and prosperity especially to this that it received to its bosom with affection all Christians persecuted for their faith, now furnishes a spectacle of savage persecutions for the faith. Deeply deplorable is it to witness such events taking place under the rule of the House of Orange-Nassau which has demonstrated so many services to the Gospel and religious liberty.[14]

The seceders bore this persecution patiently for the sake of the gospel, but its severity led many of them to immigrate to the United States. Many years later Van Raalte said,

> I am happy that I followed the voice of my conscience, even though it cost me a great deal. On the other hand, it grieves me considerably that in my own fatherland now stirred up by the Hervormde Synod and the Netherlands government and citizens, I was fined, tormented by having soldiers quartered in our home, thrown into prison, and throughout the years had filth and stones thrown at me as though I were the scum of society.[15]

The persecution eased when William II became king in 1840, but by that time many were thinking in terms of emigration, and soon two of the leaders, Scholte and Van Raalte, along with thousands of the seceders, left for the United States. Persecution was not the only factor in their departure. A potato blight had destroyed the crops in the Netherlands, and the poverty of the ordinary people led them to seek a better living elsewhere, but what they suffered was used by God to transplant the Reformed faith to the United States.

A Brief History of the *Afscheiding*

Subsequent History

Besides persecution, especially three things characterized the years following the Secession: growth, immigration to America, and divisions among the seceders themselves. In 1840, the seceders numbered more than six thousand members, but they were still a very small group in the Netherlands. The leaders of the state church and the government comforted themselves with the fact that the seceders were the poorest of the people and a minority. That would change when in 1886 Abraham Kuyper led another, larger, and more politically influential movement out of the state church, but neither numbers nor political influence have anything to do with God's approval and blessing:

> [de Cock's] followers were, for the most part, the poor, the uneducated, the despised, the ignoble of the land. For all that, they were the godly, the pious, the upright who genuinely thirsted for that one true heavenly Bread which is Christ Jesus our Lord.[16]

The seceders soon recognized the need for an educated ministry and especially for ministers who would continue to stand for the truths of God's word. Brummelkamp and de Cock were appointed in 1839 to teach those who aspired to the ministry, but de Cock died soon after and Rev. T. F. de Haan was appointed in his place. A theological school was finally established at Kampen in 1854.

Persecution by the authorities led many to emigrate, and colonies were established in Iowa, Michigan, and Wisconsin in the period from 1845 to 1880. Some thirteen thousand Hollanders went to America during that time, and the majority of them were Secession people. There they initially aligned themselves with the Reformed Church in America, but many soon left because of apostasy in that denomination. Instead they formed the Christian Reformed Church.

After persecution waned and ceased, the seceders gained government recognition, established their own Christian schools, and continued to stand for the truth. In 1886 Dr.

Abraham Kuyper led another movement, some hundred thousand people, out of the state church. Having come to recognize the Secession of 1834 as a true reformation of God's church, Kuyper and his group eventually sought union with the Secession churches, and in 1892 that union became a reality. Four hundred Secession churches and three hundred congregations that followed Kuyper joined to become the *Gereformeerde Kerken* (Reformed Churches).

This union did not come easily and was for many years incomplete in that there were serious doctrinal differences between the two groups. Individual congregations and members continued to be identified for many years as belonging to one group or the other. In fact, the churches and people of the Secession were identified as the "A" group and the Kuyperians as the "B" group within the denomination. Each maintained its own theological school and kept itself separate from the rest. The Protestant Reformed Churches owe much to both groups.

There were also divisions among the seceders themselves. The new churches and their leaders fell into two groups, a stronger and more doctrinally sound northern branch (de Cock and Van Velzen) and a weaker southern branch (Brummelkamp and Van Raalte).[17] As a result of these divisions, there was much disagreement and infighting among the leaders of the Secession and a number of permanent breaks. Scholte was deposed by the Secession churches and after immigrating to America, remained independent. Van Raalte, after immigrating, remained in the Reformed Church in America when many of those who had followed him to America joined the newly established Christian Reformed Church. In 1838 in the Netherlands, as a result of the divisions over the question of government recognition, a new denomination was formed, *De Gereformeerde Kerken onder het Kruis* (The Reformed Churches under the Cross), the churches in which the Netherlands Reformed Congregations have their roots.

The differences among the seceders were many. Scholte disagreed already in 1833 with de Cock's decision to baptize infants from other congregations. There were differences

A Brief History of the *Afscheiding*

over hymns, some being completely opposed to their use and others having a more tolerant attitude. Those who formed the Churches under the Cross believed that the Secession churches had gone too far in agreeing to government regulations that allowed them to be officially recognized. There were differences about which church order ought to be used, about clerical dress, and about lay preaching. There were serious doctrinal differences concerning the covenant and baptism, the nature of gospel preaching, and millennialism (Scholte was premillennial in his eschatology).

Of these divisions Van Raalte later wrote, "The dissensions among the believers in the Netherlands caused me constantly a deep sorrow. They were harder for me to bear than the persecution; they deprived me of all enjoyment of life and made me afraid of life."[18]

Through all these changes, God preserved and built his church, as he continues to do today and will do until our Savior returns. We who have our roots in the Secession can be especially thankful, for it is through this mighty work of grace that God has given us our own existence as churches and has given us a rich heritage of truth. May we, remembering those who fought and suffered for the faith then, continue to fight for the truth today, showing the same willingness to suffer reproach for Christ's sake and for the truth's sake.

The Character of the Movement

The Secession of 1834 was for the most part a movement among the lowest and poorest of the Dutch people. Even the ministers of the Secession were not from the higher classes, but usually from the middle class. Kromminga says,

> The National Synod of the established Church is said to have comforted itself with the numerical smallness of the secession. The seceders came then and for years continued to come from the humbler walks of life. But, though numerically and economically weak and lacking in social prestige, the group developed a

spiritual power that in course of time astounded its adversaries. The spring of that power was their common love for the Reformed doctrine and their loyalty to the Reformed formularies [creeds] as founded on the Word of God.[19]

There are at least two reasons for this. First, from a human point of view, these were the people who had nothing to lose by leaving the state church, and it was for this same reason that many later left for America. This is in harmony with the words of Jesus: "And again I say unto you, It is easier for a camel to go through the eye of a needle, than for a rich man to enter into the kingdom of God" (Matt. 19:24). Second, from the viewpoint of God's purpose, it is always the case that he gathers his church for the most part from among such people as the seceders, the lowest and poorest, "that no flesh should glory in his presence" (1 Cor. 1:29).

This was beautifully illustrated in another way at the time of the Secession. Prior to the Secession there had been men, many of them from the nobility and all of them influential in the Netherlands, who had protested the apostasy of the state church. They were part of a movement known as the *Reveil* (Revival). Among them were men such as the poet Isaac da Costa, who wrote "Grievances against the Spirit of the Age" and was Scholte's mentor; William Bilderdijk, a prominent lawyer, whose teachings de Cock was later accused of promoting; William de Clercq, poet and financier; and Groen van Prinsterer, secretary to the king and founder of the Anti-Revolutionary political party in the Netherlands.

These men, some of whom showed sympathy for the Secession or protested the persecution visited on the seceders, all remained in the state church. Just after the Secession had become a reality, Scholte wrote, "That evening, I called on my old friend and brother Da Costa, with whom I had always agreed as had many others, although now on the thing that had happened (Secession) he differed completely from me. My actions and intentions had been completely misunderstood by him."[20] Da Costa's pamphlet had stirred the Netherlands with a call for return to God's word, but he himself

A Brief History of the *Afscheiding*

would not follow when the way was that of suffering, reproach, struggle, and ignominy.

In the providence of God, it had to be that way. As one writer says, "What would have happened had the men of the Reveil, or all who looked for the Kingdom of God, joined the Afscheiding? No doubt the *organization* would have been looser, the *doctrines* less sharply defined."[21]

It was the deep spirituality—the strong piety, the thirst for the truth among the common folk—that God used to preserve his church during the dark years before the Secession and to kindle anew the flame in the hearts of men like de Cock and even to bring about their conversion. It was these poor folk who were willing to lose everything for the kingdom's sake, who suffered cruelly for their faith, but who carried the lamp of truth in their own land, on to the new world, and even to places like South Africa.

The Secession of 1834 also illustrates the teaching of Scripture regarding the preaching of the gospel as "the power of God unto salvation to every one that believeth" (Rom. 1:16), for the Secession was about the preaching of the gospel more than anything else. It was a desire for gospel preaching that brought crowds to Ulrum to hear de Cock, that made the people of the Secession endure patiently the suffering that was their lot, and that led these common folk to support their leaders in leaving the state church, in emigrating from their home country, and in struggling to establish and maintain a new denomination.

There is no evidence that de Cock was an especially gifted preacher or skilled orator. That is only to say, however, that the power of the gospel is not in excellency of speech or wisdom (1 Cor. 2:1), but in God, who sends the gospel, and in Christ, who speaks to his people through the gospel. It was not the man the people followed, but the truth as it is in Jesus.

It was this desire for the gospel that led to extraordinary efforts to preach and hear the truth. In several cases "when soldiers and the rabble made it impossible for Seceders to meet on land," they held their services on the water:

> This happened at Oud-Loosdrecht on June 9, 1837, where H.P. Scholte planned to preach and baptize. The military prevented any service from being held, and therefore it was decided to gather on the lake in the ship of brother N. Pos, who made it available. At 8 a.m. the church ship sailed with the parents on board, as well as their children who were to be baptized. They were gaped after by the soldiers who had been called to arms! From all sides the members of the congregation converged on the ship in small boats. Scholte also went on board and preached twice that Sunday, entirely without interference. A week later he preached and served Communion on board a ship on the Zuider Zee... [But] finally, even these gatherings on water were prevented.[22]

Because the gospel is the spiritual food and drink, the life and health of his people, God preserves it in every age, and when it seems that the voice of the gospel has been silenced, God raises up out of obscurity men to feed his sheep and to lead them in the green pastures of his word. The gospel is, after all, the gospel of *his* grace and glory!

The Secession, then, was a work of God, and its beginnings and survival were a miracle of grace. The Secession had its roots in the work of God's grace in the hearts of those who remained faithful and remembered the truth during the long, dark years before the Secession. It sprang to life by a work of grace in the heart of de Cock and the members of the Scholte Club. It survived persecution, internal strife, emigration, and other difficulties by grace alone, for both leaders and members showed themselves to be sinners. There was, as one writer puts it, "considerable strange fire on the altar."[23] But God uses weak means to accomplish his purpose and work his will, as was abundantly proved in those difficult years:

> Had the Secession been a work of man, surely there would have been nothing left of the delivered church but bits and pieces. But God is faithful; He kept His work alive, although He allowed Satan and man to do many things, so that it would be apparent that the liberation and preservation of the Church is *His* work, and so that whoever boasts might boast not of de Cock or Scholte, Van Velzen or Brummelkamp, but boast only in the Lord.[24]

A Brief History of the *Afscheiding*

The seceders themselves saw this and must have sung with special fervor the words of Psalm 118 from their Dutch Psalters:

> Jehovah is my strength and tower,
> He is my happiness and song;
> He saved me in the trying hour,...
> Hence shall my mouth His praise prolong.
> The voice of gladness and salvation
> Is in the tents of righteousness;
> There do they sing with adoration,
> The Lord's right hand is strong to bless.[25]

The Lessons

What are the lessons to be learned from the history of the Secession of 1834? There are many lessons. We see in the history of the Secession the importance of the lay members of the church and their love for the truth; and the importance and necessity of the preaching of the gospel; the high cost of following Christ and the word of God; the importance of creeds in the church, for it was through them that the doctrines of Scripture lived in the hearts of the faithful in the years prior to the Secession. We see the truth that the church is reformed and always reforming; that the false church always hates and persecutes the faithful; that government control of the church of Jesus Christ is never to be tolerated; and that God uses weakest means to do his will.[26]

That faithfulness to God and his word has a price was proved first in persecution and then also in the unimaginable difficulties faced by those who had immigrated. Van Raalte is said to have broken down and cried during one worship service the first winter after coming to the United States. He asked, "Lord, shall we all perish?" The question may well be asked, therefore, "How many descendants of the Secession today would endure the persecution that their ancestors endured for the sake of their confession?"[27]

The principal lessons of the Secession are two. The first lesson is that, having been graciously preserved by God and blessed by him beyond what anyone would ever ask and think, those who have been so blessed must remember what God has done for them and must cherish what he has given them, lest they lose everything. That is what has happened in many of the denominations and churches that have their roots in the Secession of 1834. In too many of them, the creeds are again neglected and forgotten, the doctrines of the creeds and Scripture despised, and the gospel changed into powerless moralizing. In the Netherlands the churches of the Secession now tolerate evils that would not have been dreamed of in the state church before the Secession, and the country is a moral ruin. That is a lesson for us as Protestant Reformed Churches: "Let him that thinketh he standeth take heed lest he fall" (1 Cor. 10:12).

The other lesson is that God, who chose his church in eternity, redeemed her in Christ, and gave her his own Spirit, will never forsake her, but gathers, defends, and preserves her by his Spirit and word from the beginning to the end of the world.[28] God preserved his church then; he will do so in these dark days. And when those darkest of all days come, as they must, then too he will not forsake his own, but will cause the light of his truth to shine in their hearts and through them in the world until that grand day when the darkness is dispelled forever and the rising Sun of righteousness comes with eternal healing in his wings.

9

The Food of Jesus
(an 1886 sermon on John 4:34)[1]

Simon Van Velzen;
translated by David J. Engelsma

OFTEN IN OUR DAY IS HEARD THE COMPLAINT OF UNemployment. Nevertheless, in many respects we enjoy great prosperity. To the present day we continue to be spared from war with the peoples that surround us. We hear of earthquakes, diseases, and similar plagues in distant places, but we continue to be preserved from them. Up till now we are not visited with famine but may speak of a beautiful harvest! Still, many in our land are deeply dissatisfied.

This must not surprise us. "Them that honour me," God says, "I will honour, and they that despise me shall be lightly esteemed" [1 Sam. 2:30].[2] Has not the Savior said, as plainly as possible, "Seek ye first the kingdom of God, and his righteousness; and all these things shall be added unto you" [Matt. 6:33]? "Take no thought, saying, What shall we eat? or, What shall we drink? or, Wherewithal shall we be clothed? (For after all these things do the Gentiles seek:) for your heavenly Father knoweth that ye have need of all these things" [Matt. 6:31, 32]. "Labour not for the meat which perisheth, but for that meat which endureth unto everlasting life, which the Son of man shall give unto you: for him hath God the Father sealed" [John 6:27].

These plain utterances are not taken to heart by the

masses. They do not work for the meat [food] that endures unto everlasting life, and the result is dissatisfaction. Groundless complaints about unemployment are heard.

Is, then, the activity commanded by Jesus so burdensome, so grievous, that there is reason to be averse to it?

On the contrary! Never has anyone who was busy in this work complained about it. People who were the most outstanding in godliness have found inexpressible satisfaction in it. Not only this, but Jesus Himself has led the way for us. He called doing the will of His Father His food. Let me point this out to you.

> John 4:34: "Jesus saith unto them, My meat [food] is to do the will of him that sent me, and to finish his work."

The Savior spoke these words at the very beginning of His ministry. In Judea, the envy of the Pharisees had already become manifest. The Lord therefore judged it good to go again to Galilee, where the sermon on the mount, as we commonly refer to it, was preached by Him. There were two ways that led thither. The one ran through the land east of the Jordan and was longer. The shorter went through Samaria but was seldom taken because the Jews and Samaritans were hostile to each other. Nevertheless, Jesus chose this way.

Accompanied by His disciples, the Lord came into the vicinity of the Samaritan city Sychar and sat down, wearied by the journey, at Jacob's well. But the disciples, who, I think, were muscular, strong men, went to the city in order to buy food. Now, while the Lord was sitting there by Himself, there came a woman to draw water. He entered into a conversation with her. And this had the result that the woman was convicted of her sins and brought to faith, so much so that she went away in great haste in order to gain also her fellow citizens to Jesus.

In the meantime, the disciples, provided with food, had returned. They set what they had bought before Him and, knowing that He had been deprived of food for a long time, urged Him to eat. "I have," Jesus responded, "food to eat that

The Food of Jesus

you know not of" [John 4:32]. The disciples said to each other, "Has anyone brought Him food?" [v. 33]. And now Jesus said to them, "My food is that I do the will of Him who has sent Me, and finish His work."

The idea of these words is that what food is for the mortal body of a man—so strengthening, invigorating, and necessary for a man—the doing of the will of His Father, who has sent Him and whose work He must finish, was for Him as Mediator and Savior, according to the spirit. These words allow us a deep look into the disposition of the Savior. We hear in them mention of the food of Jesus. This is a food:

(i) that witnesses to the inexpressible greatness of the Savior;
(ii) that is an urgent reason for the sinner to come to Jesus; and
(iii) that gives us a glorious prospect with regard to the future.

If it is given to us rightly to understand the language of the text, then at the end of our gathering for worship we will have to say, "Never have the glory and loveliness of Jesus been made more plain than by the word of the Savior."

For us, it cannot be difficult—and in any case must not be difficult—to understand what the Lord means when He speaks of the will of His Father. Two chapters later in this gospel we read that Jesus said to the Jews, when they were offended at Him, contradicted Him, and repudiated Him,

> "All that the Father giveth me shall come to me; and him that cometh to me I will in no wise cast out. For I came down from heaven, not to do mine own will, but the will of him that sent me. And this is the Father's will which hath sent me, that of all which he hath given me I should lose nothing, but should raise it up again at the last day. And this is the will of him that sent me, that every one which seeth the Son, and believeth on him, may have everlasting life: and I will raise him up at the last day" [John 6:37–40].

Also the apostle Paul has spoken many times of the will of the Father. For example, he said that God "predestinated us unto the adoption of children by Jesus Christ to himself, according to the good pleasure of his will" [Eph. 1:5].

All these passages speak of the will of the Father with the same word, so that the truth that Jesus intends is so plain that, although the theologians—as is usually the case—are offended by it, a child can comprehend the meaning.

If Jesus has come down from heaven, then He existed before He came to earth. If He has come down in order to do the will of the Father, then He was familiar with this will, has committed Himself to accomplish it, and has assumed an inexpressibly great work. This great work is not only that He gather all who were given Him of the Father, but also that He preserve them and finally raise them and bestow upon them eternal life.

What a work it is that carries out this eternal decree of God! How much must be performed in order that the good pleasure of the Father may be perfected! One thinks only of his own sins. I do not even mention that all of us have fallen away from God in Adam, our head, although Scripture does charge us with this guilt. But now let each one be convicted concerning the guilt of his own behavior. How have we behaved in our youth? Were we always obedient? How did we behave as a young man or a young woman? Was not a great deal of vanity manifest in our life? How do we behave as a man or a woman? How do we behave as an old man or an old woman? Many times we have spoken hastily and thoughtlessly of God and His service. Scripture says, "Thou shalt not take the name of the Lord thy God in vain" [Ex. 20:7]. Many times we have used the day of rest wholly or partly for our own pleasure. Scripture says, "Remember the sabbath day, to keep it holy" [Ex. 20:8]. Many times some temporal good has been obtained in a dishonorable way. Scripture says, "Thou shalt not steal" [Ex. 20:15]. Many times the desire arises in us to possess something that is our neighbor's, even if this would mean that he would suffer loss. Scripture says, "Thou shalt not covet" [Ex. 20:17].

If in addition we remember the frivolous, idle words that

The Food of Jesus

are spoken merely to pass the time of day, but that Scripture calls "corrupt communication" [Eph. 4:29]; excess in eating or drinking that according to Scripture is gluttony and drunkenness; or the shameful lusts that proceed from the heart and, as Jesus said, "defile a man" [Matt. 15:20], how terribly great, then, is the guilt that we continually pile up.

If there is someone who, like the rich young ruler, thinks, "All these have I observed from my youth" [Mark 10:20], let him ask himself whether he always has loved the Lord above all, whether he is willing to give up all his money, goods, honor, reputation, and life for the sake of his communion with Jesus, which is infinitely more than all those earthly treasures.

Let him ask himself whether he truly loves his neighbor as himself, as he ought to be loved himself. If we found our worst enemy sleeping on the edge of a giddy precipice, would we not be rightly condemned as unmerciful if we passed by without dragging him away from that dangerous place? How much more guilty is not the man who goes on living without extending a hand unto salvation, while his fellow men find themselves on a way that ends not merely in temporal destruction, but in eternal perdition—in the terror of hell!

Indeed, there are many who tempt others to sin or to continue carelessly in the way of destruction. They make themselves guilty of double murder of souls. And many parents give no thought to it, or at least make no serious effort to save their own children. They misuse the short time of life they have with their children, and the invaluable opportunity God gives to be saved by Jesus.

Well may each one of us cry out with Ezra, "O my God, I am ashamed and blush to lift up my face to thee, my God: for our iniquities are increased over our head, and our trespass is grown up unto the heavens" [Ezra 9:6].

These iniquities, not only of a single man, but of all that the Father has given to Him, Jesus has taken upon Himself. Therefore, He became their substitute, not only to make good the obedience that was demanded of us by God, but also to suffer the punishment that is threatened upon sin. God cannot deny Himself. His righteousness and the truth of His threatenings must remain undamaged.

Nevertheless, it was His will, His decree, His good pleasure to save a multitude that no man can count.

This work the Son of God has assumed and perfected.

How inexpressibly great is He!

For our salvation it was not enough that Jesus has taken the guilt upon Himself and has suffered the punishment. All who receive salvation must be gathered, head for head, because no one can enter the kingdom of God apart from regeneration. But how great an opposition must then be overcome in the case of each one! In the case of each one, how great is the ignorance, the unbelief, the blindness, the delusion, the prejudice, and the enmity!

Not only this. When the sinner has been gathered, so that he calls for grace, flees to Jesus, and entrusts himself to Him in faith with the prayer henceforth to be led by Him, he is still exposed to the greatest danger and has a constant struggle with many mighty enemies.

But Jesus does not only seek the lost. He preserves the one whom He has found and maintains His work in all of His own people, for it is the will of His Father that of all which has been given to Him, He should lose nothing, but should raise it up at the last day [John 6:39].

At Jacob's well He gave a proof of His seeking love and faithful exertions.

When He sat down there and spoke with that Samaritan woman, she continually tried to evade Him. But He did not stop until she had been fully convinced and in faith recognized Him as the Christ, so that she witnessed to others: "Come, see a man, which told me all things that ever I did: is not this the Christ" [John 4:29]?

This gathering was food for Jesus. Just as for us men, food is for strengthening in regard to the body, so for Him as Savior was it strengthening that a sinner had been saved.

But how is this? Could Jesus be strengthened?

Certainly, beloved.

The Food of Jesus

We confess with all our heart, as an incontrovertible truth, that He is the only-begotten, eternal and natural Son of God, who is, therefore, Himself called the true God and eternal life [I John 5:20]. Let all contradiction perish!

But likewise we confess that He has assumed the true human nature in the unity of His person. Therefore, He who came down from heaven in order to do the will of the Father and to perfect the work of the Father, has been strengthened for this work throughout His whole life.

Already in the Old Testament it had been said of Him, "The spirit of the LORD shall rest upon him, the spirit of wisdom and understanding, the spirit of counsel and might, the spirit of knowledge and of the fear of the LORD" [Isa. 11:2].

When at the age of twelve He was in the temple, He said to His mother, "[Do you not know] that I must be about my Father's business" [Luke 2:49]? He was, therefore, fully conscious of His relation to His Father, who had sent Him. Thereupon we read: "Jesus increased in wisdom and stature, and in favour with God and man" [Luke 2:52].

Time and time again, the Lord withdrew in order to pray when He was about to perform an especially weighty thing.

All of you remember that in Gethsemane, when He was in fierce conflict, an angel from heaven was seen by Him, who strengthened Him!

But does this not testify to His inexpressible greatness?

Oh, He was great when He said to the tempestuous winds and the furious sea, "Peace, be still" [Mark 4:39], and they were obedient to Him. He was great when those who were enslaved to evil spirits were freed by Him and when Lazarus rose from the dead at His command.

But how can we do justice to this, that He humbled Himself so deeply that He had to be strengthened?

If one of the prominent persons of this world, who is well-off with many earthly goods, leaves his warm and comfortable home in winter and visits the slums on an evening of blizzard or biting cold, entering the hovel of a destitute person in order there to cheer and refresh his needy fellow man with words and gifts, everyone would say, "That is noble."

Would that there were many such prominent persons! Would that also those who are less well-off would try to help in this way!

If it were told us that a czar of all Russians has abandoned his throne, has visited our country, and has become a laborer in one of our cities so that he himself could become experienced in manual labor and thus be able to be of profit to his people, then this extraordinary behavior would appear unbelievable, even though the proof could always be seen.

But what are all the prominent persons of the world, what are all czars and kings, in comparison with Him who is the only begotten Son of God? What is all earthly greatness in comparison with the glory that the Son of God had before the world was?

Nevertheless, he came down from heaven. He emptied Himself, having assumed the form of a slave. And it was his food.

He—He—was strengthened when a sinner was saved by Him.

At this humiliation, by which He received all power for the salvation of an innumerable multitude, heaven and earth must proclaim His greatness in amazement, in gratitude, and in worship.

At this, the universe must kneel before Him!

However, the greatness of Jesus is not preached to us so that we are terrified and would flee from Him. He who possesses the power to save is more inclined to salvation than we are able to imagine. Merely observe Him as He showed Himself at Jacob's well. That woman did not speak to Him, but was addressed by Him, even though He was very tired, and she came to consciousness of her guilt and to faith.

Why did the Lord concern Himself so much with that woman? Had she descended perhaps from the pure blood of Abraham? No, she was a Samaritan. She belonged to those

The Food of Jesus

who were descendants of the most insignificant among the Jews who had intermarried with the heathens.

Was she then perhaps one of the most prominent persons among here fellow citizens? No, although she was well along in years, she came to draw water.

Did she then perhaps stand in high esteem with others because of her moral behavior or piety? Often we see that those who are better off are friendly toward someone who has a good reputation, whether by behavior, walk, or ability. But to this woman, Jesus said, "Thou hast had five husbands; and he whom thou now hast is not thy husband: in that saidst thou truly" [John 4:18].

Such an estranged, disreputable, lewd woman was gathered by Jesus unto communion with God. For He has come to do the will of the Father, and of all that the Father had given Him to let nothing perish [John 6:39].

10

The *Afscheiding* and the Well-Meant Gospel Offer

Herman C. Hanko

THE *AFSCHEIDING* OF 1834 WAS A TRUE REFORMATION of the church. It was a work of God through the Spirit of the exalted Christ by which the true church of Christ was delivered from the apostate state church (Hervormde Kerk). However, there were some problems, differences, divisions, or disagreements among the many people and leaders who left the state church and joined the movement. One of those differences was the question of the well-meant gospel offer.

Background

It is not possible to understand this crucially important difference over the preaching of the gospel without going back more than a century earlier to developments in the Reformed churches in the Netherlands.

While the *Afscheiding* is certainly to be explained against the background of the apostate state church (the only Reformed Church in the whole of the Netherlands), that apostasy had been a long time present. Amazingly, that apostasy had begun a little over fifty years after the great victory of the Synod of Dordt in the conflict with Arminianism. Over the years, the situation worsened, until God's people could hardly bear to worship in their own or even in other congregations. The worship was sinful, and the gospel was not preached. The souls of the saints were not being fed.

The result of such a spiritual agony as the faithful people of God were enduring was the formation of *gezelschappen* (conventicles or house meetings). In these house meetings, usually held on the Lord's day, saints came together to study and discuss God's word, read old writers who were Reformed, and pray together to bring their collective needs to the throne of grace.

Not all these *gezelschappen* were equally orthodox. This could hardly be expected when the people had no leaders and the members were frequently of the uneducated lower class. One more gifted, more educated, and more fluent of speech, if such could be found, would assume a leadership role as an *oefenaar* (exhorter), who was not an ordained minister but could give the people some guidance.

In their search for sound Reformed writings, the saints came across the work of some Scottish theologians who, as it seemed to the members of the conventicles, struck the right spiritual note of genuine inner piety. The faithful in Scotland faced many of the same problems as the faithful in the Netherlands. A state church existed also in Scotland, and like the state church in the Netherlands, had become corrupt in that land in the north of the British Isles. Differences did, however, exist. The state church in Scotland was not as doctrinally apostate as the state church in the Netherlands; but the Scottish church was extremely worldly and carnally minded, and could rightly be accused of dead orthodoxy.

The faithful in the church in Scotland were gratified by the creedal orthodoxy of the church (such as it was), but the looseness of morals and the wicked lives that members lived filled them with dismay. They concluded, rightly, that the problem was a religion of the head, but not of the heart. And this they set about to correct with an emphasis on piety. Piety was defined as a genuine conversion of the heart, rooted in a deep conviction of sin and a need of Christ's sacrifice, and a life of holiness that followed on "closing with Christ," an expression much used among the godly in Scotland.

The difficulty was that these people had no true conception of the covenant and of conversion within the covenant, and so they expressed the fruit of biblical preaching in terms of evidences of conversion in the lives of people, among which evidences was conviction of sin. Here is where some introduced the idea of a well-meant gospel offer. Those who were under the conviction of sin were not yet converted and brought to Christ; in their misery and anxiety over sin they had to be urged to come to Christ. The offer of the gospel, expressing God's love for them, God's desire to save them, God's assuring them that he had done all to make their salvation possible and real, was the way to accomplish this goal and bring convicted sinners to Christ.

The piety of these men in Scotland appealed to the people in the Netherlands who faced the same problems of moral laxity and worldliness in their own churches. So the ideas prevalent among the concerned people on the other side of the North Sea were adopted in the conventicles, and the writings of Scottish theologians were avidly read. The result was that the idea of a well-meant gospel offer entered into the thinking of some of these people. Because of their emphasis on holiness, they became known as Pietists.

When the *Afscheiding* took place under the leadership of de Cock, those who rushed to form new congregations, as de Cock had done in Ulrum, were generally from the conventicles. One characteristic of the movement in its earlier years was the drastic shortage of ministers. The situation was so serious that many of those who were *oefenaars* in the conventicles now assumed the same role in newly established congregations. It is, therefore, not surprising that the idea of the well-meant offer entered into the thinking of the *Afscheiding* churches. Not all the ministers and members of the *Afscheiding* churches accepted the doctrine of the well-meant gospel offer. In her book *Son of Secession: Douwe J. Vander Werp,* Janet

The *Afscheiding* and the Well-Meant Gospel Offer

Sheeres speaks of the fact that there were serious doctrinal divisions among the seceders. Generally speaking, there were two factions in the churches: a so-called Groningen *richting* (faction) and a Gelderse *richting*. The Groningen faction, found chiefly in the provinces of Groningen and Friesland, was strongly orthodox and intent on maintaining the confessions. The Gelderse faction was primarily in the south and had leanings towards Arminianism.

The leaders of the *Afscheiding* in the north were de Cock and Van Velzen. The leaders in the south were Brummelkamp, Helenius de Cock (Hendrik de Cock's son), and to a lesser extent, Van Raalte. The story is told (I cannot vouch for its accuracy) that when Hendrik de Cock heard that Brummelkamp was preaching a well-meant offer, he said: "Hij is geen broer; hij is e'n neef" (He is no brother; he is a nephew).

When the seceders felt the need for a seminary and one was established in Kampen, both factions were represented: the northern, more orthodox faction by Van Velzen, and the southern, more liberal faction by Brummelkamp and Helenius de Cock. The graduates from the school were themselves divided, and the more orthodox congregations in the north did not want graduates who showed the influences of the teachings of Brummelkamp and Helenius de Cock.

So the well-meant gospel offer appeared in the thinking of the *Afscheiding* churches, and many within those churches came to believe this doctrine. They were committed to the idea that God desires to save all who hear the gospel and expresses his own hope that those who hear will surely come to Christ to find their salvation in Christ's blood. God assures men that, on his part, he has done all that he can to make salvation available to them. It remains the responsibility of the hearers to attend to the words of the gospel and obey the command to "close with Christ."

This Arminian strain was present in the *Afscheiding* from its very inception. It has endured in many churches who trace their origin back to the Secession of 1834. The western Michigan settlements were composed primarily of people of the Secession, and both strains of thinking could be found in the settlements. Thus the idea of a well-meant offer entered the thinking of the Christian Reformed Church.

In the Netherlands, the Secession of 1834 was followed by the *Doleantie,* led by Dr. Abraham Kuyper. One could not find the teachings of the well-meant offer in Kuyper's reformatory movement, because Kuyper himself was completely opposed to it. But when the *Afscheiding* and the *Doleantie* merged in 1892, the well-meant gospel offer came along into the merged churches, the Gereformeerde Kerken in Nederland. Since then, the Gereformeerde Kerken have merged with the old state church and a Lutheran denomination to form the Protestant Church in the Netherlands (PKN), a completely apostate denomination.

In the late 1880s and early 1890s, the Christian Reformed Church reflected the same divisions that were to be found in the *Afscheiding* churches, divisions that were made worse by the adoption of Kuyperian common grace in the denomination. The divisions were healed and peace was restored by the adoption of the three points of common grace by the Synod of the CRC in Kalamazoo in 1924. Objecting to such a settlement, many orthodox and faithful from both the *Afscheiding* and the *Doleantie* came out of the CRC to form the Protestant Reformed Churches in America.

11

The *Afscheiding*'s Commitment to Psalm Singing

Barrett L. Gritters

THE PROTESTANT REFORMED CHURCHES (PRC) ARE A Psalm-singing denomination. They sing the Psalms in worship—and little else. The families sing the Psalms (as well as good hymns) in their homes—many psalms. Their children are taught the Psalms in their Christian schools, where the Psalms have pride of place.

The PRC are gladly Psalm-singing churches. They understand what an old preacher meant when, praising the Psalms, he said, "David has for ages subdued more hearts with his harp than ever with his sword and scepter." And they believe that *one* of the ways God uses to preserve them is the singing of the Psalms. By the Psalms they teach and admonish one another. By the Psalms the word of Christ dwells in them richly (Col. 3:16).

That the Protestant Reformed Churches are Psalm-singing churches is due in part to God's work of preserving Reformed Christianity in the Secession of 1834. There is history behind the PRC's Psalm singing.

When the churches' youth ask why the church worships God by singing the Psalms, the pastor would be wise to reason from Scripture, but very quick to direct the youth to ask another question. It is what I always call the "question of history." Those interested in why the church believes or practices *anything* should always ask the question of history. That is, how did the church of the past worship? Did they sing the Psalms?

Asking the question of history is faithfulness to God. He commands, "Ask for the old paths, where is the good way" (Jer. 6:16). He instructs the church, "Hold the traditions" (2 Thess. 2:15). One of these traditions of the church is singing the Psalms.

The fathers of the *Afscheiding* contended that separation from the existing church was necessary. Though Psalm singing was not the central issue in the Secession, the requirement that the churches sing hymns may well have precipitated the schism. A substitution of hymns for the Psalms was a departure from the old paths, the good way.

The Battle for Psalms

Some three hundred years *before* the *Afscheiding*, the great Reformation of the sixteenth century restored Psalm singing. The German branch of the Reformation, under the influence of Luther, maintained the singing of many hymns, although no one may suppose that Luther did not love the Psalms and the singing of the Psalms. However, the Swiss, French, Scottish, and Dutch branches believed that faithfulness to the old paths was to sing the Psalms, and perhaps exclusively.

This was emphatically true in the Lowlands. In 1566 the reformer Peter Datheen published a volume containing his translation into Dutch of the Psalms in meter, after the pattern of the Genevan Psalter. Already in 1568 the Dutch churches at Wesel adopted this as their Psalter. This was the songbook of the Dutch Reformed churches for many years, although not without struggle. When the Great Synod at Dordt met in 1618–1619, the churches had to fight off an attempt by the Arminians to introduce hymns. Thus, Dordt adopted a church order that called the churches to sing the Psalms (Art. 69). The synod did permit a few hymns to be

The *Afscheiding*'s Commitment to Psalm Singing

sung (as well as the ten commandments, the Lord's prayer, and the Apostles' Creed), but Dordt's intent was to convey a message no one could miss: "We are Psalm-singing churches!" For 150 years after Dordt, the Dutch churches maintained the practice of singing from King David's songbook, again not without struggle. Confirming the adage "If you want a fight in the church, debate money or music," the Dutch Reformed during the 1700s fought about which version of the psalms would be used. "Datheen," as they called the psalter of Peter Datheen, was the songbook of choice, and even "went underground" when the rulers determined another would be used instead. So it is not a surprise to hear that there were riots in some of the fishermen's towns near Rotterdam over proposals to use something other than Datheen's version of the Psalter.

But soon there were moves to add hymns to the church's repertoire of worship songs. In 1789 a psalm book was published that included an appendix with hymns. These were known as the *"evangelische gezangen"* (evangelical hymns). In 1796, the provincial Synod of North Holland initiated an official adoption of hymns by proposing that all seven provincial synods in the Netherlands jointly compose a new songbook that would include the Psalms as well as hymns, a kind of Psalter-hymnal. Some of the synods were slow to sign on, but by 1805 the joint committee presented its songbook to the acting head of the Dutch republic. By 1807 it became the official songbook of the Reformed churches.

Now it becomes clear that although the matter of psalms and hymns was not the central issue in the Secession, it was an important part of the struggle to maintain the purity of the church and persevere on the old paths.

The Psalm Singing Leaders

The ministers who led their flocks out of the departing churches testified that Psalm singing was one of the reasons for secession.

Hendrik de Cock first wrote a preface to a layman's attack on hymns. Later de Cock wrote his own tract. "Will you, I say, trample and disobey and stray from the path and do away with all the decisions of the general Synods of our fathers regarding their pronouncements from God's Word against these songs?" Then de Cock's pamphlet also quotes Peter Martyr, who said that by hymns, the "Roman church received copper in exchange for gold."[1]

De Cock objected not because the hymns were bad hymns —modernistic and theologically unsound—but because they were *hymns*. One historian's analysis of the history confirms this: "They decried the introduction of hymns into worship as another channel of heterodoxy—hymns being the words of man as opposed to psalms, the words of God."[2]

A Christian Reformed historian tells of the church discipline applied to Hendrik Scholte. The reasons? "He had objections to the preparatory questions for the Lord's Supper ...and his flock objected to the use of the hymns."[3] Anthony Brummelkamp "refused to baptize children of non-confessing members...and declared that he would no longer give out the hymns since there were many objectors to them."[4] Theirs were not the only testimonies of love for the Psalms, but they are representative of the people of the *Afscheiding*.

Reasons for Hymns

Those who promoted the hymns claimed that ministers needed songs that were appropriate for the particular Lord's Day of the Heidelberg Catechism sermon. Or they suggested that the New Testament church needed a songbook that extolled the fulfillment of the gospel in Jesus Christ by his Spirit. They suggested that the hymns were the Dutch people's attempt to have a "freer church hymn in which the Christian heart should find the satisfying expression of its holiest emotion."[5] The committee proposing the hymns was so bold as to claim that the hymns were to preserve doctrine and prevent modern dangers.

The *Afscheiding*'s Commitment to Psalm Singing

The problem with these claims is, first, that hymns are not needed to sing of Jesus Christ, as Jesus himself said in Luke 24:27, 44, and as Paul said in Colossians 3:16 (see also Eph. 5:19). Second, some of the new hymns were doctrinally unsound.

One of the Reformed ministers not on the side of the Secessionists went on the offensive against Psalm singing. J. J. Van Oosterzee's criticism was sharp. First, he flayed the seceding ministers by labeling them as shepherds "who minister to the disease of the congregation." Not satisfied with promoting hymns, Van Oosterzee attacked ministers. He also assaulted the Psalms. "As the Dutch metrical Psalms now are, they are found to be...for the greater half, altogether unusable, and also actually out of use in the Church of the New Covenant; which can indeed *read* all these Psalms, but can only to a very partial extent *sing* them in public worship."[6]

The Defense of Psalms

The *Afscheiding* ministers defended psalmody primarily, but not exclusively, by an appeal to the history of God's church. The Reformation had restored Psalms. The Great Synod had so recently called the Dutch Reformed to be Psalm singers. The church must preserve this precious heritage.

Hendrik de Cock opened his pamphlet against hymns this way:

> Hymns were never introduced into the church, except to cause degeneration and contempt for the welfare of the church, or perhaps in cases of incomplete Reformation...We see as well...that in the best of times, and in the purest churches, hymns are never found or tolerated...Where Reformation has broken out in its purest form, the hymns are completely done away with.[7]

Then:

> ...not with us nor in France nor in Geneva, are hymns tolerated or found, and certainly not in Scotland. However, in England,

where episcopalian church government remains and where Romish ceremonies are still partially allowed, one will perhaps also find hymns being sung.[8]

In their appeal to history, these reformers could be sharp, too:

> Where, therefore, were the hymns, or other whorish songs ever used in the days of the apostles in the congregations of the Lord? Do we find any reference to them? Never![9]

After referring to the heretics of ancient times, de Cock said:

> These heretics...had innovations in mind, and caused congregations to become perverse, blinded through errors, and they did these things by means of new songs of human composition.[10]

Psalms in worship! The reformers of 1834 called for the Psalms. Although their concerns in reformation were more and deeper, their reform did include this restoration of the churches' pure worship.

PRC Tradition

The Protestant Reformed Churches come out of the tradition of the *Afscheiding*. They are one of the few Reformed denominations with Dutch roots that has remained true to that tradition, although there are also a few Presbyterian denominations that maintain the Psalms in worship.

The tradition of the *Afscheiding* is maintained, but not without struggle.

When our fathers, many from the *Afscheiding* churches, came to America in the mid-1800s, they sang the Psalms. But the battle that was waged in the Netherlands repeated itself in this country. When the immigrants joined the existing Dutch Reformed denomination in the States, they soon

The *Afscheiding*'s Commitment to Psalm Singing

found membership there unacceptable. One of the reasons was the use of hymns in worship.

In 1857 five American congregations seceded from the Reformed Protestant Dutch Church (known today as the Reformed Church in America) with this confession (take note what is listed first):

> We are obliged to give you notice of our present ecclesiastical standpoint, namely, separating ourselves from your denomination... with which we thoughtlessly became connected upon our arrival in America. We are uniting ourselves with the Afgescheidene Gereformeerde Kerk in the Netherlands... The reasons for this our secession... are as follows: 1) The collection of 800 hymns...[11]

This was the beginning of the Christian Reformed Church.

The CRC, too, struggled long to maintain the singing of the Psalms. In 1932, at the beginning of that struggle, that denomination prefaced their new songbook with these words: "During the 77 years of its existence, the Christian Reformed Church has sung practically nothing but psalms in public worship." The preface said,

> We were aware of the unsound or unsatisfactory character of many current hymns, and we feared that in an environment where the Psalms are seldom sung, the introduction of hymns in public worship would lead to the neglect of those deeply spiritual songs of the Old Testament which the Church should never fail to use in its service of praise.[12]

The deeply spiritual songs of the Old Testament which the Church should never fail to use in its service of praise! But today, the CRC has adopted mostly hymns.

Knowing this history may be helpful for the people of God to maintain their love for the Psalms. It may assist them to show their questioning youth that they stand in the line of godly men and women who worshiped God in this way for hundreds and thousands of years.

May the Lord Christ, *the* "sweet Psalmist [Singer] of Israel," put his Psalms in the church's heart and mouth, so she does not miss out on their depth, breadth, and God-centered focus—to say nothing of their inspired instructions and admonitions by which the people of God converse in the beauty of covenant worship (Eph. 5:19; Col. 3:16).

12

The *Afscheiding* and Christian Education

Steven R. Key

Education prior to the Afscheiding

The history of Christian education in the Netherlands is a long history. The Reformation, beginning already with Martin Luther, called for and established schools where the foundation would be the teachings of Holy Scripture. The Dutch Reformed gave the same emphasis to Christian education as early as 1574, when a Reformed synod called on preachers to see to it that there were good Christian schoolmasters.[1]

But while the schools in the Netherlands—government schools—once had significant Christian content in their instruction, this was no longer the case by the late eighteenth and early nineteenth centuries. The spirit of toleration that characterized the Enlightenment had gained the upper hand in the churches, at the expense of sound doctrine and antithetical, godly living.[2] Secular and humanistic ideas and critical views of Scripture, which were already prevalent in the universities of the Netherlands, had worked their way through the schools as well.

While there remained in many areas a certain Christian influence, including Bible reading and prayer, the foundational principles of Christian education established in the sixteenth and early seventeenth centuries were largely lost. The truth of the Reformed faith no longer permeated the instruction.

By the time Napoleon's revolutionary army made its way into the Netherlands in 1795 and uprooted the remnants of Reformed theology and practice from public life, there were few who cared.[3] All religions were given equal footing under the law, and under the banner of toleration or non-sectarianism the teaching of any distinctively Reformed perspective in the public schools was ousted, to be replaced with deistic religion.

There were, however, schools owned and operated by Reformed churches.[4] The Education Law of 1806 allowed for private schools alongside the public schools. Private schools were supported by tuition payments for the students as well as by the foundation or society that founded them. They could also be church-operated, and they could be subsidized, if necessary, by the deacons of a congregation. Private schools were not subject to the government restrictions of religious perspective or content.

But the Education Law of 1806 did forbid even private Reformed schools the right to use any doctrinal standards in the hiring of teachers.[5] The hiring of teachers was subject to the approval of the state.[6] This contributed to a further weakening of Reformed principles in Christian education. Teachers, after all, are the heart of a sound biblical and Reformed education. With the government preventing "sectarian" (read, solidly Reformed) teachers from being hired by Reformed schools, the generic instruction of the state schools continued to advance also in the private schools.

The Development of the Afscheiding

The leadership of the *Afscheiding* of 1834 came from men who had come through those schools marked by toleration and higher critical views of Scripture. They had rejected those erroneous views and presuppositions, seeking to maintain the authority of Holy Scripture as maintained in the Reformed confessions.

Prior to 1834 these young men had been members of the

The *Afscheiding* and Christian Education

so-called Scholte Club at the University of Leiden, a group begun by Hendrik Scholte and some fellow students.[7] That group proved to be an incubator of ideas that would later influence the direction of the *Afscheiding*. One matter of importance to these men was a sound education, beginning at the elementary level and continuing all the way through university studies.[8]

With the Reformation of 1834 and in the years immediately following, there was tremendous upheaval even among the new congregations of the *Afscheiding*. The unsettled nature of the movement and the persecution that ensued prevented any development of an educational system for the children.

Already on November 10, 1834, a Christian school was opened in a very humble setting at Smilde, with Douwe J. Vander Werp the first teacher. Almost immediately, however, the civil authorities closed it and fined Vander Werp a significant sum of money.[9]

Therefore, the chief focus initially, besides the care of the congregations, was upon developing a program of theological instruction for training young men for the ministry.

Within a few years, however, there arose hopes among Christian parents that immigrating to America would enable them to provide a Christian education for their children.

The Movement to America

Our interest turns to the members of the *Afscheiding* as they soon began to immigrate to the United States of America.

It is not within our scope here to develop the reasons for the emigration movement. The suffering of extreme poverty and burdensome taxes, along with the desire for a more free exercise of religion were the main contributing factors. But among some there was also the hope that immigrating to America would enable them to provide a Christian education for their children.[10]

In late 1846 a sizable group boarded a ship bound for America, accompanied by their pastor, the Reverend A. C. Van Raalte. By early 1847 they were clearing the forests of western Michigan to establish a new colony. Other companies followed, and by the spring of the following year several churches had been established and a new classis was organized, Classis Holland.

Already at the second classical meeting, held September 27, 1848, the following decision was taken:

> Art. 6. Rev. Ypma proposes that the interests of the schools shall be discussed. The discussion takes place, and the judgment is: the schools must be promoted and cared for by the churches, as being an important part of the Christian calling of God's church on earth. All lukewarmness and coldness toward that cause must be condemned and rebuked.[11]

At the meeting of Classis Holland on April 30, 1851, Rev. Van Raalte reported that there was a plan under consideration in the Board of Domestic Missions of the Dutch Reformed Church to send a man who could serve as a teacher in West Michigan.[12] The minutes then record the following:

> This purpose, or plan, aroused rejoicing, and several of the brethren endowed with insight into the importance of some such step, expressed themselves as heartily glad of what they had heard; and expressed their own feelings with regard to the supreme importance of the education of the youth, upon which depend the character, the destiny, and the prosperity of a people; (saying) that for their own posterity they sought above all else God-fearing instruction in all the branches of knowledge.[13]

As classes began in the various communities, even equipment was lacking. There were no desks, slates, blackboards, or textbooks. "Here, classes were held in a kitchen, there in a loft, somewhere else in a church."[14] Conditions were less than ideal. Students were few, partly because too many parents saw little value in formal education.

The *Afscheiding* and Christian Education

But those who understood the importance of that education recognized that the important thing was the content of the instruction and the doctrinal perspective and understanding of those who taught. By the promotion of sound education by faithful consistories and preachers, the importance of Christian education began to be more clearly understood, and the support grew—among some.

Van Raalte very soon turned his attention to higher education. Understanding that the colonists could not bear the costs of establishing a school for higher education, he turned to the established churches on the east coast for help. The result was the establishment of the Academy, initially set up as "a high school to prepare sons of the colonists from Holland for Rutgers College, and also to educate daughters of said colonists."[15]

Ministers such as Van Raalte and Vander Meulen faithfully and constantly reminded the colonists of the value of Christian education and of supporting also the school for higher education.

> We must not let the years fly by without training our children to take over the positions and responsibilities in church, school, and society. As supervisors, fathers, and leaders of the people, we can not die with a clear conscience if we do not, while it is still day, work to leave behind us successors and shepherds and if we do not see to it in time that the people grow and mature to assume, in the right way, the responsibilities God has entrusted us with in this place.[16]

These were men with vision!

Belonging to their vision was the idea, found in the above quotation, that education was critically important in taking up "the responsibilities God has entrusted us with in this place." Christian education was to be permeated with biblical truth, the truth which is applicable to all of life, and more particularly a life to be lived in the particular location and position to which God calls us.

But by 1862 the Christian grade school in the Dutch colony

had died out. With the establishment of a district public school, "the poverty stricken pioneers found it much easier to let the government bear the burden."[17]

The immigrants were not sufficiently convinced of the need of Christian schools to make the necessary sacrifices. In a letter to a certain Rev. and Mrs. VanDer Wall, Van Raalte laments, "Parochial instruction lies buried here...I am following the advice you gave me. I am doing nothing at all..."[18] So only higher Christian education continued at the time. If not seen by many as unnecessary, it was generally thought that the establishment of Christian grade schools would hinder the transition of the children into American culture. It was this attitude that took root among the people of the Reformed Church in America.

Ironically, the principled stand of Van Raalte was carried on by those who separated from him and began what would later become the Christian Reformed Church. And when numerous educated Netherlanders settled in America during the 1890s, they brought with them the influence of Dr. Abraham Kuyper's educational ideals.[19]

But it was the contribution of the *Afscheiding* to restore the significance of Reformed Christian education to the church, the education of the children according to the truth of Holy Scripture and the Reformed confessions.

What a worthy labor for us to carry on today!

13

The Secession of 1834 and the Struggle for the Church Order of Dordt

Ronald L. Cammenga

CHURCH REFORMATION ORDINARILY INVOLVES A return not only to true doctrine, but also to biblical church government. These two, it seems, almost always go hand in hand. Corresponding to departures in doctrine within the church are invariably departures also in the area of church polity. Often the errors in the government of the church serve to promote the errors in doctrine, countenancing the doctrinal deviations and protecting those who are perpetrating them. When reformation takes place, therefore, not only must the truth be restored, but ordinarily it is also necessary that proper church government be reestablished.

History has demonstrated the truth of this. The Roman Catholic Church had become both corrupt in doctrine and hierarchical in church government. The reformers of the sixteenth century championed the restoration of the doctrines of grace and worked for the restoration of biblical church government. Especially did God use John Calvin to restore proper biblical church government. What was true of the Reformation in the sixteenth century was also true of the Arminian controversy in the seventeenth century. Not only did the Arminians promote false doctrine, which was condemned by the Synod of Dordt, but the Arminians also were agitating for a church polity that was un-Reformed and unbiblical. In the

Church Order that it drafted, the Synod of Dordt responded to the Arminian errors regarding church government. In the reformation of 1924, the issues were not only doctrinal, but also church-political, particularly the autonomy of the local consistory as opposed to the hierarchical presumption of the right to suspend and depose officebearers by the broader assemblies. God used the founding fathers of the Protestant Reformed Churches for the defense of the truth of sovereign, particular grace and the defense of proper, Reformed church government, the government of the Church Order of Dordt.

What has been true of reformation movements generally throughout the history of the New Testament church was also true of the Secession of 1834 in the Netherlands. Significant doctrinal issues were at stake in the Secession movement. Without question, the Secession represents a genuine return to the truth of the word of God and to the Reformed confessions. But the Secession also represents a return to proper church government. An important aspect of the Secession of 1834 was its struggle for the restoration of a biblical polity in the churches. Matters of church polity were a significant factor leading up to the Secession, and matters of church polity led to intense internal struggles within the churches of the Secession in their early history. Through these struggles, God led the Secession churches to a return to the Church Order of Dordt.

Church Political Struggles Leading up to the Secession

The Napoleonic era in the history of the Netherlands ended with the return from exile of King William I. On November 30, 1813, William returned to the Netherlands after eighteen years of absence. He returned at the request of the Dutch after Napoleon's defeat at Leipzig in October 1813. In 1814 William gained sovereignty over the whole of the Low Countries, and on March 16, 1815, he proclaimed himself king of

Secession of 1834 and Struggle for Church Order of Dordt

the United Kingdom of the Netherlands. As part of the sweeping reforms that he introduced in the wake of the departure of the French, William reconstituted the Reformed churches in the Netherlands. By a royal decree issued in January 1816, the king imposed a new hierarchical, collegial system of church government that dismantled entirely the classes and synods of the Dutch Reformed churches. William replaced the Church Order of Dordt with a new church order called *Het Algemeen Regelement* (General Regulations). The General Regulations placed the Reformed churches of the Netherlands under the control of the state. The Department of Education, Arts, and Sciences was charged with administering the affairs of the Reformed churches in the Netherlands. Executive boards took over the government of the churches, whose officers were appointed by and subject to the government. Although William's reorganization of the churches was radical, very few protests were voiced. The churches were so relieved to be delivered from French rule that they were willing, for the most part, to yield control over their affairs to the restored monarch.

But by their acquiescence the Dutch churches had relinquished the cherished Church Order of Dordt. That proved to be a costly concession indeed. Not only did the churches become subject to the dominance and interference of the state, but because of this the churches were also unable to stem the growing tide of liberalism that swept through the Dutch churches. Time and again, the state boards protected the heretics, and time and again the state boards came down with a heavy hand to crush ministers and consistories who voiced their objections to those who were promoting wrong doctrines and practices in the churches.

From the very beginning, the Secession of 1834 expressed a determination to return to the Church Order of Dordt. Already the "Act of Secession or Return" formulated by the consistory of Ulrum made reference to this resolve. In this document, the consistory expressed that the "Netherlands Ecclesiastical Board has now made itself equivalent to the

Popish Church rejected by our fathers." And the document closes with the resolution "to order our public religious services according to the ancient ecclesiastical liturgy; and with respect to divine service and church government, for the present to hold to the Church Order instituted by the aforementioned Synod of Dordrecht."[1] At its root, therefore, the Secession of 1834 was not only a return to right doctrine, but also a return to proper church government—a return to proper church government in the form of the reestablishment of the Church Order of Dordt in the churches. The church would not any longer be subject to the intrusion of the state, but would be governed by the principles of God's word as those principles were articulated in the Church Order of Dordt.

Internal Struggles over the Church Order of Dordt within the Secession Churches

Although the Secession of 1834 began with an interest in restoring the Church Order of Dordt to its rightful place in the Dutch Reformed churches, this did not immediately happen. Soon internal struggles erupted over this very issue, struggles that threatened to and eventually did splinter the reform movement. Differences of opinion divided the leaders of the Secession movement, some favoring the restoration of the Church Order of Dordt, others supporting a new church order that, while it might borrow from Dordt, would be unique to the Secession churches. Those who favored the restoration of the Church Order of Dordt were de Cock and Van Velzen especially. It was particularly Scholte who favored a new church order.

In 1837, Scholte presented to the second synod of the Secession churches, meeting in Utrecht from September 28 to October 11, the draft of a new church order. This new church order borrowed from the Church Order of Dordt, but was

Secession of 1834 and Struggle for Church Order of Dordt

at the same time a radical revision of the Church Order of 1618–1619. The new church order was adopted after lengthy discussion and some modification.

But hardly had the synod recessed before opposition to the new church order was raised. The main objections were the following. First, it was objected that the new church order was too much the work of one man. Even though the synod had approved it, the church order was primarily the work of Scholte. There was a strong sentiment that if the Secession churches were going to adopt a new church order, many more of the leaders of the new denomination should be involved in its formulation. Second, there were those who opposed setting aside the Church Order of Dordt in favor of a new church order because this negated the Secession's claim that they were not only seceding from the apostate state church of the Netherlands, but also returning to the old paths and the time-honored traditions of the Dutch Reformed churches. Many felt that by setting aside the Church Order of Dordt, the Secession's claim to be a return to Dordt was compromised. Third, the new church order was opposed because it gutted the broader assemblies of any real authority. Following Scholte's fear of hierarchy, the broader assemblies had no binding powers in the new church order. All decisions of the broader assemblies had to be ratified by the local consistories, and the decisions of the broader assemblies were to be only advisory. In his new church order, Scholte manifested the streak of independentism that would plague him in his labors among the Secession churches in the Netherlands, and later in his work in Pella, Iowa.

After much debate and heated exchanges, and after extensive wrangling in the assemblies, the churches of the Secession finally put the controversy over church polity to rest at the Synod of Amsterdam in 1840. At this synod it was decided to rescind the new church order and to establish the Church Order of Dordt as the church order of the Secession churches. At this same synod Scholte was reprimanded and subsequently deposed for refusing to accept the original

Church Order of Dordt. At a considerable cost, the issue over church polity was resolved, and the peace of the churches was restored. The Secession churches returned to the biblical principles and polity of Dordt.

The Significance of the Church Political Struggles of the Secession Churches

The history of the struggle of the Secession churches over issues of church polity underscores the importance of biblical church government. Without question, one of the monuments of the Secession was that it restored to the Dutch Reformed churches proper church government. This is part of the heritage of the Secession to those who count themselves heirs of the Secession. The Secession restored not only the doctrines of Dordt, but also the polity of Dordt.

The Secession was a return specifically to the Church Order of Dordt, its principles and provisions. Opposition to the Church Order of Dordt from without and within was put down. In the end the Church Order of Dordt was confirmed in the churches of the Secession. The struggle to restore this document ought to endear it to Reformed churches that count it their own.

The Secession's struggle over the Church Order of Dordt makes plain the conviction of the Reformed that proper church government belongs to the being (*esse*) of the church, not merely to the well-being (*bene esse*) of the church. This is the settled conviction of the Reformed, a conviction reinforced by the history of the Secession. In the end, the churches of the Secession came to see that this is the confessionally Reformed position. That position is expressed in Article 30 of the Belgic Confession of Faith: "We believe that this true Church must be governed by the spiritual policy which our Lord hath taught us in his Word..." Article 32 adds, "In the mean time we believe though it is useful and beneficial that those who are rulers of the Church institute and establish certain ordinances among themselves for maintaining the body of the Church; yet they ought studiously to take care that they do not depart from those things which Christ, our only master, hath instituted."[2] The restoration of the Church Order of Dordt rested squarely on the conviction that proper church government pertains to the very being of the true church of Jesus Christ. That conviction must motivate those who are the spiritual descendants of the Secession of 1834 to maintain the Church Order of Dordt.

14

The Covenant Doctrine of the Fathers of the Secession

David J. Engelsma

At the beginning of that reformation in the Netherlands, the fathers of the Secession of 1834—Hendrik de Cock, Simon Van Velzen, Anthony Brummelkamp, and perhaps others—were agreed that election governs the covenant of grace. They differed in other respects, especially whether children of unbelieving members of the congregation should be baptized and concerning the meaning of the phrase "sanctified in Christ" in the first question of the baptism form. But with one voice they confessed that election determines the covenant promise, covenant membership, the enjoyment of covenant blessings, and the realization in some baptized children of covenant salvation.

For the fathers of the Secession, the covenant is a covenant of *grace*. God establishes his covenant unconditionally with the elect, and with the elect only. The reason was not that those benighted men had not as yet been able to free themselves from the fetters of "scholasticism," as C. Veenhof contends. The "liberated" Reformed theologian dismisses Van Velzen's covenant doctrine, which Veenhof correctly describes as the doctrine that has election governing the covenant, as a "typically scholastic method of reasoning."[1]

Rather, the leaders of the Secession formed their doctrine of the covenant according to the gospel of sovereign grace that they found in the Bible and in the Reformed confessions.

The Covenant Doctrine of the Fathers of the Secession

It was this gospel of sovereign grace that gave birth to the Secession. The Secession of 1834 had its origin in Hendrik de Cock's heartfelt conviction of the truth of salvation by the almighty grace of God. By reading Calvin's *Institutes of the Christian Religion,* de Cock came to know the truth of the confession of one of his parishioners, Klaas Kuipenga: "If I must add even one sigh to my salvation, then I would be eternally lost."[2]

The Canons of Dordt played a powerful, indeed decisive, role in launching the Secession. With good reason, one scholar has called the Canons the credo of the Secession. De Cock discovered the Canons after his ordination to the ministry. Previously this Reformed confession was unknown to him, even though he was a graduate of a Reformed seminary (as is the case with many graduates from Reformed seminaries in North America today). At the beginning of the Secession, de Cock had the Canons reprinted at his own expense and then distributed copies far and wide throughout the Netherlands.

Hendrik de Cock preached the gospel of grace as confessed and defended by the Canons. To this, God's people responded by a living faith, as they always do, so that the Secession became a mighty and nationwide reformation of the church. Algra tells us that in the early days of the Secession, people traveled half a day on foot to Ulrum (where de Cock preached), in order to hear a sermon that did not teach that one is saved "by 'doing and permitting,' but by the eternal wonder of unmerited free grace."[3] The first sermon de Cock preached after the Secession had taken place in Ulrum was on Ephesians 2: "By grace ye are saved," and the afternoon sermon was on Lord's Day 1 of the Heidelberg Catechism. The date was October 19, 1834, and it is worthy of remembrance.

In his biography of his father, Helenius de Cock acknowledged Hendrik de Cock's embrace of the gospel of salvation by sovereign grace. Reading Calvin's *Institutes,* Hendrik de Cock

> now recognized... the great truth, that later shone through in all his preaching and writing, that it is God who seeks man, who must

first love us, if we shall be able to love Him; and who has known and loved His people from before the foundation of the world, so that He would sanctify them. Now it was God alone and He in everything, to whom the honor of redemption belonged.[4]

The enemies of the Secession understood well that the Secession was church reformation by means of and for the sake of the gospel of grace as confessed by the Canons. Early in the Secession, when Van Velzen pleaded with the leaders of the state church to defend the confessions, one of the ministers replied, "I'd rather have my neck wrung than subscribe to the Canons of Dordt."[5]

Men gripped by the truth of sovereign grace must teach a covenant of grace, that is, a covenant governed by election.

This was the covenant doctrine of the fathers of the Secession.

Fundamental to the doctrine that the covenant is governed by election is the truth that the covenant promise refers to the elect children of believers in Jesus Christ, and to the elect children only. Regarding these objects of the covenant promise to Abraham—that God will be the God of Abraham and Abraham's seed—Hendrik de Cock wrote, "That promise did not refer to all the children of Abraham's family, head for head, but to all the elect children, which God would later indicate" (Rom. 9:7, 8). He added,

> For a child that went lost circumcision could not be a sacrament sealing the promise to this child, because the promise was not made to that child, but to Abraham, not with respect to every child head for head, but with respect to the elect children, to whom that reprobate child did not belong (Rom. 9:7, 8; Gen. 17:10).[6]

Simon Van Velzen, the outstanding Reformed theologian of the Secession, also taught that the covenant is governed by election. Curiously, Canadian Reformed theologian Dr. Jelle Faber overlooked Van Velzen when he listed the representatives of the two contending covenant views in the churches of the Secession in the late nineteenth century. As a represen-

The Covenant Doctrine of the Fathers of the Secession

tative of the doctrine that election governs the covenant, Faber could only think of H. Joffers, whose personal reputation suffers among Reformed scholars (thanks in no small part to the "liberated" Reformed, who never fail to lament his narrow-mindedness and stubbornness), and who, in any case, does not belong to the fathers of the Secession. However, Faber could give a long list of Secession ministers who, according to Faber, taught a doctrine of the covenant from which election is strictly banished.[7]

Another vitally important element of the covenant doctrine of those Reformed theologians and churches that confess that election governs the covenant is the explanation of the phrase in the baptism form, "our children...are sanctified in Christ," that identifies these children as the elect in Christ among the physical children of believers. In 1857, Van Velzen explained this phrase as follows:

> We know that everyone who is sanctified in Christ is infallibly saved, that the covenant, of which Baptism is sign and seal, is called an eternal covenant of grace, so that they, who are included in it, cannot perish. How then must we understand it, when at Baptism the little children are said to be "sanctified in Christ"? Must we conceive this of all children who are baptized, of all children head for head who have believing parents? Neither the one, nor the other! It is incontrovertible, I think, that the words in view cannot be understood definitely of every child who is baptized. Rather, they have reference to the seed of the promise, and here the elect are counted for the seed.[8]

Eight years later, Van Velzen availed himself of his privilege as editor of the magazine *De Bazuin* to respond to the covenant doctrine of his colleague Rev. K. J. Pieters. By this time, Pieters was introducing into the churches of the Secession, and defending, a radically different doctrine of the covenant than that held by the fathers of the Secession. Pieters taught that at baptism God extended his gracious covenant promise to every child alike. According to Pieters, God assured every child that he or she was now in possession of the grace of the covenant. He said that at baptism, every child participates in covenant grace, although this by no means assures the salvation of any, for the covenant is conditional. Pieters argued that only this doctrine does justice to God's assuring all the children that they are heirs of the covenant and its blessings. Pieters charged that the other doctrine of the covenant, which has the covenant governed by election, makes God a liar and is, in fact, "blasphemous." But this doctrine of the covenant was that of the fathers of the Secession, particularly that of Van Velzen, as Pieters was well aware. And Van Velzen was editor of the magazine in which Pieters was defending his new doctrine of the covenant, and condemning the covenant doctrine of Van Velzen.

Incidentally, Pieters' violent assault on the doctrine of the covenant that has election governing the covenant exposes the error, if not the foolishness, of those today who plead for the tolerance in one church federation of both doctrines of the covenant that struggled for the heart, mind, and confession of the churches of the Secession in the latter part of the nineteenth century. These two doctrines of the covenant are mutually exclusive. They detest each other, and necessarily so. They are, in principle, two different gospels with specific reference to the grace and salvation of the covenant.

Van Velzen's response to Pieters' outrageous charge clearly revealed the covenant doctrine of this father of the Secession.

> By circumcision, God had given assurance to Israel that they were in possession of the righteousness of faith in the most solemn and earnest manner, and many Israelites have not obtained this righteousness and have not participated in it. But God's assurance nevertheless does not fail. For the children of the promise, those who are brought to faith out of the power of God's election and promise, are counted for the seed.[9]

Anthony Brummelkamp, whose teaching of a "well-meaning offer" of salvation would contribute to a radically different doctrine of the covenant, was originally one with de Cock and Van Velzen in teaching that election governs the cove-

The Covenant Doctrine of the Fathers of the Secession

nant. Brummelkamp maintained that election determines the true seed of Abraham, the true children of believers to whom the promise is made and who alone are included in the covenant of grace. Replying on behalf of the important, early Secession Synod of Utrecht (1837) to questions raised by Hendrik de Cock, Brummelkamp said this about the holiness of children taught in 1 Corinthians 7:14 ("now are they [your children] holy"), and by implication the sanctification of children in the first question of the baptism form, and about the relation of election and covenant:

> The word "holy" used by the apostle [in] I Cor. VII:14, concerning the children of believers, has the same meaning in this passage as it does at the beginning of the epistle [in] chapter 1:2 when the apostle addresses the congregation as sanctified in Christ Jesus, called saints, since the children of the congregation as well as the adults are included in the covenant of God, and the Lord has shed His blood as well for them as for the adults and has adopted them as His children and taken them into the covenant of grace (Bel. Conf., Art. 34 and the form of infant baptism). Giving this explanation, we must at the same time observe that we most vehemently deny that we are thereby saying: *that each and every child of the congregation head for head possesses or will possess a holiness worked in their heart by the Holy Spirit* (Dutch: *eene inklevende heiligheid*), as little as we would give such an explanation concerning every one of their parents, who show themselves to us as sanctified in Christ, although we treat them as such. For not because they are produced from the congregation according to the flesh are they all children of God, but the children of the promise are the holy seed (Rom. IX:7, 8). This holy seed, as well as all the other elect, is taken into the covenant of grace, in which covenant nothing is included that is unholy.[10]

Conclusive is Brummelkamp's appeal to Romans 9:7, 8. The appeal to this passage in a discussion of the covenant promise indicates that one views the covenant, particularly the membership of children in the covenant, as governed by God's sovereign predestination. This, of course, is precisely the doctrine of the apostle in the passage.

Two synods of the Secession churches expressed the judgment of the fathers of the Secession that election governs the covenant. The first was the Synod of Utrecht (1837). Among other decisions, this synod declared that

> the children of believers are included in the covenant of God and His congregation with their parents by virtue of the promises of God. Therefore, Synod believes, with Head I, Art. 17 of the Canons of Dordt, that godly parents must be admonished not to doubt the election and salvation of their children, whom God takes away in their infancy. Therefore, Synod, with the Baptism Form, counts the children of believers to have to be regarded as members of the congregation of Christ, as heirs of the kingdom of God and of His covenant. Since, however, the Word of God plainly teaches that not all are Israel who are of Israel, and the children of the promises are counted for the seed, therefore Synod by no means regards all and every one head for head, whether children or adult confessors, as true objects of the grace of God or regenerated.

The synod added that it denied "a falling away of saints or a falling out of the covenant of grace."[11]

These statements by the Secession Synod of Utrecht express the covenant doctrine of the Protestant Reformed Churches in America.

The other synod was the Synod of Leiden (1857). This synod treated a protest against the preaching of Brummelkamp, who was universalizing the saving grace of God in Jesus Christ by a "well-meaning offer" of salvation. Significantly, the synod was compelled to declare that the three forms of unity "rejected universal atonement." But the synod also made a statement concerning the doctrine of infant baptism: "That the children of the congregation must be baptized as members; but just as not all were Israel who were of Israel, that likewise also among the children of believers there are unconverted and reprobates."[12]

From the very beginning of the Secession in 1834 through the 1840s and 1850s, the fathers of the Secession, and therefore the churches of the Secession, proclaimed a doctrine of the covenant that has the covenant governed by election (not: "oppressed by," "stifled by," "burdened with," "identified with," or any of the other pejorative phrases used by Reformed theologians who oppose this doctrine of the covenant)—election as an eternal, gracious, sovereign decree. There were other differences concerning the covenant, particularly how the holiness of the infants was to be explained. But on the vital matter, the fathers of the Secession agreed. They agreed because they read, rightly interpreted, and loved the covenant gospel of grace taught in Romans 9. E. Smilde was right when he said that the "Churches of the Secession lived in Rom. 9 and held fast the connection of election and the covenant of grace without wavering."[13]

In the 1860s, two Secession ministers, K. J. Pieters and J. R. Kreulen, introduced a radically different doctrine of the covenant. This doctrine denied any relation of election and covenant. The two ministers were so bold as to declare that every thought of election must be banished at the baptism font. This new doctrine of the covenant—new to the churches of the Secession—found a reception. This is the covenant doctrine of the Reformed Churches in the Netherlands ("liberated"). This is the covenant doctrine that now comes to full development in the heresy of the Federal Vision.

The Radical Departure of Pieters and Kreulen: Banishing Election

Pieters and Kreulen introduced into the Dutch Reformed churches of the Secession of 1834 a doctrine of the covenant that was both new to these churches and a radical departure from the accepted doctrine of the fathers of the Secession, setting forth their novel doctrine in 1861 in a book titled *Infant Baptism*.[14]

The purpose of the book and the fundamental characteristic of the covenant doctrine it advocated was the cutting loose of the covenant from God's decree of election. The book denied that election governs the covenant of grace, particularly with regard to the baptized children of believing parents. Election does not determine membership in the covenant of grace, the objects of the gracious covenant promise, inheritance of the blessings of the covenant, or abiding in the covenant so that the baptized child at last enjoys eternal life in heaven.

According to the covenant doctrine of Pieters and Kreulen, God establishes the covenant of grace with all the baptized children alike, so that all alike are in covenant communion with God. He extends his gracious covenant promise to all the children alike. All the children alike are heirs of the covenant blessings. But all the baptized children alike can fall out of the covenant, separate themselves from covenantal union with God in Christ, become objects of the dreadful curse of the covenant instead of the gracious promise, forfeit the covenant blessings, and perish everlastingly in hell.

For election does not govern the covenant.

Already on page 6 of their book, the two preachers in a denomination that was then called the Christian Separated Reformed Church[15] denied that the Reformed baptism form speaks of "an eternal covenant membership on the part of the elect, in the head, Jesus Christ," and they denied that the phrase, "sanctified in Christ" in the first question of the baptism form refers to "the elect in Christ."[16]

Election simply has no place in this supposedly Reformed doctrine of the covenant and infant baptism.

So much is this the case that when the authors were compelled by their theological foes in the churches of the Secession to reckon with the teaching of Romans 9:6–13, they explained Romans 9 in such a way that election has nothing to do with the salvation of some baptized children in distinction from others who go lost. Pieters and Kreulen posed the question this way: "Is not the universality of the promise for the entire visible church in conflict...with that which the apostle Paul teaches in Romans 9:6–13?" Their answer was that there is no conflict between the universal, gracious promise taught by themselves and the apostle's doctrine in

The Covenant Doctrine of the Fathers of the Secession

Romans 9, because "the gracious promise given by God to Abraham's seed in His covenant did not absolutely and unconditionally guarantee participation in the blessings of the covenant."[17]

The problem both for Paul and for Pieters and Kreulen was the perishing of so many Israelites in light of the covenant promise of God that he would be the God of Abraham's seed. Search the passage as they might, the two Dutch theologians could not find election in Romans 9 as the solution to the problem, although election accompanied by reprobation is the apostle's solution: "For the children being not yet born, neither having done any good or evil, that the purpose of God according to election might stand..." (v. 11). Rather, they found the solution in a conditional promise, about which the apostle says not one word. The implication is that the reason why some children of Israel were saved was not election, but their own performance of the condition upon which the promise depends for its fulfillment.

The covenant doctrine of Pieters and Kreulen utterly banished divine election from the baptism of children and therefore from the covenant. "Let us then regarding Baptism forget about eternal election and establish that the promise of the covenant is bestowed and offered as the revealed counsel of God and refers to every baptized [child] in the visible church without any exception."[18]

Universalizing Grace

The goal of this rigorous rejection of election, as also the necessary implication, was the universalizing of the grace—the *saving* grace—of the covenant. In the covenant theology of Pieters and Kreulen, God is gracious to all the baptized children alike, indeed to all the members of the visible church, including many who nevertheless perish. This doctrine is, on its very face, a contradiction of the fundamental Reformed doctrine of irresistible, or efficacious, grace, as authoritatively confessed in Heads 3 and 4 of the Canons of Dordt—the doctrine that is at the heart of the Reformed controversy with Arminianism.

Desperately trying to maintain some semblance of Reformed orthodoxy in a denomination of churches that only twenty-seven years earlier had separated and suffered on account of the gospel of sovereign grace, Pieters and Kreulen concocted a distinction between "objective" grace and "subjective" grace. "Subjective" grace, they argued, is the inner working of the Holy Spirit in one's heart. The two Dutch ministers assured their readers that they denied "subjective" grace in all baptized children.

But they vehemently affirmed an "objective" grace of God toward all baptized children without exception. Although they never defined this "objective" grace, it is clear from their writings that God's "objective" grace is his attitude, or disposition, of loving favor toward all baptized children. In this attitude of favor, God wills and desires the salvation of all children without exception. He expresses this will of salvation, and thus his "objective" grace, by promising and offering covenant salvation to all the children alike at their baptism.

God's "objective" covenant grace does more, according to Pieters and Kreulen. It bestows covenant salvation upon all the children "objectively." By the sacrament of baptism, the "objective" grace of God makes all the children heirs of the salvation that is in Christ, especially the forgiveness of sins. Those who eventually perish therefore "disinherit" themselves. They "disinherit" themselves of the inheritance of covenant salvation that had very really been theirs.

Pieters and Kreulen were bold in their assertion that the (saving) covenant grace of God in Jesus Christ, be it "objective," is toward and upon all the baptized children without exception.

Regarding the statement in the Reformed baptism form concerning the infant children of believers, "so are they again received unto grace in Christ," the two Dutch Reformed ministers insisted that the reference is to all the baptized children without exception, those who perish as well as those who are saved. They explicitly denied that this gracious reception of children is governed by "election in Christ."[19]

All of the baptized children without exception are "heirs of the kingdom of God and His covenant in this sense that they possess this [the kingdom and its riches] in the promise and one day would possess it in actuality, if they do not despise this promise by unthankfulness and thus disinherit themselves by unbelief."[20]

So rich and real is the covenant grace of God toward all baptized children, according to Pieters and Kreulen, that the wonderful blessings for which the prayer after baptism of the Reformed baptism form gives thanks to God are the possession "objectively" of all the children without exception. These are the blessings of the forgiveness of sins, reception by God through the Holy Spirit, and adoption unto children. Implied is that Christ has died for them all, for the prayer thanks God that "Thou hast forgiven us and our children all our sins *through the blood of Thy beloved Son Jesus Christ,* and received us through Thy Holy Spirit as members of Thine only begotten Son, and adopted us to be Thy children."[21] In this prayer the congregation thanks God "for the benefits which the Lord *objectively* gave and promised to her and to her children in His covenant." Pieters and Kreulen meant *all* of the baptized children of the congregation without exception.[22]

As circumcision testified to all Israelites in the Old Testament, Esau as well as Jacob, so baptism seals and assures to all baptized children without exception that God "will[s] to give them... the benefits of salvation."[23]

Resistible Grace

Although the covenant grace of Pieters and Kreulen is very broad—universal within the visible church—it is strikingly, and ominously, ineffectual. It assures the salvation of no one. Many baptized children to whom God is thus gracious lose this grace, fall out of the covenant of grace, and "disinherit" themselves of the riches of salvation bestowed on them by the gracious promise. Even though, in the language of the prayer after baptism of the Reformed baptism form (which Pieters and Kreulen applied to all baptized children), God forgave all their sins through the blood of His Son Jesus Christ, they perish everlastingly in hell.

A Conditional Covenant

The reason for this resistible grace and lack of assurance, according to the covenant doctrine of Pieters and Kreulen, is that the covenant, the covenant promise, membership in the covenant, and covenant salvation are conditional. They themselves raised the question "Why," in view of the universality of the covenant promises, "does it then happen that the great promises which are signified and sealed by Baptism remain unfulfilled in the majority of those who are baptized?" Their answer was the conditionality of all the promises:

> The cause why this is the case [namely, that the covenant promises go unfulfilled most of the time] must absolutely not be sought in this, as if on God's part the promises were given to the one and not to the other. But the cause is found in this, that the divine promises are not given, signified, and sealed *unconditionally* in Baptism.

The condition is the "demand" upon the baptized child that he believe and repent. "Without this [the performance by the child of the demanded condition], God is not held to His promises, to fulfill them."[24]

Significantly, Pieters and Kreulen declared that conditionality is the very "nature of the covenant."[25] Since the covenant with believers and their seed is essentially the same as the covenant with Abraham, also Jehovah's covenant with Abraham was conditional. "This promise [to Abraham in Genesis 17:7]: I am your God and the God of your seed...as a *covenant promise* include[d] a demand and condition... [It

The Covenant Doctrine of the Fathers of the Secession

was not] *absolute,* so that it had to be fulfilled in Abraham's descendants..."[26] For Pieters and Kreulen, the covenant was a contract between God and Abraham, between God and the believer, and between God and the baptized child—*every baptized* child—consisting of the conditional promise on God's part and faith as the demanded condition on the child's part. And the fulfillment of the promise depended upon the performance of the condition.

A few years after the publication of his and Kreulen's book *Infant Baptism,* Dominie Pieters wrote a series of articles in *De Bazuin,* magazine of the churches of the Secession, on the meaning of baptism according to Question and Answer 69 of the Heidelberg Catechism. In this explanation of the Catechism, Pieters taught that all baptized children alike are "in God's covenant of grace...according to God's gracious ordinance." In his grace to all the children, God promises salvation to all the children alike "without distinction and without reservation." "God," Pieters continued, is "faithful and true," so that he "does not speak empty words, but always surely and certainly fulfills what He promises, *unless the baptized child upon growing up despises and rejects this divine promise by willful unbelief.*"[27]

The covenant promise of God often goes unfulfilled!

In all these instances, God does *not* "surely and certainly" perform what he promises!

By his failure to fulfill his promise, he shows himself unfaithful and false!

The reason for this appalling state of divine affairs is that in the covenant the saving grace of God in Jesus Christ is conditional. Salvation in the covenant depends not upon the electing God, but upon the willing sinner—in this case, a totally depraved infant child.

This is the Arminian heresy, condemned as heresy once and for all by the Synod of Dordt, applied to the covenant.

Pieters and Kreulen themselves recognized that their covenant doctrine inevitably drew the charge of "Remonstrantism," or Arminianism. They attempted to ward off the charge by distinguishing "condition" in their covenant doctrine from "condition" in Arminian theology. They contended that in their theology of the covenant, "condition" is merely the means by which the covenant child receives salvation. They added that it is the grace of God that enables a child to perform the condition.

> Does someone say, in this manner there comes a condition into the covenant of grace, without which one does not become a partaker of the salvation promised in the covenant? Be it so, still the question really is, what does one here understand by a condition? If you take this word in a legal sense for something that man does by his own power, something that gives him a merit, upon which and because of which he would become partaker of the benefit contained in the covenant of grace, who would then give his assent to such an idea? But if one understands by a condition the means that God ordained by which man becomes partaker of the salvation of the covenant in God's way, and without which he shall never enjoy this [salvation], then faith is surely a condition in the sense of the means by which (not: because of which or on the basis of which) the member of the covenant becomes partaker of the blessings of the covenant of grace. It is only in this sense that we believe and teach, as the Reformed church has always done, that faith is the condition of the covenant of grace.[28]

It is true that orthodox Reformed theologians have referred to faith as the "condition" in the covenant, although the three forms of unity, which were the creeds of Pieters and Kreulen, not only do not speak of faith as a "condition," but also explicitly reject this teaching. The Canons of Dordt deny that faith is a condition either of election or of salvation. When orthodox Reformed theologians spoke of faith as the "condition" in the covenant, they meant that faith is the means by which God realizes his covenant promise to the elect and by which he gives the elect the blessings and salvation of the covenant.

But it is false that in the covenant theology of Pieters and Kreulen "condition" functions only as a means. On the contrary, "condition" functions radically differently from a means. In the covenant theology of Pieters and Kreulen, the condition (which is faith) renders a general, or common, or

The Covenant Doctrine of the Fathers of the Secession

universal, gracious promise, effectual in a few children. It is the reason why some remain in the covenant in distinction from many others who fall out of the covenant and fall away, and it accounts for the salvation of some, in the context of a gracious will or desire of God for the salvation of all.

In the covenant theology of Pieters and Kreulen, as in that of the Reformed Churches in the Netherlands ("liberated"), the Canadian Reformed Churches, and the men of the Federal Vision, covenant grace, which is wider than election and indeed cut loose from election altogether, becomes effectual in the salvation of baptized children not by the efficacious power of the grace itself, but by the performance of a condition by the child. Thus, the covenant, the covenant promise, and covenant salvation do, in fact, *depend upon* the condition, that is, upon the will and work of the child.

It makes absolutely no difference whether the child performs the condition in his own strength or with the help of God's grace. In both cases, the covenant depends upon the will and work of man.

In his biography of Anthony Brummelkamp, Melis te Velde notes that critics of Pieters and Kreulen in the churches of the Secession condemned the doctrine of the covenant of the two ministers as "attributing a decisive role to the believing of man," which is "Remonstrantism."[29] The critics were right.

Orthodox Reformed covenant theology, that is, a covenant theology that is faithful to the truth of sovereign grace as confessed by the Canons of Dordt, holds that God has a favorable covenantal attitude toward ("objective" grace) and works his covenantal salvation within ("subjective" grace) the elect children of godly parents. The means by which they know his favor and receive his saving operations is faith, which is itself a benefit of the covenant promise and is worked in them by sovereign, particular covenant grace.

The covenant does not depend on the will of the covenant child, whether with or without the help of grace. Rather, the covenant depends squarely and wholly on the electing God.

The covenant is a covenant of *grace*.

It is not a covenant of *condition*.

"A New Opinion"

"Liberated" Reformed theologian C. Veenhof acknowledged that "with the publication of their book, the two Frisian preachers [Pieters and Kreulen] ... opposed Van Velzen concerning the doctrine of covenant and baptism."[30] But Van Velzen's doctrine of covenant and baptism was that of the fathers of the Secession, and, therefore, that of the churches of the Secession for almost thirty years, from the very beginning of the Secession.

A colleague of the two ministers, H. Joffers, opposed the covenant doctrine of Pieters and Kreulen and charged that it was "a new opinion" in the churches of the Secession. The reason for his own book on infant baptism, he informed his readers, was that

> in recent years a new opinion about infant baptism and the [Reformed Baptism] form has surfaced in our church [the Christian Separated Reformed Church], namely, that all children at baptism are objectively in the covenant of grace, which pernicious opinion seeks to rob the parents of the comfort and certainty that they are able to have from the baptism of their children.[31]

Joffers referred, of course, to the covenant doctrine of Pieters and Kreulen, recently introduced into the churches of the Secession by their book *Infant Baptism*.

Readers might have challenged Joffers' charge that the covenant doctrine of Pieters and Kreulen was "pernicious," but Joffers was confident that none could challenge his description of the covenant doctrine of his two colleagues as a "*new* opinion" in the churches of the Secession.

In the person of Simon Van Velzen (Hendrik de Cock was dead by this time), the fathers of the Secession defended their and the churches' covenant doctrine, and condemned the novel view of Pieters and Kreulen. The doctrine of the covenant of Rev. Pieters and Rev. Kreulen, wrote Prof. Van Velzen, is "in conflict with all our godly fathers, in conflict with the confession of the church, and in conflict with the Holy Scripture."[32]

Covenant and Election

Writing in the January 20, 1865, issue of the magazine of the Secession churches, *De Bazuin*, Van Velzen grounded the covenant of grace in an eternal "covenant of redemption" between the Father and the Son. Van Velzen's understanding of the source in eternity of the covenant of grace is not now our concern. What is important is Van Velzen's insistence that there is in eternity "a covenant between Jehovah and the Lord Jesus...concerning the elect" and that this eternal covenant is the "origin" and "ground" of the covenant of grace in history. Since the covenant of grace originates in this eternal covenant, the covenant of grace is with the elect and with the elect only.

> The covenant of grace and our covenant relation with God in Christ have their origin and their ground in this covenant of redemption between God and Christ. From this proceeds the beginning, continuance, and end of the salvation of men. Before one existed, before the gospel was preached to him, it was already decreed and arranged in this covenant when he would be born, when and by what means he would be delivered [from sin], how much grace, comfort, and holiness, how much and what kind of strife and cross he would have in this life—all of this was decreed and comes to each one from this covenant. The elect have then, on the one hand, to do nothing and let the Lord work...By the power of this covenant, the Lord Jesus is the one who carries out the salvation of the elect.[33]

Although Van Velzen did not mention Pieters and Kreulen, there can be no doubt that he was opposing the covenant doctrine they had introduced four years earlier in the book *Infant Baptism*. Van Velzen was defending the orthodox doctrine that eternal election, which was reflected in, and virtually identical with, the eternal "covenant of redemption," is the source and ground of the covenant of grace. Van Velzen was earnestly contending that the covenant of grace with believers and their children is governed by election.

> Here a matchless love reveals itself, which surpasses all understanding. In this covenant [of redemption in eternity], to be known and thought of; to be given by the Father to the Son; to be written by the Son in His book; to be an object of the eternal, mutual delight between the Father and Christ to save you—that is blessedness! that is a wonder! Here was no foreseen faith, no good works, by which the parties were moved to think of certain persons in this covenant. Here was no necessity, no constraint, but only eternal love and sovereignty. "Yea, I have loved thee with an everlasting love" (Jer. 31:3).[34]

Baptism as a Certain Seal

In the same issue of the magazine, Van Velzen condemned Pieters and Kreulen—his colleagues in the ministry in the churches of the Secession—by name. Van Velzen used his editorial prerogative to give a running criticism of an article by K. J. Pieters on infant baptism and the covenant. In one of his long editorial comments, Van Velzen expanded the scope of his criticism to include the book that Pieters had written with J. R. Kreulen. Because of their insistence that baptism is a sign and seal of God's grace and salvation for all the baptized children alike, Pieters and Kreulen were forced to weaken drastically the significance of baptism. They had written that in the baptism of infants Christ merely testifies that all the children "can find in Me a rich righteousness, salvation, and honor in the way of faith."

Van Velzen responded:

> "Can find...in the way of faith?"! Merely this? The believer says more, much more. As certainly as our children have been washed

with water, they have the forgiveness of sins, for to them is promised redemption from sins by the blood of Christ, no less than to the adults (Heid. Cat., Q. 74)...Therefore they ought to receive the sign and the sacrament of that which Christ has done for them (Bel. Conf., Art. 34).[35]

Those who deny that election governs the covenant are forced to view the baptism of infants as an uncertain sign of what the Savior is willing to let the children do ("find in Me a rich righteousness," etc.), rather than as the sure sign of what Christ has done and will do for the children, namely, shed his blood for them, forgive their sins, and sanctify them unto life eternal.

Turning his attention back to Pieters' article in *De Bazuin*, Van Velzen answered Pieters' charge that those who maintain that the true covenant children are the elect children of believers strip the sacrament of its meaning in the case of the other children who are baptized. Without naming him, Pieters had directed this charge against Van Velzen, editor of the magazine in which he made the charge. Pieters wrote: "Most administrations of Baptism happen to those who are no members of the covenant [by election, on the view of Van Velzen]. What then does Baptism signify and seal regarding them? Must not the answer to this question be, 'Nothing, absolutely nothing'?"

Van Velzen's answer was brief and conclusive:

> What Baptism signifies and seals to those who are no members of the covenant? It is the same in this case as with the Lord's Supper. "The ungodly indeed receives the Sacrament to his condemnation, but he doth not receive the truth of the Sacrament" (Bel. Conf., Art. 35).[36]

A "Common and Powerless Grace"

Striking to the very heart of the error of Pieters' conditional covenant with all the baptized children alike, Van Velzen charged that Pieters' covenant doctrine made the covenant promise of God false and ineffectual. In the words of the apostle in Romans 9:6, in Pieters' doctrine "the word of God hath taken none effect." For Pieters taught that God promises the forgiveness of sins and eternal life to all the baptized children without exception. Regardless of this promise, however, many of the children perish, unforgiven and damned.

Van Velzen contended for a true and effectual promise—a promise that *saves,* a promise that God not only makes, but also *keeps.*

> If God gives them this promise, a promise that is not empty and useless, then He will not impute their sins to them, then they have forgiveness with Him, and they are partakers in "the strongest sense of the word" of saving grace [Pieters had suggested understanding the grace promised to all the children in a strange, obscure, weak sense—DJE].[37]

Closely related to Van Velzen's objection to the false and impotent promise of Pieters' conditional covenant was Van Velzen's condemnation of Pieters' doctrine of covenant grace. Pieters taught that God is gracious to every child at baptism. Because this covenant grace is conditional, it fails to save many of the children. Covenant grace can be lost. Covenant children can very really fall away from the grace of God in Jesus Christ once bestowed upon them. In what was a damning indictment of the new doctrine of the covenant in the churches of the Secession, Van Velzen condemned it as a doctrine of a "common and powerless grace."[38] The indictment was damning because the doctrine of common, resistible grace was the heart of the Arminian heresy condemned by the Canons of Dordt, official and beloved creed of the Christian Separated Reformed Church.

This father of the Secession saw clearly the implications of Pieters' and Kreulen's doctrine of a gracious, conditional covenant promise of salvation to all the children alike. At the conclusion of Pieters' series on baptism and the covenant in *De Bazuin,* Van Velzen summed up Pieters' doctrine this way:

The Covenant Doctrine of the Fathers of the Secession

> In Baptism, the forgiveness of sins is promised to the entire visible church, to all the members of the visible church without distinction, to children and adults, head for head. In the promise, the benefits of salvation are given to each and every one of them. But the promise of forgiveness and of the other benefits is not saving.

Van Velzen added this ominous prophecy:

> It is easy to perceive that this opinion must have great influence on the preaching and that by necessary logical consequence the idea of the covenant of redemption, election and reprobation, limited atonement, and such truths [the doctrines of grace as confessed in the Canons of Dordt] must undergo enormous change.[39]

Van Velzen's prophecy has been fulfilled in all the Reformed churches that have embraced Pieters and Kreulen's doctrine of a conditional covenant of grace with all the children alike. The preaching does not magnify the sovereign grace of God in the salvation of the covenant children. It proclaims a grace for all the children alike that does not save, but merely makes salvation possible. Refusing to find the source and ground of the covenant of grace in election, it necessarily finds the source of the covenant in a will of God for the salvation of all, and the ground in the faith and obedience of the children.

That these churches are well aware of their apostasy from the Reformed and biblical truth of sovereign grace is evident from their readiness to strike out against the preaching of sovereign grace in the covenant with the slander "hyper-Calvinism!"

The prophecy of the father of the Secession is fulfilled with a vengeance today in the theology and preaching of the Federal [Covenant] Vision. The men of the Federal Vision openly teach justification by faith and works and the doctrine of universal, resistible, losable grace—*in the covenant.*

Their heresy is the necessary development of the doctrine

of a conditional covenant that cuts the covenant loose from God's election.

That was the covenant doctrine of K. J. Pieters and J. R. Kreulen.

It was emphatically *not* the doctrine of the covenant of the fathers of the Secession of 1834.

Simon Van Velzen was not the only minister in the churches of the Secession to oppose the new covenant doctrine of Pieters and Kreulen. Joffers, a younger colleague who had embraced the doctrine of the covenant of the fathers of the Secession and was zealous for the gospel of grace also condemned Pieters and Kreulen's covenant doctrine as heretical. While minister of the Christian Separated [Dutch: *Afgescheidene*] Reformed Church at 's Gravenhage, Joffers criticized the doctrine of Pieters and Kreulen in a little book titled *De Kinderdoop, met zijn Grond en Vrucht* (Infant Baptism with its Ground and Fruit).

With reference to the teaching of Pieters and Kreulen that many children to whom God makes his gracious, solemn promise of salvation are, in fact, not saved by the promise, Joffers charged that "these expositors fall into one of these two evils: [either] that God has bound the blessings of the covenant to conditions; or that these expositors present God as a deceiver, who promises something to many, but does not give [it to them]."[40]

To Joffers, as to the fathers of the Secession, the teaching that the covenant depends upon conditions was as grievous an evil as making God a deceiver.

Joffers pointed out that the doctrine of Pieters and Kreulen implied the falling away of those who were once in the covenant:

> According to their view, members of the covenant fall out of the covenant and perish, which is not possible according to Isaiah 54:10, "For the mountains shall depart, and the hills be removed; but my kindness shall not depart from thee, neither shall the covenant of my peace be removed, saith the LORD that hath mercy on thee."[41]

The Covenant Doctrine of the Fathers of the Secession

Fundamental in the controversy over the covenant in the churches of the Secession, as it is fundamental in the controversy over the covenant in Reformed churches today, was the explanation of the phrase in the Reformed baptism form, "our children...are sanctified in Christ." With all defenders of a conditional covenant, that is, a covenant that is not governed by election, Pieters and Kreulen explained the phrase as referring to all baptized children without exception. The holiness, therefore, cannot be the inner cleansing and consecration to God worked in the hearts of the infants by the Holy Spirit. Nor can it be the unique covenant holiness of the elect children in Jesus Christ, their head, as Van Velzen taught. Nevertheless, it is a real covenant holiness bestowed upon every baptized child by virtue of the gracious covenant promise. Therefore, according to the covenant doctrine of Pieters and Kreulen, it is a covenant blessing that can be lost. Pieters and Kreulen called this an "objective" holiness.

Joffers charged that this explanation of the first question of the baptism form sins against the firmness of the covenant of grace and therefore against the faithfulness of the covenant God, for "an *objective* holiness that can be lost contradicts the firmness of the covenant of grace, according to Isaiah 54:10."[42]

Joffers condemned as heresy the covenant doctrine of his two colleagues, which suspended the covenant and its salvation on conditions, taught the falling away of saints, and made God a liar. The covenant doctrine of Pieters and Kreulen, wrote Joffers, is "something new, introduced by the devil, and [it] opens the way to a real and total apostasy from the covenant of grace, which is impossible according to Is. 54:10 and Jer. 31:33."[43]

What especially distressed Joffers was that the covenant doctrine of the two ministers robbed God's people of all comfort of salvation. It did so, particularly, by explaining the second principal part of the Reformed baptism form as referring merely to an objective covenant salvation. The determination of Pieters and Kreulen that the covenant not be governed by election forced them to explain the second principal part of the doctrine of baptism in the Reformed baptism form as teaching that baptism merely seals to all baptized persons, adults as well as infants, an *objective* membership in the covenant, an *objective* redemption, and an *objective* sanctification. But these "objective" blessings of the covenant are non-saving and losable. In the theology of the two Dutch ministers, baptism no longer functioned to seal covenant salvation to anyone, infant or adult. Baptism was no longer a means to give precious assurance of covenant salvation in the *experience* of the believer and the child of the believer.

Against this destruction of the assurance of salvation in the covenant, Joffers responded with indignation, comparing the covenant theology of Pieters and Kreulen to the mouth of Nebuchadnezzar's fiery furnace.

> That view [of the covenant] yawns wider than the furnace of Nebuchadnezzar, through the mouth of which the three young men were thrown into the fire of that fiery furnace. For according to their view, they throw the members of the covenant through the door of "objective" out of the right to life, out of life itself, and out of the possession of any blessings of salvation into or under the wrath of God.[44]

Let no one miss the significance of this objection. Every doctrine of the covenant that separates the covenant from election makes assurance of salvation impossible for the baptized members of the covenant. Only election affords assurance of salvation.

Joffers warned his two colleagues "that they not continue with such a way of treating [baptism and the covenant], so that it not happen to them that they be killed by the fire of God's wrath, as happened to those men who threw the three young men into the fiery furnace and were killed by the sparks of that fire."[45]

In a devastating paragraph, Joffers responded to the mockery of Pieters and Kreulen that the covenant doctrine of Joffers and Van Velzen was hardly a "hundred years old." Suppose this is true, said Joffers;

The Covenant Doctrine of the Fathers of the Secession

then they [Pieters and Kreulen] are still obliged to acknowledge that that view is a hundred years older than their "objective" view, which [Pieters and Kreulen] have drawn from their novelty-producing pen now four years ago [with the publication of their book, Infant Baptism]. They are also obliged to acknowledge that the view which they mock has more support in the history of the church than their "objective" view. For that view, that all baptized children of the church are "objectively" in the covenant of grace, is an "unchurchly" and unbiblical doctrine.[46]

No one could deny that the covenant doctrine of Pieters and Kreulen was a new doctrine in the churches of the Secession, indeed a new doctrine in the tradition of the Reformed churches in the Netherlands.

The main purpose of Joffers' book was not the exposure of the false doctrine of Pieters and Kreulen. The main purpose was a positive explanation of the orthodox, biblical, and Reformed doctrine of infant baptism and the covenant. Joffers was defending the doctrine of the fathers of the Secession.

Fundamental to this doctrine is the close relation between covenant and election.

> The covenant... is secured to eternal election as is evident from Rom. XI:7, "What then? Israel hath not obtained that which he seeketh for; but the election hath obtained it, and the rest were blinded."[47]
>
> The covenant of grace is established by God with the elect, with them alone, emphatically with them alone.[48]
>
> The non-elect have no part in the covenant of grace.[49]

"Secured to eternal election," the covenant is unconditional, that is, does not depend upon the faith and obedience of the baptized child.

> Against [the teaching that God makes His covenant conditionally with all the baptized children], we assert that God has not made the covenant of grace with man under conditions, properly so called, or that this covenant depends upon the faith and conversion of man. Rather, God has established His covenant of grace

with the elect without conditions, properly so called, and promises unilaterally to give everything that is promised in the covenant of grace as pure grace.[50]

Especially dear to the heart of Joffers was the truth that the promise of the covenant is certain and trustworthy to every one to whom God makes the promise.

> Everything He promised, He gives. To this, the elect assent in the time of love, and this assent the Lord has promised, and that He will operate upon the hearts of the elect to this end, as is written in Jer. XXXI:33, "But this shall be the covenant that I will make with the house of Israel; After those days, saith the LORD, I will put my law in their inward parts, and write it in their hearts; and will be their God, and they shall be my people." This operation upon the heart unto the assent to, or reception of, the covenant of grace and its promise God promises and gives, not to the entire [nation of] Israel and their children head for head; nor does God promise and give this to the entire, external, evangelical church with their children. But God promises and gives that only to His elect, who are the "children of the promise, who are counted for the seed," according to Rom. IX:8.[51]

This doctrine of the covenant assures every member of the covenant, in whom the promise of the covenant creates a true and living faith in the promising God, that he or she will be preserved unto everlasting life. There is no falling out of the covenant, no falling away of covenant saints unto perdition.

> As certainly as the fire of the furnace of Nebuchadnezzar had no power upon the three young men, to destroy them, so certainly also has the fire of God's wrath lost its power upon the baptized children who are in the covenant of grace, so that it cannot destroy them to all eternity.[52]

Joffers presented his view of infant baptism and the covenant as the prevailing, if not the *only* doctrine of the churches of the Secession prior to the publication of the book by Pieters and Kreulen in 1861. He had no doubt that his readers would acknowledge this, including Pieters and Kreulen.

Nevertheless, Joffers recognized the popularity of the doctrine he was opposing. In the brief period of four years, "that view has much influence in our church."[53] Joffers expected strong opposition to his doctrine: "Although I have fully anticipated that my view, set forth in this little work, will meet with much opposition and many adversaries in our church at first, nevertheless this has not deterred me from responding to the pernicious view referred to [that of Pieters and Kreulen]."[54]

Joffers was hopeful regarding the doctrine of an unconditional covenant of grace, which has its source in and is governed by God's eternal election of grace: "[I] expect that my view will remain standing firm in God's church."[55]

God has not put his expectation to shame. The covenant doctrine of the fathers of the Secession has always been maintained in the Reformed churches of the Dutch tradition. That it remained the dominant view in the Dutch Reformed churches standing in the tradition of the Secession is plain from Herman Bavinck's treatment of the covenant in his *Reformed Dogmatics*.[56] It is boldly and joyfully confessed today by the Protestant Reformed Churches in America.

Opposition to the new covenant doctrine of Pieters and Kreulen was not limited to a war of books and magazines. A ruling elder in the churches of the Secession, named G. Vos, protested the doctrine of his colleagues in the ministry to a Secession synod. This was the Synod of Franeker (1863).

Vos' protest charged the two Dutch preachers with "heterodoxy" in their book on infant baptism and the covenant. Their doctrine of a covenant of grace with all baptized children alike, dependent on a condition the children must perform, was, in Vos' judgment, a denial of the gospel of grace: "I may not tolerate that grace must be bought from God by a condition, and, therefore, the covenant of grace is to be compared with a business contract for buying a house or some other property."[57]

The Synod of Franeker rejected Vos' protest. By no means, however, did it enthusiastically adopt the covenant doctrine of Pieters and Kreulen. Deliberately it cautioned the members of the Secession churches that it did not want to be judged as holding that the covenant doctrine of Pieters and Kreulen "is in all respects the most correct expression of the sentiments of the Reformed Church." Nevertheless, the synod decided that it "is not able to condemn the brothers [Pieters and Kreulen] as being in conflict with the confessions of the Church."[58]

E. Smilde was right that this synodical decision was a "compromise."[59]

"Liberated" Reformed theologian C. Veenhof was also right that the decision recognized the new covenant doctrine of Pieters and Kreulen as "confessional."[60]

The compromise-decision of the Synod of Franeker, no doubt taken in the interests of peace in the churches—always a powerful force at the major assemblies—was destructive. It sanctioned a doctrine of the covenant that cut the covenant, the covenant promise, covenant grace, covenant perseverance, covenant salvation, and the covenant faithfulness of God loose from election. It set the covenant on the basis of children's performance of a condition.

By refusing to judge between the two radically different and mutually antagonistic conceptions of the covenant, it opened up the Reformed churches to fierce controversies and agonizing schisms. One thinks of the schism in the Reformed Churches in the Netherlands in the 1940s and of the schism in the Protestant Reformed Churches in the 1950s.

By tolerating, if not approving, the conditional covenant doctrine, it paved the way to the heresy of the Federal Vision, which denies justification by faith alone and all the doctrines of grace as confessed by the Canons of Dordt, now troubling many of the Reformed and Presbyterian churches in North America.

In the minutes of the Franeker Synod, "father" Van Velzen had recorded that the decision of synod on "this weighty matter" was contrary to his advice. Joffers saw to it that the minutes contained the notation that he "protests against the [decision of synod], that a little book with a strange doctrine, which...is in conflict with the first question of the Baptism form concerning the infant children of believers, shall be tolerated in our Church."[61]

As is invariably the case with compromising major assemblies—miserable creatures!—the Synod of Franeker neither settled a fundamental doctrinal issue (as synods are duty-bound to do), nor brought peace to the churches (as synods are peculiarly privileged to do). The strife over infant baptism and the covenant continued unabated, as is evident from the fact that the articles by Pieters and Van Velzen in *De Bazuin* and the little book by H. Joffers appeared *after* the decision of the Synod of Franeker in 1863.

The issue of infant baptism and the covenant appeared again on the agenda of the Synod of Amsterdam in 1866. The Reformed churches of North Holland overtured that "synod declare itself concerning the doctrine and practice of Holy Baptism, so that there come an end to the strife between its objective and subjective meaning and sealing."[62]

Unable to reach agreement and unwilling to decide between the two opposing views, the Synod of Amsterdam contented itself with a decision that called on all the ministers to restrict themselves to the language of the confessions in treating of infant baptism and the covenant.

How unsatisfactory, indeed impossible, this decision actually was appears in the treatment of it by the "liberated" theologian C. Veenhof. He celebrates the decision as allowing both of the conflicting doctrines a place in the Reformed churches, whereupon he promptly interprets the language of the confessions as teaching a gracious, conditional covenant promise to all, that is, the covenant doctrine of Pieters and Kreulen.[63]

Scholars of the Secession of 1834 have spoken of the "tragedy of the Secession." They referred to the doctrinal controversies that racked the Secession churches.

The scholars are mistaken. The controversies were not a tragedy. They were the necessary, if painful, struggles of living churches, recently brought to life out of the spiritual death of Arminianism and modernism, growing to maturity and developing in the "knowledge of the Son of God" (Eph. 4:13).

There was a "tragedy of the Secession." The tragedy was that churches born of the gospel of sovereign, particular grace were so soon bewitched by a doctrine of the covenant that made the grace of God powerless, the will of man decisive, salvation uncertain, and the promising God deceptive.

The tragedy was the acceptance of the conditional covenant doctrine of Pieters and Kreulen.

Upheld and Confessed Today

"[I] expect that my view [of the covenant of grace] will remain standing firm in God's church," wrote Christelijke Afgescheidene Gereformeerde Kerk minister H. Joffers in his defense of the doctrine of the covenant of the fathers of the Secession in 1865.[64]

Christ has not put the hope of the fiery defender of sovereign grace to shame.

The doctrine of the covenant of the fathers of the Secession, particularly Hendrik de Cock and Simon Van Velzen, is confessed today by the Protestant Reformed Churches.

God's eternal, gracious decree of election, accompanied by the just decree of reprobation, governs the covenant of grace with believers and their children, as it governed (and still governs) the covenant with Abraham and his seed, being one and the same covenant. Election is the source of the covenant of grace, of the gracious covenant promise, of the bestowal of all the blessings of the covenant, of covenant salvation, and of the preservation of covenant saints.

Accordingly, the covenant grace of God in Jesus Christ is particular and irresistible, or efficacious. God's grace in the covenant is not universal, that is, wider than election, which is the source of covenant grace, or more extensive than the cross of Christ, which is the judicial ground of the covenant.

The Covenant Doctrine of the Fathers of the Secession

The grace of the covenant is not resistible and losable, as it must be if it is universal in the sphere of the covenant. Because the covenant has its source in election and is governed by election, the covenant is unconditional. For its establishment, maintenance, and perfection, it depends upon the almighty grace of God in Jesus Christ. The covenant does not depend upon the will, work, or worth of the baptized child, whether the will, work, or worth of the child is aided by grace or is the child's own unaided contribution.

The faith of the covenant child is certainly the necessary means by which the child receives and enjoys the covenant and its blessings, as it is the power of the demanded covenant life of obedience. But faith is the gift of God in the covenant, with regard both to the power of faith and to the activity of faith (Canons of Dordt, Heads 3 and 4, Art. 14). This gift of faith to the child is determined by predestination (Acts 13:48; Canons of Dordt, Head 1, Art. 6).

The faith of a baptized child does not make covenant grace, supposedly offered to all alike and even bestowed on all alike, effectual in some. The faith of a child is not the cause of the *fulfillment* in a few of a promise supposedly *made* to all the children alike. The faith of a child is not the reason why some children remain in the covenant in distinction from others, who once were in the covenant as truly as those who abide, but eventually fall out of the covenant.

On such a view, faith is a human work upon which the covenant, indeed the covenant God himself, depends. And the inheritance and salvation of the covenant are, in fact, of him that runs and wills, rather than solely of God who shows mercy (Rom. 9:16).

Official Condemnation of the Doctrine of Pieters and Kreulen

Publicly, officially, decisively, and at huge cost of reproach, scorn, and exclusion in the Reformed community (not unlike the reproach borne by the Secession in its early days), the Protestant Reformed Churches have rejected the doctrine of a conditional covenant made in grace with all the children of believing parents alike. Thus, the churches have maintained the covenant doctrine of the fathers of the Secession.

They rejected the doctrine of conditional, resistible covenant grace to all the baptized children alike, first, in their repudiation of the well-meant offer of the gospel in 1924. The "well-meant offer" of Christ as adopted by the Christian Reformed Church was the doctrine of preaching that arose out of Christian Reformed theologian Prof. William Heyns' teaching of a covenant grace of God towards and in all baptized children without exception. Repudiating the well-meant offer—the doctrine that God is gracious in the preaching to all hearers without exception, that is, the doctrine that election does not govern the preaching of the gospel—the Protestant Reformed Churches also, in fact, rejected the doctrine of universal, conditional, resistible grace in the sphere of the covenant. As the history of the Secession of 1834 illustrates, the doctrine of a well-meant offer and the doctrine of conditional grace to all baptized children go hand in hand.

The Protestant Reformed Churches rejected the doctrine of a conditional covenant a second time in 1951. This rejection was explicit. It had to be explicit, for just as in the churches of the Secession in the early 1860s, some ministers within the churches themselves introduced the new and different doctrine of a covenant cut loose from election. Unlike the churches of the Secession at their synods of Franeker (1863) and Amsterdam (1866), the Protestant Reformed Churches responded to the erroneous teaching as a Reformed denomination confessing the Canons of Dordt is bound to do. By synodical decision they condemned the doctrine of a divine covenant dependent on human conditions as contrary to the Reformed creeds, including the Reformed Form for the Administration of Baptism. They affirmed the covenant gospel of sovereign, particular grace.

The Protestant Reformed Synod of 1951 adopted a statement that simply applied the teaching of the three forms of

The Covenant Doctrine of the Fathers of the Secession

unity and the baptism form to the controverted issue of the covenant. The statement is titled "Declaration of Principles of the Protestant Reformed Churches." The Declaration affirms that "all the covenant blessings are for the elect alone" and that "God's promise is unconditionally for them only: for God cannot promise what was not objectively merited by Christ."[65] The Declaration denies that "the promise of the covenant is conditional and for all that are baptized."[66]

The covenant doctrine that the Protestant Reformed Churches repudiated in 1951 was that of the Reformed Churches in the Netherlands ("liberated"). Ministers in the Protestant Reformed Churches had become enamored of the doctrine of the covenant taught by K. Schilder, B. Holwerda, and C. Veenhof. But the covenant doctrine of the "liberated" Reformed was, and is, that of the Secession ministers Pieters and Kreulen. This is the case not only because all forms of covenant doctrine that cut the covenant loose from election are essentially one and the same, but also because the "liberated" Reformed theologians deliberately patterned their doctrine of the covenant after that put forward by Pieters and Kreulen in their book on the covenant and infant baptism in 1861. Veenhof, leading architect of the doctrine of the covenant of the "liberated" Reformed, tells us this: "[The 'liberated' doctrine of the covenant] was drawn up in conscious connection with that which was taught by men such as Pieters and Kreulen..."[67]

Indeed, "drawn up in...connection with" fails to do justice to the dependency of the "liberated" doctrine of the covenant upon Pieters and Kreulen. One who has read Pieters and Kreulen's *De Kinderdoop* (Infant Baptism) concludes that the "liberated" Reformed theologians simply made Pieters and Kreulen's doctrine their own.

The dominant feature of the "liberated" doctrine, like that of the doctrine of the two Secession ministers, is its cutting loose of the covenant from election. It was the avowed purpose of the "liberated" Reformed theologians that election *not* govern the covenant of grace. "With regard to what was taught [by the Reformed Churches in the Netherlands ("liberated")] concerning covenant, covenant promise, and Baptism, very consciously this was *not* placed under the control of election."[68]

All of the other elements of the doctrine of Pieters and Kreulen make up the doctrine of the covenant of the "liberated" Reformed: a gracious promise to all the children alike, dependent for its realization upon the condition of faith; the failure of the promising God to keep his promise in many instances, because of the failure of the children to perform their condition; a covenant grace to every baptized child without exception, which grace can be resisted and lost; the bestowal of covenant blessings upon all the children at baptism, which blessings can be lost; the very real possibility of apostasy from the covenant in which one was once included as truly as were those who persevere unto eternal life; and even the characteristic attack on the teaching that God establishes his covenant with Christ as head of the covenant and the elect in him, consisting of the charge that this doctrine robs baptism of its meaning in the case of reprobate children.

By the Protestant Reformed condemnation of the conditional covenant doctrine of the "liberated" Reformed Churches, therefore, Reformed churches carrying on the tradition of the Secession of 1834 condemned the covenant doctrine of Pieters and Kreulen as contrary to the Reformed confessions. What the Secession churches failed to do at their synods of 1863 and 1866, the Protestant Reformed Churches did in 1951.

Election and Covenant in Light of the Federal Vision

The fundamental issue between the two contending covenant doctrines in the Dutch Reformed tradition, indeed in the history of Reformed Christianity from Calvin and Bullinger to the present day, is not, as Veenhof thought, the conditionality or unconditionality of the covenant promise: "the central question, namely, the nature of the covenant promise [whether conditional or unconditional]."[69]

The nature of the covenant promise—whether a gracious, conditional, resistible promise to all the children alike, or a gracious, unconditional promise to the elect children only that effectually realizes itself in all to whom God makes it—is indeed important. The promise of the covenant is a chief concern of the Declaration of Principles, just as it is a great concern of the apostle in Romans 9:6–29, that the word of God's covenant promise to Abraham and his seed not be ineffectual in any to whom it referred: "Not as though the word of God hath taken none effect."

Nevertheless, the fundamental issue in the controversy between the two contending doctrines of the covenant is not the nature of the covenant promise. Rather, the fundamental issue is the relation of election and covenant: Does election govern the covenant?

If election governs the covenant, as the fathers of the Secession taught in the nineteenth century and as the Protestant Reformed Churches confess today, the covenant, the covenant promise, covenant union with Christ, the gift and possession of covenant blessings, perseverance in the covenant, and covenant salvation are unconditional. They depend not upon the believing and obeying child, but upon the free, sovereign, electing grace of the covenanting God in Jesus Christ.

The issue is the gospel of (covenant) salvation by (covenant) grace alone.

That this, and nothing less, is indeed the issue in the longstanding controversy over the covenant, the heresy of the Federal Vision now makes plain in the community of Reformed churches. The men of the Federal (that is, Covenant) Vision are, by their own testimony, developing the covenant theology of Schilder, Holwerda, and Veenhof, and therefore the covenant doctrine of Pieters and Kreulen. This development of the covenant doctrine of the "liberated" Reformed Churches brazenly denies justification by faith alone and every one of the five grand truths of the gospel of grace confessed, explained, defended, and adopted by the Reformed churches in the Canons of Dordt. I have demonstrated all of this in a full-length book, and need not argue or prove these incontrovertible statements here.[70]

It is not enough, therefore, not nearly enough, that Reformed churches affirm non-binding propositions gainsaying some of the more egregiously heretical teachings of the men of the Federal Vision.

It is certainly not enough that Reformed seminaries and theologians, under pressure, distance themselves from the men of the Federal Vision.

The God of Reformed church history, whose mills of judgment upon error grind slowly but exceedingly fine and whose advancing of the truth of the gospel to victory moves similarly slowly but surely, now puts all of Reformed Christianity to the test by means of the theology of the Federal Vision, his unwilling servant.

A conflict over the covenant that has continued, and repeatedly raged, over hundreds of years now must and will be resolved.

From the full, bitter fruits of the doctrine of a covenant cut loose from election, the Reformed churches must now recognize that this doctrine is the denial of the gospel of grace as confessed in the Canons of Dordt.

In light of the dreadful judgment of God on the doctrine of a conditional covenant in the form of the theology of the Federal Vision, Reformed churches are called to renounce the doctrine of a conditional covenant and to confess that God's gracious, sovereign, eternal decree of election in Christ governs the covenant of grace.

They are called to return to the covenant doctrine of the fathers of the Secession.

Thus, in the great matter of covenant salvation they will return to the Canons of Dordt, which was the credo of the Secession of 1834.[71]

So that to God alone may be the glory of salvation—in the covenant!

Part 3

The Reformation of 1886 in the Netherlands

15

Abraham Kuyper: A Short Biography

Herman C. Hanko

Childhood and Youth

Abraham Kuyper was born on October 29, 1837, to Rev. and Mrs. Jan Frederik Kuyper in the small fishing village of Maassluis, the Netherlands. It was a time of great apostasy in the Reformed Church, and modernists occupied thousands of pulpits and all the important posts in the schools. Kuyper's own father was somewhere between liberal modernism and being mildly Reformed.

Two reform movements had swept the Netherlands—one a mere gesture towards reformation, the other a genuine reform of the church. The first, called the *Reveil* (Renewal), had spread throughout Protestant Europe, was more humanistic than ecclesiastical, and hoped to bring reformation into the church from within. The second, called *De Afscheiding* (The Separation), was led by Hendrik de Cock and was composed of thousands of godly and pious people among the lower classes, whom Kuyper himself was later to call *de kleine luyden* (the little folk). These had separated from the false state church to re-establish the church of Christ. Kuyper was not touched by either movement.

Bram (as he was called) was home-schooled and early learned French and German. He was a promising student from the outset and not only showed an aptitude for languages, but also quickly mastered whatever was put in his way.

He studied in Middelburg and Leiden when his family moved to these cities, to prepare himself for university work. He graduated from "gymnasium" in 1855 and delivered the valedictory address in German on the subject "Ulfilas, the Bishop of the Visigoths, and His Gothic Translation of the Bible." His post-graduate studies were at the University of Leiden, a 280-year-old school with an enrollment of about five hundred students. All the instruction he received was thoroughly modernistic. He graduated in 1858 *summa cum laude* and entered the divinity school in Leiden to prepare for the ministry. No wonder that when Kuyper graduated from divinity school in 1861 and earned his doctorate in 1863, he was a thorough-going modernist of no use to God or man.

Conversion and Early Ministry

But God had other plans for this young man; he was destined to become one of the greatest and most influential Reformed preachers of the past few centuries. To fashion him in the proper mold required his conversion. Kuyper tells us that three elements played a part in humbling him and bringing him to God.

The first experience took place in his university days and did not bear its fruit until later. While working on an essay that dealt with a comparison between Calvin's and à Lasco's views of the church, Kuyper could find none of à Lasco's works, though he searched throughout the libraries of Europe. An old minister, the father of one of his liberal professors, had a complete set, perhaps the only one in Europe. Kuyper considered this almost miraculous and a special evidence of God's providential direction of his life.

The second experience was brought about by a complete nervous collapse due to overwork, during which time Kuyper could do nothing but build a model ship and read light fiction. In reading Charlotte M. Yonge's book, *The Heir of Redclyffe*, he was so moved by how God had humbled the arrogant main character of the book that he later wrote, "What my soul experienced at that moment I fully understood only later. Yet, from that moment on I despised what I used to admire and sought what I had dared to despise."[1]

The third experience took place in his first congregation where were a few genuine Christians. One, a peasant girl of thirty, Pietronella Baltus, refused to shake his hand and explained her actions by telling him that he was unconverted and not fit to be a minister. Kuyper was stunned by this but had the humility to inquire further from these humble folk, who sent him back to Calvin and the Reformed fathers to learn the Reformed faith.

The Preacher

After his conversion, Kuyper became a powerful and effective preacher of the Reformed faith and was used by God to bring a revival of the Reformed faith to the Dutch church. He was an extraordinary exegete, a forceful orator, and a fearless critic of modernism. He moved many to love the Reformed faith, and he moved many enemies of the gospel to hate him passionately.

His first congregation was the small church of Beesd, from which he moved to Utrecht, a church of 35,000 members and eleven ministers. In Utrecht he had his first confrontation with the ecclesiastical hierarchy, which was to lead in the future to a split. After three years he moved to Amsterdam, the most influential, the largest, and the most prestigious church in the Netherlands. It had 140,000 members, 136 office bearers, 28 ministers, 10 sanctuaries, and 4 chapels.

Kuyper was not only a superb preacher, but also an effective liturgist. His prayers were eloquent and brought God's people to the throne of grace. His reading of Scripture was so powerful that one of his colleagues once said that hearing Kuyper merely read Psalm 148 was clearer exposition than most sermons on it and brought him to tears.

How effective he would have been if he had remained a preacher is impossible to say, but it was a loss greater than can be described that Kuyper resigned from the ministry in 1874 in the interests of entering politics. That marked the beginning of the decline of his effectiveness as a Reformed man.

The Journalist and Writer

Kuyper's works fill a large shelf and are on such a variety of subjects that one marvels at his vast learning and extensive knowledge of almost any subject to which he applied himself. Already while in Utrecht he became editor of *De Heraut* (The Herald), a weekly, and he remained in this post until the end of his life. In 1872 he became editor of *De Standaard* (The Standard), a Christian daily newspaper, and he held that post for almost fifty years, until he was eighty-two years old. He published a Dogmatics, a three-volume exposition of the Heidelberg Catechism, a three-volume work on theology entitled *Encyclopaedie der Heilege Godgeleerdheid,* a three-volume work on common grace, and hundreds of meditations published in various books.

Kuyper made use of countless illustrations, some of which he used to prove his point rather than illustrate it. Kuyper's writings have been largely responsible for his influence in Reformed circles to the present.

The Church Reformer

After his conversion Kuyper became an implacable foe of modernism, which had captured the universities and divinity schools, and which had sapped the church of its spiritual life. His Reformed preaching and writing were blessed by God to turn a significant part of the church back to the faith of their fathers. This brought him into conflict with the state church.

The first confrontation took place in Utrecht when Kuyper's consistory refused to answer a questionnaire sent out in the place of classical visitation. This refusal aroused the fury of the authorities and was finally to become an issue in the split.

As is so often the case in the church, confessional integrity was also an issue. The church was no longer requiring subscription to the creeds in many instances, but was satisfied with a vague promise. Kuyper and the consistory of Amsterdam would have none of this.

Young people who showed in doctrine and walk that they were unbelievers were admitted to membership in the church and the Lord's table. In Kuyper's thinking this was intolerable.

The hierarchy acted against Kuyper and deposed office bearers in the congregation. The result was that about two hundred congregations totaling 100,000 people left in 1886 to form a new denomination called *De Doleantie* (The Aggrieved Ones). In time, also with Kuyper's support, these people came together with *De Afscheiding* of 1834 to form what is now the Gereformeerde Kerken in Nederland (GKN). Though once Reformed, that church and two others merged in 2004 to form the Protestant Church in the Netherlands (PKN), which is as apostate as the state church in Kuyper's day had ever been.

The Politician

While to some Kuyper's greatest glory came as a politician, it nevertheless remains a fact that his involvement in politics did great harm to the cause of the Reformed faith.

Early in his ministry Kuyper had joined the Anti-Revolutionary Party founded by Groen Van Prinsterer. After resigning from the ministry and standing for election to the Second Chamber of Parliament, and after twice being defeated, he was elected in 1874.

He was re-elected a year later, suffered a nervous collapse a second time, which removed him from action for fifteen months, returned with renewed energy to reorganize and revitalize the party, and finally came to the point where he saw the possibility of becoming prime minister.

To become prime minister, however, was possible only by forming a coalition with the Roman Catholic party. The justification for forming such a coalition was in large part the motivation of Kuyper's development of a thoroughly unbiblical and wholly philosophical theory of common grace.

Kuyper's tenure as prime minister was short, but Kuyper the politician and proponent of common grace is often the Kuyper remembered and adored.

The Educator

Kuyper was always interested in Christian education in general and Reformed higher education in particular. His love for children was great; he cared tenderly for his own children, and he took every opportunity to visit the orphanage in Amsterdam to spend time with and speak to the children there.

Although he fought long and hard to make Christian education available to all the common folk whose financial burdens were too great to bear, his greatest achievement was the establishment of the Free University in Amsterdam. This university remains to the present, although it has become a hotbed of liberal and socialistic thought.

It was as an educator that he was invited to Princeton University where he delivered his "Stone Lectures" in 1898.

The Christian Man

Kuyper was a godly man who loved and cared for his family. While in Beesd he married Johanna Hendrika Schaay, a girl from Rotterdam. With her he had five sons and two daughters. The life of his covenant family was dear to him; family devotions were held regularly, to which the servants were invited; Scripture was explained and prayers were made. Mealtimes were times of discussion, argumentation, fellowship, and laughter. The old year never passed away, and the new year never arrived, except Kuyper could be found with his family reading Scripture and in prayer. This custom was preserved to the end of his life.

Kuyper was a man of vast learning who knew and spoke many of Europe's languages, who wrote on countless subjects, who lectured and wrote in Latin, but who also was deeply mystical, though in the Reformed sense. No one can read, without being moved, Kuyper's book *Nabij God te Zijn*, translated under the title *Nearness to God*.

Kuyper was a man of God with many flaws—as we all are. He was often intolerant even of friends who might disagree with him. He became increasingly crusty and belligerent with the passing of the years. When he was gently eased aside because the infirmities of old age made his work less effective, he became bitter. But God does not use perfect men in his church, and the Reformed faith owes more to Kuyper than it realizes. It is with sadness that Reformed men see the Kuyper of common grace extolled by today's apostate church, while the Kuyper of sovereign and particular grace goes unremembered.

Dr. Abraham Kuyper died on November 8, 1920. The funeral, attended by thousands, was simple and without flowers. The climax was the thunderous singing of Kuyper's favorite, Psalm 89:7, 8. On his tombstone were engraved the words: "Dr. A. Kuyper / Born October 29, 1837 / And fallen asleep in his Saviour November 8, 1920."

16

The *Doleantie*

Ronald L. Cammenga

Cracks in the Dike

By the mid-nineteenth century there were gaping cracks in the dike of Dutch Reformed orthodoxy. The Hervormde Kerk, the state Reformed church of the Netherlands, bore few similarities to the church of the Synod of Dordt that had stood so firmly against the Arminian heresy at the beginning of the seventeenth century. Not only had Dordt been undone, but the Arminianism of the early 1600s had also given way to full-blown modernism by the mid-1800s. This was cause for great grief among those still committed to the truths of Holy Scripture and the Reformed confessions. The loudest of the voices raised against the departures of the church was that of Abraham Kuyper—minister, professor, statesman, journalist, pamphleteer, and church reformer.

Kuyper himself had received a thoroughly modernistic education and early in his ministry promoted the tenets of modernism. Recalling the days of his theological training at the University of Leiden, he wrote,

> Orthodox books I neither had nor knew. So it was in those days among the theological students at Leiden. The orthodox faith was presented to us in such a ludicrous, caricatured way that it seemed a luxury and waste of money for students of modest means to spend anything on such misbegotten writings.[1]

The *Doleantie*

Although Kuyper was at first a disciple of liberalism, God in his grace led Kuyper, through various circumstances, out of the wasteland of modernism to the Eden of God's truth. This conversion took place especially during the time of Kuyper's first pastorate in Beesd. From that time forward Kuyper set himself to oppose with all his might the modernism that he was convinced had a stranglehold on the church of his day.

> Modernism is not even new. All through the centuries it has brought about sorrow in the church of Jesus and it will continue to ferment till the Day of the Lord. Yet it has never ruled as now, never achieved the central importance it has today. Only in our age could it become what it really is. Today it stands at the zenith of its power.[2]

Much like the modernists of our day, the modernists of Kuyper's day denied every major doctrine of Holy Scripture. The Trinity was impugned. The deity of Christ was set aside. Jesus' literal, bodily resurrection from the dead the third day was scoffed at. The infallibility and reliability of the Bible was ridiculed. In the area of salvation, predestination, limited atonement, and man's natural depravity were denied by the crassest universalism. Contrasting modernism and the Reformed faith, Kuyper wrote,

> In matters of faith Modernism chooses human authority as its starting point, the very thing against which Protestantism raised its mighty protest. It forfeits the right to adorn itself with the honor of the Reformation if for no other reason than that it never knew the desperation, brokenheartedness, and mental anxiety from which Luther cried out to his God. The Reformation sought redemption for the troubled heart, Modernism only the solution to an ingenious problem. This is why Modernism only knows the reality of visible things and misses the reality of the other kind, which is much higher and much more firmly established, which speaks to us of the "immovable" kingdom of God even in the fact of sin.[3]

In another place Kuyper sketched the main tenets of modernism.

Tell me, with what else but unproven premises and therefore (from their own viewpoint) cheap dogmas does Modernism start in all its preaching? Its confession can be broadly sketched as follows: "I, a modernist, believe in a God who is the Father of all humankind, and in Jesus, not the Christ, but the rabbi from Nazareth. I believe in a humanity which is by nature good but needs to strive after improvement. I believe that sin is only relative and hence that forgiveness is merely something of human invention. I believe in the hope of a better life and, without judgment, the salvation of every soul."[4]

This is what it had come to in the Reformed churches in the Netherlands in Kuyper's day.

Coupled with the doctrinal errors rampant in the state church was the grievous yoke of a hierarchical church government. The reform movement under Kuyper, as is so often the case with church reformation, would not only call the church back to the doctrine of the Scriptures, but also restore biblical church government.

The Hervormde Kerk was firmly under the control of the state. This was the result of the reorganization of the Dutch church in 1816 under King William I. The Church Order of Dordt had been set aside. The autonomy of the local church had been replaced with synodical hierarchy, the broader assemblies with church boards. The domination of the church by the state made reform of the church from within well-nigh impossible. The liberals occupied the seats of authority and controlled the universities, and an entrenched hierarchy shielded them from ecclesiastical censure.

The Dike Bursts

Matters came to a head for Kuyper and the consistory of the church in Amsterdam in which he served towards the end of 1885 and the beginning of 1886. Kuyper and his consistory insisted on strict confessional subscription among both prospective ministers of the gospel and church members. Agree-

The *Doleantie*

ment, they said, must be expressed with the Reformed confessions. On this basis the consistory refused to accept the confessions of faith of (and admit to the Lord's supper) a number of young people.

Voices of protest were raised. The classical board intervened. When pastor and consistory remained adamant in their position, the board took action against them. Kuyper and approximately eighty members of the Amsterdam consistory were suspended from office in December 1885. Kuyper and his followers appealed to the provincial board of the Dutch Reformed Church. On July 1, 1886, the provincial board issued its decision. The suspension of Kuyper and the other elders of the Amsterdam consistory was upheld. They were stripped of their offices in the Hervormde Kerk.

Kuyper refused to recognize the validity of his deposition. On Sunday, July 11, 1886, the first Sunday after his ouster from the state church, he preached to the faithful in his congregation in the Frascati auditorium in Amsterdam. The theme of his sermon was "It Shall Not Be So Among You," based on Matthew 20:25, 26. In the sermon he lamented the departures in the state church.

> The good are not supported so that evildoers may tremble, but the deniers of the deity of the Lord occupy the seats of honor. Drunkards and fornicators go scot-free, while the faithful witnesses of the Lord are being threatened with ecclesiastical death.
> Thus the deeply sinful, unspiritual, worldly striving runs its course to its own shame. And what is most appalling of all, the unholy business wraps itself in the robes of piety.[5]

In rejection of modernism, Kuyper insisted that the church must return to Dordt.

> For many years did not the Arminian have the upper hand so that the confessor of the free sovereignty of the Lord was almost completely marginalized? Did not the Arminian glory in the fact that the old fable of Dordt had been done to death by the speech of some and the silence of the rest? Were not their voices crying

throughout the land: "Though the Lord is powerful, I am the master of my own soul!"[6]

The old confession had to be revived: "God the Lord is almighty also in the work of grace."
And the oppressive yoke of the ecclesiastical hierarchy had to be thrown off. The church must be free under Christ to govern itself without the interference of the state.

> Brothers and sisters, every one of us is jointly responsible for the emergence of alien "lordships" and "powers" in the church of God. If the people of the Lord in this city had consistently held high the power of the Lord, had honored all power and government only for the Lord's sake, had strictly maintained the power entrusted to them and not arrogated power that did not belong to them, there would everywhere have been a clear sense of the difference between a false invasive power and the powers instituted by God.[7]

The saints who left the state Hervormde Kerk under Abraham Kuyper called themselves the *Doleantie*. The Dutch word means "lament" or "grief," and is expressive of the deep sorrow of these saints over the apostasy in the church of their forefathers. With heavy hearts they found it necessary to leave that institute and, through separation, to reform the church.

Rebuilding the Dike

There were many throughout the Netherlands who were sympathetic to Kuyper and the Amsterdam consistory. As is always the case in church reformation, many disappointed. When the break finally came, a number of ministers and theological professors who supported Kuyper failed to join the *Doleantie* and remained in the Hervormde Kerk. Kuyper's friend and colleague at the Free University, P. J. Hoedemaker, would not support Kuyper in leaving the mother church. Undoubtedly many were motivated by the security of earthly po-

The *Doleantie*

sitions and the reluctance to share in the lot of the despised *Doleerende* (members of the *Doleantie* churches). Nevertheless the movement grew rapidly. The result was the organization of *Doleantie* churches throughout the Netherlands. These congregations established a new church federation known as the Nederduitsche Gereformeerde Kerken. By 1889 the new denomination included some two hundred congregations, more than 180,000 members, and approximately eighty ministers.

From the beginning, Kuyper and the *Doleantie* sought contact with the churches of the *Afscheiding*, the Secession of 1834 that had taken place under the leadership of men like de Cock, Scholte, and Van Raalte. That was natural because they had so much in common. Many of the same doctrinal and church political issues that precipitated the *Doleantie* had been at the heart of the *Afscheiding* as well. Kuyper worked tirelessly to bring about union. His efforts met with success. In 1892, only six years after the expulsion of Kuyper and his followers from the state church, union was effected. The new denomination took the name Gereformeerde Kerken in Nederland.

It took time for the union to become more than merely formal and institutional. Some of the *Afscheiding* churches refused to go along with the joining. They continued as the Christelijke Gereformeerde Kerken. Among the churches participating in the merger, ongoing tensions between the two groups resulted in the formation of "A" churches and "B" churches, often worshiping side by side in the same city. The "A" churches were those of *Afscheiding* extraction, the "B" churches from the *Doleantie*.

The bold stand for the truth taken by Kuyper and the *Doleantie* serves as a model for Reformed Christians today.

Sad to say, Kuyper's legacy is not much appreciated by many in the Reformed churches, even in those churches that he was instrumental in founding. If he is remembered, he is remembered as the Kuyper of common grace and the Kuyper of politics.

But there is another Kuyper: the Kuyper who championed

sovereign grace against modernism, the Kuyper who refused to knuckle under to ecclesiastical hierarchy, the Kuyper who was willing to jeopardize prestige and position for the sake of truth, the reformer Kuyper. God grant that the legacy of that Kuyper may enrich the Reformed church world until the Christ of Kuyper returns.

17

Abraham Kuyper and the Union of 1892

Russell J. Dykstra

> Brothers, if the Lord Jesus were in our midst, we would not dare to stay where we are. Let us convene this day as if the Lord Jesus really were among us. Thank you, brothers, that you have come here from your cities and villages. You did not say: "Leave those 'Doleantie churches' to rule their own affairs." You did not act that way, but you came.[1]

These are the words of Dr. Abraham Kuyper addressed to a delegation of men from the Christelijke Gereformeerde Kerken (CGK) in 1888. He spoke at a joint conference of theologians from the CGK and the *Doleantie*. The purpose of the conference was to work toward unity, even a union, between the CGK and the *Doleantie* churches. By 1892, the union was a reality, and the two groups of churches fused into one new denomination, the Gereformeerde Kerken in Nederland (GKN).

The union of the CGK and the *Doleantie* is striking because the churches at large, not to mention the Reformed church world, are more accustomed to church schism and splits than to proper unions. This union is even more remarkable in light of the differences that existed between the two groups of churches. How did this union come about? A study of the history indicates that Dr. Abraham Kuyper was a driving force behind the movement toward unity.

As noted above, the two groups were very different in many

respects. They were different in their relative ages. By the time of the union, the CGK were fifty-eight years old as churches, having been organized out of the Secession (*Afscheiding*) of 1834. The *Doleantie* came out of the state church in 1886 and thus were only six years old at the time of the union.

The two groups were different in their origins. The CGK was the result of a secession. Led by such men as Hendrik de Cock, Hendrik Scholte, Simon Van Velzen, and Albertus Van Raalte, thousands pulled out of the state church (Nederlandse Hervormde Kerk, NHK). The Secession repudiated the state church and labeled it the false church. They viewed the Secession as a work of reformation in which the true church of Christ was re-formed, that is, formed again. In contrast, the *Doleantie* viewed itself as the continuing Hervormde Kerk in the Netherlands and insisted that all the members of the NHK were members legally under the consistories of the *Doleantie*. They hesitated to call the NHK a false church. They desired to continue reforming the local churches.

The two groups had their own distinct characteristics. Generally speaking, the Secession drew its membership from the poorer and less educated members of society. In addition, the Secession churches were severely persecuted for their stance over against the state church. They also tended to be less precise doctrinally, although they had an outstanding theologian at the time of the union in Herman Bavinck. The *Doleantie*, on the other hand, appealed to the higher classes of society. The members were often better educated and tended to be more doctrinally precise, especially under the leadership of Dr. Abraham Kuyper.

The two churches also had significantly different viewpoints on the matter of the training of ministers. On the one hand, the CGK had established its own theological school at Kampen. They were convinced that the churches must have their own school to train their own ministers. On the other hand, Abraham Kuyper and other leaders had established the Free University in 1880 exactly for the training of ministers in an institution not governed directly by the church. They con-

Abraham Kuyper and the Union of 1892

sidered this necessary in order that theology maintain its high position of scholarship among the other sciences.

There were also serious differences in doctrine in the two churches. These differences included significant doctrines regarding the church, baptism, the covenant, and eternal justification.

These real and distinct differences had been the cause of conflict in the past. While the members of the *Doleantie* were still in the state church, they had definitely looked down upon the Secession. They despised these churches and refused to join with them.

Nonetheless, when the *Doleantie* formed, everyone recognized that the two groups also had much in common. In general they had a common heritage in the Reformed faith. They represented the cause of the reformation in the Netherlands. They both maintained the same creeds—the three forms of unity. They maintained the same Church Order, that of the Synod of Dordt. They used the same liturgical forms.

Additionally they shared the important element that they both had come out of the state church. Both formed because of apostasy in the NHK. Therefore, even though they came into existence under radically different circumstances separated by some fifty years, the Secession and the *Doleantie* were both church reformations.

In spite of the many differences between the two groups of churches, the union was realized, and that within a mere six years after the *Doleantie* churches formed.

Our interest is in the part that Abraham Kuyper played in this union. As will become plain, he took a leading role.

It should be noted first that this union of the *Doleantie* and the CGK was Kuyper's great desire. At the same conference referred to above, he said,

> Of the grand wish that we might come to dwell together in one tent, something has now been fulfilled. I had not dared think it: I did not even expect to see it by the time I became an old man. To be on the road to unity already—never, never had I dared predict this. The Lord is amazing.[2]

He had worked for this union from the beginning of the *Doleantie*. He promoted it in *De Heraut* (The Herald). In typical Kuyperian style, he not only advocated the union, but he also set forth straightforwardly what problems he saw in the CGK which, he maintained, would keep the two parties separate until they were resolved.

The synodical convention held in 1887 faced the question of what should be the relationship between the *Doleantie* and other churches that had left the NHK. It adopted the following advice of the committee of which Abraham Kuyper was the reporter:

> Our starting point ought to be the undiminished and resolute confession that all those who are committed to the same confession of the truth and who follow the same church order when it comes to church government, may not, in the long run, remain separate ecclesiastically, and may not rest until all the sons from the same house are again united in a single bond of ecclesiastical fellowship.[3]

In addition, this convention encouraged individual consistories to "take up contact with the nearby consistory of their church in order to give expression to fraternal unity in all humility . . . and also to assure them of our hearty willingness to walk with them down paths of unity on the basis of the Three Forms of Unity and the Church Order as accepted by both sides."[4] Abraham Kuyper was asked to draw up a letter for the consistories' use.

Within a month, Dr. Kuyper had sent out a draft copy to the consistories of the *Doleantie*. It sounded this humble note:

> So we have come out [of the NHK] as those who left later, and thus as greater sinners. We now turn to you as our brothers to testify that there is great joy in our hearts. We are joyful because, after a period of sinful waiting that continued too long, our eyes have finally been opened so that we could see that the path down which we were walking led nowhere.[5]

This letter also expressed "the deep desire within us that cries out for the day on which, through God's gracious favor, all the people of His inheritance in this good land may be brought together under one and the same administration of the Word and the holy sacraments." In the letter Kuyper pleaded for "an end to all that now must grieve the Holy Spirit in terms of the relationship between us. Let us see to it that a divided life on the part of all the Reformed people in this country is recognized as sin before God." He called on the CGK to join the *Doleantie* "in finding the spiritual maturity of love and of mercy, which will in the end break down every barrier and remove every stumbling block."[6]

As one of the deputies appointed by the *Doleantie* convention, Kuyper pressed for a meeting between the deputies and the faculty of the Theological School in Kampen. When this became a reality, Kuyper wrote in *De Heraut,* "May the prayers of the churches now go up without ceasing to the Throne of grace as we plead for the unity of the Confessions."[7] Kuyper frequently expressed this sentiment in *De Heraut*. As editor, he used the paper as a means to promote the union as well as to provide information on the progress.

At the meetings between the *Doleantie* men and the CGK men, Kuyper continued to promote unity. His speeches were powerful and encouraging, and were very well received by the men of the CGK.

Kuyper had a hand in the writing of documents in the process of unification. He and Dr. F. L. Rutgers were appointed by the first provisional synod of the *Doleantie* (1888) to draft a letter to the synod of the CGK calling for unity.

When (in 1888) the respective synods of the two groups failed to agree on the basis for union, Abraham Kuyper persevered. He wrote up an Act of Union and presented it to the deputies of the CGK for discussion. From the viewpoint of the CGK deputies, the Act of Union seemed to require far too many concessions from them, and too few from the *Doleantie*. The synod of the CGK at Kampen (1889) agreed. It adopted the Act of Union only after significant amendments were made. In contrast, the *Doleantie* provisional synod of Utrecht adopted the document without change.

Abraham Kuyper promoted the union in other ways. One

of the burning issues for the CGK was the matter of the school for training ministers. They resisted the proposal that their school in Kampen be closed or incorporated into the Free University. When a position in faculty of theology became available in the Free University in 1889, Kuyper thought he knew a way to take care of the problem. He pressed for the appointment to go to Herman Bavinck, a professor in Kampen. Although Bavinck eventually declined the position, Kuyper's hope was to bring Bavinck into the Free University, and thus over to the *Doleantie* theological school.

Eventually the CGK synod of Leeuwarden (1891) adopted a new proposed basis for union. It called for union based on the three forms of unity (the Reformed confessions) and the Church Order of Dordt. This proposal, along with some specifications on the practical working out of the union, was brought to the third *Doleantie* provisional synod (the Hague) by appointed CGK deputies. Abraham Kuyper, as president of the synod and member of the negotiating committee that studied the proposal and conferred with the CGK deputies, guided the deliberations carefully and skillfully. Compromise was worked out to the point that the *Doleantie* synod adopted the proposed basis with amendments agreed upon by the CGK deputies.

The final version was adopted also by the CGK synod of Amsterdam in June of 1892, and the union was realized. The GKN was born.[8] Certain it is that this was the desire of many members and leaders in both the churches. It is also certain that Abraham Kuyper, zealous for the unity of the church, was an instrument of God to bring about the union of 1892.

Several observations must be made about this slice of history. First, it is noteworthy and commendable that Dr. Abraham Kuyper and the *Doleantie* sought out the older CGK. This stems from a twofold realization. First, the *Doleantie* recognized that the Secession was a legitimate reformation of the church in the Netherlands. Since the *Doleantie* also considered itself a true reformation, consistency demanded that the *Doleantie* churches explore the possibility of unity with the earlier movement. Second, this move stems from the confession that the church is one and must manifest the oneness institutionally as much as possible.

A second noteworthy feature is that the union was based simply on the three forms of unity and the Church Order of Dordt. Even though some significant differences in doctrine existed, these theological issues were not discussed and resolved. Later the GKN passed judgment on some of the issues in the Conclusions of Utrecht (1905). Yet it was a compromise document, and it did not settle the issues.

This lack of unity in doctrine stands connected to the final observation. The sad fact is that this union really did not work. Although one denomination was forged, the differences between the *Doleantie* and the Secession churches remained. Throughout the Netherlands, "A" churches and "B" churches existed, often within the same city. Everyone knew that the "A" churches were from the Secession, and the "B" churches were from the *Doleantie*. No "A" ministers would take a call to a "B" congregation, or vice versa. They were different in doctrine, preaching, and worship. These differences remained until the time that Dr. Klaas Schilder was deposed by the GKN in 1943, and the GKN "Liberated" was formed. Far and away the majority of the Liberated were the "A" churches of the Secession.

The lesson is plain. True unity is not established merely on the basis of the three forms of unity and the Church Order of Dordt. This is not to denigrate the unspeakable value of the Reformed creeds as forms of unity. Rather the point is that in the providence of God, the truth develops in and through the history of the church. The truth develops beyond the confessions—not outside their boundaries, understand, but beyond them in the sense that the truth is better defined, becomes sharper, more in focus. To ignore that development and declare merely, "On the basis of the Three Forms!" is not realistic.

Significant differences in doctrine have developed since the Reformed confessions were written, and conflicting views on certain doctrines have been proposed within the Reformed camp, all of which are defended on the basis of the confessions. It cannot be, obviously, that two opposite views are both correct. Only one can be. One position stands within the boundaries of the confessions; the other does not. However, when two denominations are considering union, if they are serious about true unity, they must nail down which position on a particular doctrine they will consider to be within the boundaries of the confessions and which is not. Not to do so is to build schism into the union.

This was not totally overlooked in this process of union in the Netherlands. A few men here and there called for discussions on theological differences. Sadly, these voices were drowned out by the mighty chorus for unity, admittedly a good and proper goal. But true unity is in Christ, who is the Truth.

18

Abraham Kuyper as Defender of Particular Grace

Marvin Kamps

DR. ABRAHAM KUYPER WAS A MASTER THEOLOGIAN. By means of his writing, lectures, and preaching, the truth of sovereign, particular grace in Christ Jesus for the elect of God was once again restored to the confession and preaching of many thousands in the Netherlands. His work was above all a work of reformation of the church. It was reformation because it was a return to the Scriptures as confessed by the Reformed church. But this was not without a great price that had to be paid by Kuyper. He had many enemies. He was accounted a pariah and charged with heresy and perversion of the truth. His enemies cut him off from their fellowship, and what was worse, they denied him the fellowship of the Spirit and brought down on his head the curse.

One of the books published by Dr. Kuyper is entitled *That Grace is Particular*.[1] Dr. Kuyper exposed the unbiblical character of the doctrine of *Christus pro omnibus* (Christ for all), a theology that permeated the Reformed church of his day.

> By "Christ for all" is meant that Christ, according to the purpose and extent of his self-sacrifice, died for all men without exception.[2]
>
> The universalists, or advocates of general grace...maintain this position: When Jesus died on the cross, it was God's will and

Christ's purpose to bring about the kind of atonement, that, if need be, was sufficient for all men. In addition, they contend that this atonement, offered in Jesus' name to all men, would be a blessing to as many as, according to Jesus' intention, desired to accept this salvation, while the atonement would remain unused only by as many as did not believe, even though it was so appointed for them and even though Jesus had intended and expected that they would believe.[3]

When Kuyper refers to those who defend a "Christ for all" as universalists, he is not identifying them as those who believe that all will eventually be saved, but as those who claim that Christ died for all. Against this false doctrine Kuyper maintained that the Scriptures teach particular grace:

On the other hand, there are the *particularists,* or advocates of special grace, who teach this: The church must preach to all creatures that there is atonement obtained through Christ's death for everyone who believes, has believed, or will believe; that is, because all believers are elect, atonement is only for the elect, not according to the [foreseen] result, but according to Christ's purpose and God's counsel. Particularists also teach concerning the application of this salvation that it is not concerned with possibly but as yet unconverted persons; on the contrary, it has to do with persons whom the Lord loves with an *eternal* love, even before they were born, and whom he *calls by name.*[4]

Kuyper's task was formidable. Humanly speaking we would say it was impossible. The Reformed church for many years had not received solid preaching on the subject of particular grace. The state church of Holland had been made nearly oblivious to what was the truth of the gospel in that regard. The common people had been so misled by the preachers of the day that they just took for granted that God's gospel of grace in Christ, the cross, was for every man, that God loved all men in Christ, and that God wanted to save all men head for head. To stem the tide and to call the church back to the gospel of Scripture and the creeds would require all the strength and determination and dedication a man could

Abraham Kuyper as Defender of Particular Grace

muster. Kuyper says in regard to the church's lack of sensitivity to the truth and the unwarranted criticism that he received for his position that God's grace is particular: "But how could this be otherwise with the defense of an aspect of the truth that has not been heard from the pulpits for fifty years, and that under foreign influences has died out of the confession of the greater part of the church?"[5] In other words, even good people of God lacked spiritual discernment and were easy prey for unfaithful men.

But Kuyper was motivated and inspired by one all-encompassing responsibility: "the honor of God's holy name."[6] The false doctrine of a Christ for all, general grace, or universalism, was for Kuyper a God-dishonoring doctrine that robbed the church of the essence of her calling, that is, to worship. How can the believer worship when the preaching presents a God who cannot accomplish his will, whose Son is made a beggar, and whose grace is made in most instances insufficient to save, or when sinners are made to believe that their salvation is dependent on their own efforts?

In refuting the error of "Christ for all," Kuyper first felt obligated to demonstrate that the texts which the proponents of general grace always present as conclusive proof of their position do not teach what they claim. These texts are 1 John 2:2, 1 Timothy 2:4, and 2 Peter 3:9. The explanation of these texts shows how completely Rev. Herman Hoeksema's exegesis of these passages echoes that of Dr. Kuyper. When it came to the subject of particular grace, Hoeksema's instruction did not differ from that of Kuyper. In addition, Kuyper rejected the well-meant offer of salvation theory that is undeniably linked to the general grace theory as an idea that denies the total depravity of the fallen sinner:

> If what the proponents of general grace teach is true—namely, that grace is offered to all persons individually on the ground that actually and essentially the ransom already *has been* paid for them—then it certainly *must* be supposed that the sinner still rightly carries in his soul a power and an ability to *accept salvation* if it is offered to him.[7]

Later he concluded,

> In light of the above, one thing is certain: that whoever teaches a general grace supposes and accepts that in every sinner there are faculties that by nature enable him to choose Jesus as his own. And it is also certain that we oppose the doctrine of general grace on the very sound basis that it fails to appreciate what the Bible has revealed to us concerning the depth of the corruption of sin.[8]

There are many different aspects of Dr. Kuyper's refutation of "Christ for all," but two aspects of his masterful defense of particular grace and refutation of general grace are presented here. First, Kuyper made the charge that general grace ought to be rejected because "it is unreconcilable with what holy Scripture reveals concerning *the essence and the attributes of the living God.*"[9] After establishing that even the proponents of general grace have to acknowledge that not all men are in fact actually saved, but that many—if not most—perish in unbelief and that God knew this fact eternally, Kuyper writes,

> Nevertheless, some preachers imagine, write, and teach that the very same holy, glorious, all-discerning, and all-knowing God, in connection with the devising of his plan of salvation, had the will, the purpose, and the intention to let his only begotten Son at Golgotha pay "the ransom" for all them also who would perish in hell. They teach, therefore, that the Lord God certainly knew of some that they *cannot* be saved, yet that the very same God made a plan of salvation as though he really could save them, as though their salvation were conceivable, and as though he designed, according to the intention of his plan, the actual salvation of *all*.
>
> These are two viewpoints that, of course, absolutely exclude one another and that cannot for a moment coexist, at least not in the mind of a rational man, much less in the mind of God!
>
> In this way the universalist sets forth the possibility in the being of God that he, the Holy One, would have devised something approximately in this manner: "They will certainly perish; but who knows. I so much want with all my heart to save all of them! Let me act for a moment as if I did not know that they will die in their sins, and let me present a plan of salvation in which I set

aside my divine thoughts and forget what I nevertheless know and see."[10]

The essential attribute of God is to be God... [but] the doctrine of general grace teaches this: God certainly knew from eternity, for example, that Judas would not be saved, and yet God thought when devising his plan of salvation, "Who knows whether something will not happen whereby he is indeed saved?" For that reason God really had the purpose in his plan, and Christ really had the intention in his death, to pay the ransom price for Judas also.

We very earnestly resist this notion, and do so with all the strength that is in us. This idea infringes upon the Godhead of the Divine Being. It abolishes God's essence in the Divine Being.[11]

Kuyper also demonstrated that the doctrine of general grace is a denial of God's attribute of righteousness:

The doctrine of general grace clashes with nearly all God's attributes that the sacred Scriptures reveal to be in the Divine Being. To mention only one, it is at variance with God's inviolate and inviolable *righteousness*.

Everyone will agree with this: that nothing more contradicts every conception of *righteousness* than the refusal to free the slave for whom the ransom *has been* paid.

If Jesus fully paid the debt, the ransom for every person—even as men pretend and the proponents of *Christus pro omnibus* acknowledge (but let us in deep sorrow also acknowledge that *the majority* die in their sins)—how would one be able, then, to maintain the *righteousness* of a God who first allowed the ransom for the lost to be paid and then counted the sin against them, nonetheless, as if it were not paid?[12]

Second, Kuyper turned to the matter of Christ's foreordination and the blessed reality of the mystical union of Christ and his people, in order to disprove the notion of "Christ for all." The truth and reality of the mystical union of Christ and his people rests upon the truth that specific persons were eternally known to God in love and given to Christ as his responsibility for their redemption, sanctification, and preservation. This mystical union may be expressed as the "sweet whisperings" of the Spirit of Christ to his own. The Spirit testifies to the repentant sinner and to him alone, "There is therefore now no condemnation to them which are in Christ Jesus" (Rom. 8:1); to those who patiently endure his just chastisements, "But if ye be without chastisement, whereof all are partakers, then are ye bastards, and not sons" (Heb. 12:8); and to the weary in well-doing, "Eye hath not seen, nor ear heard, neither have entered into the heart of man, the things which God hath prepared for them that love him" (1 Cor. 2:9).

Dr. Kuyper addressed the question, When does this mystical union begin? After faith, or long before faith? His point is illustrated by the question, When does the bond begin between mother and daughter? Only after birth and after the child has developed self-consciousness? Or did the mother have a bond with this child before birth and before the child's self-consciousness? Every mother knows the answer: The mother took responsibility for the child long before, loved her long before, and did all that was possible to make the child's entrance into the relationship one of health and unspeakable joy. This is but a faint picture of God's loving care of his own chosen in Christ from before the foundation of the world.

Having demonstrated that the doctrine "Christ for all" is an attack on the being of God, Kuyper proceeded to the subject of the person of the Mediator. He showed that the person of the Mediator is impoverished and the matter of Christ's foreordination is neglected by those who promote the notion of general grace. Kuyper writes as follows:

> As often as we seek in quiet reverence to understand the *person* of the Redeemer in the depths of his being, we have to deal, naturally, not only with his divine and human natures, but also with his *foreordination*.
>
> By the "foreordination" of the Christ is understood the firm and unshakable stipulations that from all eternity were made binding in God's counsel concerning the calling the Christ would have to accomplish, the task he would have to fulfill, and the place he would have to take in history.
>
> ... Crib and cross and crown were the direct consequence and

the effect of a devised plan, of a previously established decree of the will of a foreordaining God.

...We do not for a moment hesitate, on the basis of the sacred Scriptures, to express firmly and plainly that to present a Redeemer who only *accidentally* would be suited to his work of redemption is an idea that is thoroughly false, ungodly, and absurd. No Christian who lives uprightly can or may confess anything else than that the Mediator's *person* and the Mediator's *work* inseparably belong together; are foreordained for each other in the "decree" from all eternity; and in connection with the execution of this "decree," were prepared for one another from the beginning.[13]

Dr. Kuyper, having reminded his readers of this foreordination of the Son of God to be the Christ, then asserts that "grace can be no other than particular."[14] He advances his argument with the question,

Does the relationship between the Mediator and the redeemed begin at exactly the moment that the faith of the redeemed becomes active, or has the bond between the Redeemer and his redeemed existed even before their birth, taking its origin in God's eternal decree?

If one pleads for a general grace, of course, only the *first* can be true. Then it is first decided and established through someone's own faith, at the moment that he enters into faith, *whether he is a redeemed person and that he is a redeemed person.* Until that moment it could just as well have happened that he never would have come to faith and, therefore, never would have become "one redeemed in Jesus."

...However, we know from the clear statements of prophet and apostle, and also from what was heard from Jesus' own lips, that the redeemed are given to him by the Father and that only such can "come" to him. Clearly and forthrightly the Bible states that the bond of love, the relationship between Christ and his members, is grounded in the eternal and rooted in the decree from before the foundation of the world. By this we can come to no other conclusion than that the *person* of the Mediator is foreordained and prepared for those specific persons who one day will appear as his redeemed.[15]

Dr. Kuyper went on to explain that Christ is the head of his body, the church, and that Christ Jesus was prepared for certain specific persons with specific names, who together constitute the body of which he is the head. Kuyper rejected with all his soul the idea that the Mediator was prepared for a certain number of persons unnamed: "The person of the Mediator becomes a phantom, an imaginary image, an abstract conception without reality, if you make him a Redeemer of N.N., and that an injustice is done to him unless you frankly confess that he is the Mediator, Guarantor, and Redeemer of A, B, C, etc."[16] Kuyper realized why this is so important:

> A person would carelessly fail to appreciate the sensitivity and depth of the Christian faith if he, in a supernaturalistic manner, should remove from our confession the *mystical union* with Christ, defined as the soul's communion and the fellowship of life of the redeemed with their Lord. This mystical union, this communion, this togetherness, and this belonging to one another of Jesus and his redeemed must be acknowledged, professed, confessed, and firmly maintained, or your Christianity is gone.
>
> But what is this mystical union? Is it a handful of undifferentiated straps and ties and cords that Jesus displays so that you can grasp this one, and I can grasp that strap or tie or cord, according to our own choosing, in order to be joined to Jesus for an anchor?
>
> No, certainly not! Everyone has his *own* tie with which he is bound unto his Jesus. *You* would have no use for the strap that I grasp, the tie that surrounds *me*, the cord that binds *me*, and I would not be able to gain anything from the tie that binds *you* to Jesus.
>
> Everything in the work of redemption is personal, individual, and prepared for each person. Everything has its own address and name and title. It is not a retail store where things are sold and, therefore, everyone can take according to his own choosing. It is a palace where gifts are distributed and the gift is designated, therefore, for each one for whom it is intended.
>
> The bond of the mystical union with Jesus *has to be* personal, also for the reason that the bond penetrates to the depths of our life, of our character, and of our existence. And precisely because that bond of the mystical union with Christ is so completely personal, so also must there be in Jesus' person, in the person of the

Mediator, *one's own, special point of contact* for each redeemed person. This means that there must be something in that person of Jesus for me that only I can find in him, and also for you, there must an attracting power that draws not *me,* but only *you.*[17]

After having established the fact of Jesus' foreordination of specific elect persons with specific names and needs, Kuyper contrasted this biblical fact with the superficiality and unbiblical character of a general grace doctrine.

> In this way it is conclusively proven that the doctrine of general grace can in no way be reconciled with the true reality of the person of the Mediator.
>
> On the untenable position of general grace, the redeemed comes into existence only at the moment when he comes to faith by a choice of the will; the birth of a relationship between him and Jesus begins only at that moment; there is neither in him anything that previously was prepared as to the Mediator nor anything in the Mediator prepared personally and specially for him...
>
> With this notion not only all foreordaining is lost, but likewise the reality, the fullness, and the glory of the person of the Mediator. Thus people produce a representation of the Savior so offensive, annoying, and scandalous that it is for us truly comforting to be able to add that not even one universalist has ever dared to present this blasphemous image of the Mediator, and that all, to the very last one, prefer to remain superficial and illogical rather than to cause the image of their Mediator to appear so empty and shallow.[18]

Then Kuyper turned with great urgency to his reading audience who had been misled by general grace preachers and who had been inclined to disregard the counsel of God, the decree of election, and the foreordination of the Christ to be the Mediator of specific persons with specific needs, and Kuyper asked them,

> But if the Bible shows you a more excellent way, and history tells you that your own fathers walked that excellent path, why, why, I pray you, is that much more glorious way always avoided and brought into discredit as an errant path of abomination?[19]

19

Abraham Kuyper, Developer and Promoter of Common Grace

Charles J. Terpstra

THE LEGACY LEFT BY DR. ABRAHAM KUYPER TO THE Reformed faith and churches is for the most part a great and beneficial one. A significant exception to this is Kuyper's development and promotion of the doctrine of common grace. As much as we appreciate what Kuyper gave to the Reformed churches, including our own, in many areas we must criticize, condemn, and cast away his teaching on common grace.

It is no secret that the Protestant Reformed Churches (PRC) in America have their origin in a rejection of the doctrine of common grace as it was officially adopted by the Christian Reformed Church (CRC) in 1924. The Protestant Reformed Churches have always maintained that God has but one kind of grace, namely, his saving grace in Jesus Christ, and that this grace is particular, that is, only for those whom God chose in Christ in his eternal decree of election. It is the position of the PRC that God never has or shows any grace to the reprobate wicked, for they are outside of Christ and as such are the objects of the holy hatred of God and under his just wrath. The good gifts God bestows on the unbelieving reprobate do indeed reveal the inherent goodness of his being. But they are also expressions of his sovereign displeasure with and disfavor toward the ungodly, serving to leave them without excuse as they despise and abuse God's gifts, thus increasing their condemnation.

The CRC inherited much of her doctrine of common grace from Kuyper. Not indeed all of it, for the CRC went beyond Kuyper in some aspects of its teaching on common grace. But much of her doctrine is rooted in Kuyper's development of common grace. An understanding of Kuyper's doctrine will better enable us to understand the CRC's doctrine. At the same time it will lead us to see that a rejection of the doctrine of common grace as adopted by the CRC means a rejection of its source in Kuyper.

Kuyper's Development of Common Grace

As a Reformed church theologian, Kuyper well knew and properly held to sovereign, particular grace. Standing on the Scriptures and the Reformed confessions, he believed and taught that God's saving grace in Jesus Christ was only for the elect. He referred to this as God's "special" grace. He even reserved a special word in the Dutch for it—*genade*. He was adamant that this saving grace is in no sense common or general, that is, for all men. It is limited to the elect by God's sovereign decree and by Christ's atoning death. This grace is also limited in the preaching of the gospel. The preaching is an expression of God's favor only to the elect, and, in fact, through the preaching God gives grace only to them. In this respect Kuyper's teaching on common grace is markedly different from that which the CRC adopted in 1924. She went beyond Kuyper in her first point of common grace, teaching that even God's saving (special) grace is common, claiming that in the preaching of the gospel God shows his favor (grace) to all who hear, elect and reprobate, believing and unbelieving. This Kuyper rejected.

But Kuyper did believe and teach that besides God's special grace for his elect, he has a common grace for all men.

He used the Dutch word *gratie* to distinguish it from saving grace. The doctrine of this "grace" Kuyper developed in his three-volume work, *De Gemeene Gratie* (On Common Grace), published in 1902–1904.[1]

Ironically, Kuyper developed his views on common grace in connection with two solid, Reformed doctrines: the absolute sovereignty of God over all things and the total depravity of mankind through the fall of Adam in paradise. These, he said, form the basis for God's general favor to all men. Because God rules over all creation and all men, he gives them grace to live in his world and carry out their calling. And because man is radically and totally depraved, God shows all men favor by holding their sin in check so that they are able to live together in society and so that his church can live and grow in the world.

But Kuyper's motivation for developing the doctrine of common grace was not solely theological; it was also very practical. For one thing, he sought to answer the growing effects of modernism in the church world. He noted that modernism had a broad vision of the world and for the world, but that this vision was grounded in humanistic rationalism. He wanted the Reformed faith to have the same broad vision, but to be grounded in the sovereign work of God. Common grace gave him the answer, he thought. Further, Kuyper had become involved in a political career in the Netherlands and needed some justification for his programs and for his cooperation with other religious and secular groups in these programs. Again, he believed that common grace provided him the support he needed. Still more, in connection with these two things, Kuyper had developed a growing aversion for what he believed was an "Anabaptist" spirit in the churches of the Netherlands. There were Reformed Christians who believed that being true to the Reformed faith meant living a godly life of separation from the world. That meant no cooperation with the world in any realm, whether it be labor, religion, or politics. Kuyper's common grace sought to reprove this narrow view of the Christian's life in this world and to create a full-orbed world view.

Abraham Kuyper, Developer and Promoter of Common Grace

The doctrine of common grace that Kuyper developed and promoted consists of two main elements, a negative element and a positive element. The negative is God's favorable restraint of sin in the wicked. Kuyper taught that, because of the fall, man is totally depraved, given over to all wickedness in nature and in deed. If this sinfulness was not held in check, man would quickly destroy himself and there would be no human race. But this would make the development of creation, mankind, and the church impossible. For this reason, said Kuyper, God bestows on all men a certain grace that restrains their wickedness, preventing them from being as wicked as they could be and from walking in all the vile sins they would. This restraint of sin in man is not just external, but also internal. God by his Holy Spirit works in the wicked, even in their hearts, holding them back from sin. Because of this "grace," the wicked can live together in society, creation is prevented from being ruined by mankind, and the church can live and grow in the world among evil men.

But Kuyper did not stop with this merely negative element. He went on to teach that there is a positive element in God's common grace to all men. By means of common grace the natural man can also do good and positive things in this world. He becomes creative and can develop the powers in God's creation for good and useful purposes. He uses his God-given abilities and God's creation gifts for the benefit of mankind. He is able to fulfill the original "cultural mandate" of Genesis 1:26–28. He can develop a culture that is good before God, approved by him and pleasing to him. This is, to be sure, not saving good, but only civil good. Nevertheless, it is real good, because it is the fruit of God's general grace working in natural man. It is another irony in Kuyper's teaching that he believed that man's ability to develop himself and his world under God's common grace would nevertheless ultimately result in the development of the antichristian kingdom. The fruit of God's general grace to men would be the greatest kingdom of evil in the history of the world!

An important implication that Kuyper drew from common grace is that the Christian who is saved by God's special grace can and ought to cooperate with the wicked who are benefited by God's common grace. According to Kuyper, there is a close relation between these two graces. Not only does common grace make it possible for believers to live among the wicked, but it also makes it possible, even obligatory, for them to join with the wicked and work together for the development of a creation culture that glorifies God. This was the vision that Kuyper had for the Netherlands in his political career. And it was the vision he had for the whole world, as God's common grace worked universally in every nation and among all peoples.

Kuyper's Influence on the Reformed Churches

Kuyper's teaching on common grace has had a powerful and wide influence on the Reformed church world. This influence is not restricted to the Reformed churches in the Netherlands, where Kuyper's work and writings were obviously known and widely accepted. It has spread throughout the world, wherever Dutch Reformed churches have been established and have done mission work, and wherever those in the Kuyperian tradition have established Christian schools. Perhaps especially in North America (the U.S. and Canada) Kuyperian common grace has had a major impact. Many of those who immigrated to North America from the Netherlands during the twentieth century came with a firm belief of common grace as defined and developed by Kuyper. These immigrants further disseminated his views when they arrived in these new lands. Ministers promoted it via the pulpit and catechism room. Church members advanced it via discussions and the spread of his writings. And Christian school teachers taught it and applied it to the children in the classroom.

This is how the common grace of Kuyper found its way into the CRC. In her three points of common grace adopted in 1924, the CRC reflected the influence of Kuyper. Particularly

Abraham Kuyper, Developer and Promoter of Common Grace

in her second and third points is this revealed. In her second point the CRC stated her belief that there is a "restraint of sin in the life of the individual man and of society in general . . . God by a general operation of His Spirit, without renewing the heart, restrains the unbridled manifestation of sin, so that life in human society remains possible."[2] This is Kuyperian common grace pure and simple. In her third point the CRC expressed her belief that "the unregenerate, though incapable of doing any saving good, can do civil good."[3] This too is nothing but Kuyper's doctrine. And the CRC has continued to develop and promote this teaching throughout her history. It is the doctrine that dominates her theology and practice. And, sad to say, it has borne an evil fruit in her midst. Because of her adoption of common grace, the CRC has steadily departed from the historic Reformed faith and practice. Due to her belief in God's general favor toward the unregenerated and their good work in the world, she has imported the "blessings" of higher criticism of the Bible, evolutionism, feminism, unbiblical divorce and remarriage, rock music, and movies.

The influence of Kuyper's common grace spread to North America also through a personal visit he made to the United States in 1898. That year he was invited to present the Reformed world view in a series of lectures at Princeton Theological Seminary in Princeton, New Jersey. Kuyper gave six lectures, known as the "Stone Lectures on Calvinism." In these lectures Kuyper defended a Calvinistic worldview based on his doctrine of common grace. Not only were these lectures influential when he gave them, but they have continued to be so due to their publication and wide distribution in this country and beyond. On the occasion of the one-hundredth anniversary of these lectures, Kuyper's world view of common grace was celebrated and praised by many in the Reformed camp.[4]

Because of this wide acceptance and appreciation of Kuyper's doctrine of common grace, it has become the prevailing view in most Reformed and Presbyterian circles. This is the doctrine that accounts for the efforts to redeem all of culture for Christ, including the most pagan parts of it. This is the teaching that accounts for the efforts to bring about the kingdom of Christ here on earth and make this world a better place for all. This is the doctrine that accounts for the efforts to cooperate with the world of unbelief to achieve these goals. This is the doctrine that prompts Christian college graduates to teach in public schools to help unbelievers be good citizens, to infiltrate Hollywood to make better movies, and to enter politics to work for the improvement of society. This is the doctrine that accounts for the church's attempt to make herself more relevant to the world by importing drama and dancing and contemporary music into the worship of God.

Indeed, Kuyper's doctrine of common grace has had a tremendous impact on Reformed faith and practice, but not for good.

Rejection of Kuyperian Common Grace

Subjecting Kuyper's doctrine of common grace to the test of Scripture and the Reformed confessions, it fails miserably and must be rejected. This doctrine of common grace usurps a position above the truth of sovereign particular grace, burying it and destroying it in those churches that hold to it. Kuyper's doctrine carries with it a blatant denial of the truth of the antithesis between the church and the world and leads inevitably to full-blown worldliness in practical living. It creates a dualism in the work of God, teaching that God really has two great works going on in the history of the world: the work of the redemption of the church by special grace and the work of the redemption of society by common grace.

The weight of history supports this criticism. More than one hundred years of Kuyperian influence by means of this doctrine have not resulted in the strengthening of the Reformed faith and practice but in its severe weakening and demise. The Reformed churches are not better because of Kuyper's teaching, but worse. Reformed Christians are not spiritually richer because of Kuyper's views, but profoundly poorer. There has been no solid development of Reformed doctrine due to the doctrine of common grace. There has been no real growth in spiritual godliness because of the teaching of common grace. Quite the opposite is true. There has been departure from the most fundamental of Reformed doctrines. There has been a growing worldliness and ungodliness in Christian living.

This weakening is why the Protestant Reformed Churches have rejected Kuyperian common grace. It is a serious error that has produced corrupt fruits. Instead of being praised and promoted by Reformed Christians, the doctrine of common grace needs to be rooted out of the Reformed faith and practice. Who will stand and strive to be faithful to the God of sovereign, particular grace?

20

Abraham Kuyper's View of Presupposed Regeneration

James A. Laning

MANY TIMES THE PROTESTANT REFORMED CHURCHES (PRC) have been accused of holding to Kuyper's false doctrine of presupposed regeneration. Many say that since they tell all their children that God loves them and that Christ died for them, they are presupposing that all their children, head for head, have been chosen by God and are actually in the covenant of grace. Although some who accuse the PRC of this are simply taking a delight in falsely representing the PRC, there are others who do not really understand what Kuyper's view actually was, and how the view of the PRC is to be distinguished from his.

Kuyper's View

Kuyper's view consisted of two parts. First, he maintained that Christians are to presuppose that all infant children of believers are actually in the covenant. Second, he taught that this presupposition is the basis upon which we baptize them.

What did Kuyper mean when he said that we are to presuppose that all children of believers are actually in the covenant? He did not mean that Scripture teaches that all children of believers are actually saved. Repeatedly he made

Abraham Kuyper's View of Presupposed Regeneration

clear that he was not saying that God saves all children born to believing parents. Godly parents, he said, cannot know with certainty that all their young children are actually regenerated. But, he went on to say, they do "presuppose the possibility" that all their children are saved.[1] And, presupposing this, they view and speak to all their children as though they have been chosen by God and regenerated.[2] They tell them that God loves them and that they belong to his covenant people.

Kuyper illustrated his position as follows. A gold miner treats everything that might contain gold as though it were gold, even though he knows that later only a fraction will be found actually to be gold. Similarly, according to Kuyper, we are to treat all our children as though they were actually children of God, even though we know that later we will find out that many were not.

To prove his position Kuyper cited Article 17 of the first head of the Canons of Dordt, which states that godly parents ought not to doubt the election and salvation of their children whom God calls out of this life in their infancy.[3] The church, he argued, confesses that many of these children are saved, but not that all of these are saved head for head. But even though we do not know for certain that a particular child is saved, we are to suppose that he is saved, and we are to think and speak of him this way.

Kuyper maintained that this presupposition of regeneration is the basis upon which we are to baptize our children. His argument goes like this. The sacrament of baptism, for the infant of believers as well as for the adult believer, is a seal of the righteousness of faith. Since this seal serves to strengthen the faith of the infant being baptized, it must be the case that faith is already present in the infant before the sacrament is administered. When an adult believer is baptized, his conscious faith is strengthened. Although the infant does not have conscious faith, he does have the power of faith, and it is this power of faith that is strengthened in the infant by the sacrament. Since this faith must be present in the infant before the sacrament of baptism can strengthen it, the church can baptize infants only on the ground of the presupposition that God has already worked this faith in the child's heart and has regenerated him.

Protestant Reformed View Contrasted with Kuyper's

Kuyper was striving to counter the error of many in the church of his day who were presupposing that their children were unregenerate until they grew up and it was clearly manifested that God had performed a work of grace in them. Although the PRC agree with Kuyper that this is a serious error, we disagree with the doctrine of presupposed regeneration that he set forth against this error.

Members of the PRC are not to presuppose that all their children, head for head, have actually been regenerated. As Rev. Herman Hoeksema was wont to say, we cannot presuppose to be true that which we know from Scripture is not true. Scripture makes clear that not all of our physical children are children of the promise, but rather that there are Esaus born into the sphere of the covenant (Rom. 9:6–8).

Some may argue that Kuyper merely meant that we are to view all our young children as regenerated until they show themselves to be otherwise. Insofar as Kuyper meant this, the PRC do indeed agree with him. They regard their young children to be children of God unless they grow up and clearly manifest themselves not to be. In other words, they view them just as they view everyone else in the congregation. They regard all members in a true church to be children of God. They think of them as such and treat them as such. They do this even though they know that there are always reprobate in the sphere of the covenant. Viewing the members of the church individually, we regard each of them as a child of God, whether they be infants or aged saints, unless they clearly manifest themselves not to be. But viewing the congregation as a whole, they do not presuppose that all in

Abraham Kuyper's View of Presupposed Regeneration

the instituted church, head for head, are regenerated children of God.

But what, then, are we called to believe with certainty with regard to our children? What are we called to hold to be certainly true? We are called to believe that all our real children, the children of the promise, are elect of God, and that God can and does regenerate them—at least often—when they are very young, even in the womb. These are the children members of a Protestant Reformed church are speaking about when they read the baptism form, which says that all the sins of our children have been forgiven, and that they are "sanctified in Christ."[4] These are the real children, the children who have been born again by the power of God's unconditional promise.

Some may question Protestant Reformed parents referring to their elect children as our real children. But this truth is taught, among other places, in Genesis 22:2. There God referred to Isaac as Abraham's only son, even though he also had Ishmael as a son. This same truth is taught in Galatians 3:16, 29, which says that Abraham's seed was only Christ, and those who are in Christ. Applying this to members of the church today, they can say that their real seed consists only of those who are in Christ.

Protestant Reformed parents do not baptize their children on the basis of their own words, but on the basis of the word of God. If a man "presuppose" something, that presupposition is his own thoughts, not the word of God. But if parents are to do anything good, it must proceed from faith, from a faith that is firmly based solely on God's word.

According to Question and Answer 91 of the Heidelberg Catechism, for the baptizing of our children to be a good work, it must proceed from faith, and must be done according to the law of God and to his glory. Infant baptism, just like any other good work, must proceed from a certain faith, a faith which is firmly based, not on man's presupposition, but solely on God's infallible word. The specific word of God upon which baptism is based is the unconditional promise of

God to establish his covenant with believing parents and their real seed (Gen. 17:7; Acts 2:39). The activity of baptizing our infants proceeds from a faith in this unchanging promise of our covenant God.

Since this promise of God is not only for believing parents, but also for their children, the parents are commanded to baptize them in the name of the triune God. This means that the activity of baptizing our infant children proceeds from faith in God's promise and that it is done according to God's law.

Parents must not baptize their children, or do anything else, on the basis of an uncertain presupposition in their minds. They must baptize them on the basis of the promise of God, according to the law of God. Only then will the baptizing of infant children be done also for the glory of God and the edification of his covenant people.

21

Dr. Abraham Kuyper, Politician— A Critique

Kenneth Koole

D R. ABRAHAM KUYPER WAS A THEOLOGIAN OF THE "first water," as they say; but he was also a politician, and in his day in the Netherlands it could be argued that he was the foremost politician in the land. In fact, a case could be made that in terms of time and energy, not theology but politics became the primary focus of Kuyper's life. Not politics rather than Christianity (there is no question concerning Kuyper's sincere and Reformed Christianity), but politics more than theology. Nor can there be a question that Kuyper's Calvinistic theology had tremendous impact on his political perspective. The question and concern is, to what extent did his political involvement and commitment affect even his theology? In the end, we are convinced, far too much.

Kuyper did nothing by halves. When he threw himself into politics, he did so with greatest energy, as is evidenced not only by his becoming editor-in-chief of *De Standaard*, but also his turning this weekly Christian newspaper into a daily. This required no small commitment on Kuyper's part, considering that he continued as editor-in-chief of the weekly religious periodical *De Heraut* at the same time.

The Reverend Abraham Kuyper entered the political arena earlier than one might think. At the age of thirty-three (1871) he stood for office (while minister in Utrecht), and at the age of thirty-six he was elected to the lower chamber of the Dutch Parliament. Already in the late 1860s he was corresponding with Groen van Prinsterer, his political mentor and founder of what was known as the Anti-Revolutionary Party (originally the least significant of the four main parties in the land). The party was so named in reaction to the anti-religious and revolutionary spirit that just decades earlier had spawned the anarchy of the French Revolution, and which, van Prinsterer was convinced, now threatened the Netherlands.

In our assessment of Kuyper's involvement in politics, we lay aside the question of whether a minister of the gospel is justified in resigning from the active ministry in order to serve in political office. Due to Dutch law, Kuyper had to do precisely that. Dutch law forbade ministers active in the office from holding political office at the same time, so Kuyper resigned from the active ministry, sought emeritation, and was counted as such from that point on.

Nor do we criticize Kuyper simply because he was active in politics and sought office in government. In the Christian life certainly there is room for more political involvement than simply being registered to vote, going to the voting booth, and voting against the candidate one thinks poses the greatest threat to life, liberty, and the pursuit of godliness. The indisputable fact is that in both the old and new dispensations many a God-fearing man involved himself in government, functioning in various offices in the land, whether as prince under Pharaoh, as adviser to Nebuchadnezzar and Darius, as a judge and a prince in reformation Europe, or even as duly elected member of the parliaments and congresses of the later western world. Kuyper counted himself as one in the line of such illustrious and conscientious men, and so he became involved in the hurly-burly of politics.

Kuyper's perspective was that it is not enough simply to protest evil legislation and complain about bad laws and policy once they are in place; rather, we are to be actively involved in government and politics, attempting to set the agenda to begin with. There is some truth to that.

Dr. Abraham Kuyper, Politician—A Critique

Kuyper's pull towards political activism was understandable. His beloved Netherlands was at a crossroads of national policy. It was a nation more and more faced with a thoroughgoing modernism and the pernicious spirit of revolution (a spirit that was intrinsically anti-religious and anti-authoritarian). Detesting such a spirit, Kuyper determined to be actively involved in doing what he could to prevent this spirit with its laws from dominating Dutch government and life. He would do what he could to set Calvinistic, biblically based policy in its place—a praiseworthy and honorable intention, to say the least.

The question arises, however, whether politics will allow such idealistic intentions to survive in any functionally useful way; how long can one resist the temptation of political "necessity," which invariably means compromise in the interests of attaining one's cherished legislation and advance in power? The ideal is one thing; the actual involvement in politics to achieve "Christian," biblically consistent legislation has proved to be quite another.

Politics, it has been said, is "the art of the possible." How true. As a Christian one might propose a piece of legislation of the highest ideal, but what is really possible (garnering enough support and votes to enact it) is another thing altogether. Political savvy bows to reality (what is possible in present circumstances) and satisfies itself with this "less than we would like, but better than nothing at all" mentality. Policy becomes entangled with reality, and legislation is the result of negotiation with those who expect some considerations in return.

This is what faced congressman Kuyper, and later, from 1901 to 1905, Prime Minister Kuyper. This is what opened him to criticism from within the Reformed camp in his day, and legitimately so.

We do not take issue with the commitment Kuyper and the Anti-Revolutionary Party had to setting right various social evils, but with how in the end they determined to go about it. They had many legitimate concerns, chief among which were the "school issue" and the grievous abuse of the common working man (and of working children in particular).

Dutch government was dominated by the Liberal Party. This party enacted legislation which made it all but impossible to establish Christian schools, levying a tax on every home for the support of the government-run (public) schools, and providing no support for the non-public schools. While such policy is not by any means foreign to us in America, the simple fact is that the great majority of Reformed households in the Netherlands were simply too dirt poor to support the government-controlled schools and finance their own as well. The economics of public policy forced many to educate their children in schools that were becoming more anti-biblical and anti-authority all the time. This injustice was the original issue behind the formation of the Anti-Revolutionary Party.

Because the Liberal Party derived support mainly from the middle to upper class, it was little interested in extending voting rights beyond that of property owners. It was a party that had little regard for the plight of the common working man—what happened to him and his family when injury or sickness disabled him—or for the plight of working children, many of whom worked sixty to seventy hours per week at the most minimum of wages. A voice for the disenfranchised was necessary! Who can fault a man like Kuyper for raising his powerful voice and sharpening his eloquent pen for such causes. We do not!

But what happens when for all your righteous, crusading zeal, you and your party do not have the votes—when, though there be much sound and fury, next to nothing is accomplished? And then consider that just across the aisle may sit men who in certain vital areas share common concerns but are a world apart theologically and have their own agenda in other social areas as well, yet whose support would give you the majority in parliament and turn you into a force to be reckoned with. Such was the case for Kuyper and his party. The smaller Roman Catholic party offered just such a golden opportunity.

They too, for instance, wanted their constituency to be free from carrying a double financial burden when it came to education and their own schools. Surely, if legislation dear to

Dr. Abraham Kuyper, Politician—A Critique

one's own heart had any hope of being enacted, a political union with such was the only way to accomplish it.

And so it happened. By 1887 the Anti-Revolutionary Party had become large enough to convene a national, pre-election convention. Power, that golden apple of all but irresistible appeal, political power to govern the nation, stood almost within their grasp. It was this gathering that

> ...received overtures from the Catholics, which at one stroke brought the two parties much nearer together. It was now distinctly possible for the leaders to provide a basis for co-operation by perfecting a mutually acceptable agreement.
> Calvinists and Catholics? What a team!
> What was it, then, that produced rapprochement? Simply this. Neither party had, or could in the foreseeable future expect to have, a majority in the Second Chamber of Parliament. If they were to achieve any legislative success, they must practice a policy of mutual assistance. They must inexorably cooperate. The exigencies of the political situation drove them together and made joint ventures mandatory. Cooperate or fail![1]

This unholy alliance sent tremors through the Reformed camp. Kuyper certainly was not alone in promoting this union, but it fell to Kuyper almost alone to justify the coalition from a biblical perspective; he had to justify it to his own conscience, which (I am convinced) vexed him, and to the Reformed community that was the grass roots of his party's support. This he did in his theology of common grace. He developed his justification in a series of articles in *De Heraut* that ran for some six years, from mid-1895 to mid-1901. No less sympathetic a biographer than Louis Praamsma, in his book *Let Christ Be King*, heads his treatment of this stage in Kuyper's life as "A Shift in Emphasis."[2] Politics had affected Kuyper's theology, and in a profound way.

I call common grace Kuyper's "theology" because common grace becomes a primary revelation of the very character and virtues of God, especially as he wants to be known by the unbelieving, rebellious, yet not-so-revolutionary-as-Kuyper's-party-at-first-declared, human race. In short order this theory was seized upon by Reformed theologians dazzled by the scientific discoveries and culture of the age, and this common grace, rather than antithetical, saving grace, became the primary revelation of the being and virtues of God. Kuyper, who set out as theologian and even politician of the antithesis, lost this emphasis in his grasp for political influence. We rue the day. And for all Kuyper's energetic involvement in political reform and social action, is the Netherlands today any better for it? Is the Reformed church? What enduring good remains of Kuyper the energetic, and in the end, compromising social-reformer? The consequences of his attempt to justify his course of action live on with us to this day. It is a bitter fruit.

What happened to Kuyper is not without precedent in church history. One is reminded of Solomon and his expedient alliances, of Jehoshaphat joining forces with Ahab, and of Hezekiah and the Babylonians. They were men of spiritual stature all, beneficial to the church, but apparent political exigencies proved to be a fatal flaw. The problem is not a matter of wanting to do the King's business in the realm of government; it is a matter of with whom you are willing to try to do it.

We mention one other danger that faces Christians who become deeply embroiled in politics in order to press their Christian agenda, which danger Kuyper's involvement in politics served to underscore. Men who identify with the same Reformed and Christian faith will inevitably disagree on some political policies, legislation, or strategy, and sometimes vigorously. There are fallings-out. The public disagreement and criticism between Christian brothers easily lends itself to becoming an occasion for the world and the enemies of righteousness to revel in the perceived disunion and division even among these Christians. "And we (the world) should become one with these Christians who obviously cannot even get along with each other? And they preach forgiveness and love!" The testimony of the unity of the believers in Jesus and biblical truth is seriously compromised.

Such divisions and disagreements showed themselves in Kuyper's party again and again, Kuyper himself often taking

Dr. Abraham Kuyper, Politician—A Critique

the lead due to his forceful character, and also because he had pen and press so readily available. When he was bypassed by his party as prime minister in 1908 (due to his age and inflexibility), sorely hurt, Kuyper used his pen to call into question the motives of Christian brothers and to subject most of his own party's policies to sharp criticism. A sharp rejoinder followed, highlighting all of Kuyper's perceived character flaws and questionable tactics over the years followed.[3] A most unedifying (but deliciously savory) display of any "Christian" spirit. How the enemies of righteousness lapped it up! And Kuyper, the leading preacher and spiritual figure in Christ's church besides! To his credit, Kuyper later, with grief, apologized in print, but the damage was done. The hurly-burly of politics is a most seductive and dangerous mistress.

If anything, the Reverend Dr. A. Kuyper's political career underscores the truth of the King's words: "Not by might, nor by [political] power, but by my spirit, saith the LORD of hosts" (Zech. 4:6).

Kuyper was indeed by any measure a giant, yet sadly flawed.

22

"Father" Abraham, or The Indebtedness of the Protestant Reformed Churches to Abraham Kuyper

David J. Engelsma

A<small>BRAHAM</small> K<small>UYPER IS NO LONGER HELD IN HIGH ES</small>teem in the Reformed churches. In his day—some one hundred years ago—he bestrode the Netherlands like a colossus. He cast a long shadow across much of the Reformed world. That shadow lingered for many years. But today Kuyper the Reformed theologian is rejected, if not despised.

There are still theologians and churches that honor Kuyper the theoretician of a Christian culture, the man of social action, and the successful politician. But no one speaks out in appreciation of Kuyper the Reformed theologian. When his name comes up (as it did for the one-hundredth anniversary of his 1898 lectures on Calvinism at Princeton Seminary), it is to honor him as a champion of cultural influence and dominion.

The Reformed world acknowledges Abraham Kuyper, if they acknowledge him at all, as the philosopher of common grace. About Kuyper the Reformed theologian they are silent. For them Kuyper is the man of only two books: *Lectures on Calvinism* and *De Gemeene Gratie* (Common Grace).

This is a perennial perversity in the church. Luther noted it in his controversy with Erasmus. Men are eager to collect all the dung that they can find in the fathers, while carefully

"Father" Abraham

overlooking the gold. Luther was commenting on Erasmus' examination of the church fathers to gather many quotations favoring the free will of the sinner, while ignoring their statements on the enslaved will.

I honor Abraham Kuyper as a Reformed theologian. His theology, although imperfect, was solid, sound, biblical, and creedal Reformed doctrine. By this theology and on behalf of this theology, Kuyper reformed the church of Christ in the Netherlands at the end of the nineteenth century. In its fundamentals, his theology was the gospel.

The Protestant Reformed Churches (PRC) are indebted to Kuyper the theologian. We might speak of him as "father" Abraham in acknowledgment of the use that Jesus Christ made of him in giving existence and life to these churches.

The indebtedness of the PRC to Kuyper is a fact of history. The founding members of the PRC were men and women who were put out of the Christian Reformed Church (CRC). Many members of the CRC were Dutch immigrants who had left the apostate national church in the reformation of 1886, the *Doleantie* of which Kuyper was the leading reformer. Many members of the PRC today are direct descendants of men and women who were delivered from the darkness of Arminianism and modernism into the light of the Reformed faith by means of Abraham Kuyper.

Some years ago I myself stood before a small, red-brick church building in Joure, Friesland. The church belongs to the denomination founded by Kuyper. In this church my paternal grandfather was baptized and then reared until as a young man he emigrated to the United States, where he joined the Hope CRC of Grandville in western Michigan. I thanked God for "father" Abraham on behalf of myself and my own family.

The debt that the Protestant Reformed Churches owe to Kuyper as a servant of Christ is doctrinal. Because doctrine is the main thing for the church, the debt of the PRC to Kuyper is great.

The members of the PRC themselves may not be aware of their doctrinal indebtedness to Kuyper. Usually Kuyper's name comes up among us as a father of common grace, which teaching we repudiate as erroneous. In addition, Herman Hoeksema seldom indicated his own dependency on the theology of Kuyper. He almost never quoted Kuyper with approval. His many references to Kuyper are critical.

This is unfortunate and misleading. Although Hoeksema corrected, developed, and put his own stamp on the theology of Kuyper, the theology of Hoeksema is essentially that of Kuyper. As Kuyper faithfully confessed and developed the theology of Calvin and the Reformed tradition on the basis of the confessions, so Hoeksema received and worked with the tradition as it came to him in large part through Kuyper.

Herman Hoeksema was heavily influenced by the theology of Abraham Kuyper.

Early in his ministry Hoeksema readily acknowledged this influence. In the foreword of *Van Zonde en Genade* (Concerning Sin and Grace), co-authored with Henry Danhof in the heat of the common grace controversy, Hoeksema wrote, "The great Netherlands leader (Abraham Kuyper) has written much with which we heartily agree. When we read his *Dat de Genade Particulier Is* (That Grace is Particular), we feel ourselves thoroughly one with him."[1]

In 1930, in an article in the *Standard Bearer* on "Dr. Abraham Kuyper and Common Grace," Hoeksema spoke highly of Kuyper and his theology:

> Although we refuse to worship him or to make him the court of last appeal in Reformed theology, as is often done...and although it is our conviction that he departed from the line of Reformed thinking in his development of the theory of Common Grace; yet, it must not be forgotten that he was instrumental to a great extent in the restoration of Reformed theology.[2]

What, in briefest summary, is the theology of Kuyper that has come to the Protestant Reformed Churches by way of Herman Hoeksema?

First, there is the heartfelt conviction (on which everything is staked) that sound doctrine is necessary and primary for the church; that this doctrine is the historic, confessional Reformed truth; that this doctrine is God-centered; and that this doctrine is a system. Herman Bavinck described Kuyper's theology this way:

> Avoiding all Apologetics, Dr. Kuyper proceeded in a thetical manner. He chose his standpoint not on the outside but within faith, planted himself squarely on the basis of the infallible Scriptures and the Reformed Confession...
> While thus embracing the Reformed doctrine he revives the same in its most strict type. To him the line marked by the names of Calvin, Voetius, Comrie represents Reformed theology in its most correct development. For it is characteristic of the Reformed doctrine, that it deduces all things from God and makes all things return to God. Hence Dr. Kuyper is not satisfied until every dogma has been traced to its deepest roots and set forth in its inner connection with the divine decree...The various Reformed doctrines are to him... one world of ideas, one strictly coherent system.[3]

Second, at its heart this theology is the confession that the grace of God in Jesus Christ is sovereign and particular. The theology of Kuyper (in distinction from his philosophy) is found in his *Dat de Genade Particulier Is;* his commentary on the Heidelberg Catechism (*E Voto Dordraceno*); *De Leer der Verbonden* (The Doctrine of the Covenants); and the *Dictaten Dogmatiek* (Kuyper's dogmatics lectures at the Free University).

Dat de Genade Particulier Is is a grand, moving defense of particular, sovereign grace against the heresy of a universal, ineffectual grace of God in Jesus Christ and his gospel. Kuyper began by explaining the three main texts that open and secret Arminians always raise against particular grace: I John 2:2; 1 Timothy 2:4; and 2 Peter 3:9. All have the elect, and the elect only, in view. Mentioning that his own colleagues in the national church cursed him from the pulpit for teaching it, Kuyper insisted that Christ died only for the elect. He also taught that God's grace in the gospel is intended for and directed to the elect alone. God desires the salvation of the elect only.[4]

Kuyper taught eternal, unconditional election accompanied by eternal, unconditional reprobation. In his *De Leer der Verbonden,* he asserted that one who refuses to confess reprobation thereby refuses to confess biblical election: "Election is always accompanied by its dark shadow. Without confessing reprobation, you also do not confess election. To suppose that you could be able to have the one without the other is playing with words."[5]

For Kuyper the order of the eternal decrees is supralapsarian. This order, he thought, was more biblical, as well as more glorifying to God.

The actual saving of the elect sinner is the sovereign work of God alone apart from any cooperating activity on the part of the sinner. This was Kuyper's doctrine of immediate regeneration. Only the teaching that the Spirit regenerates without the means of the preached Word explains the regeneration—and salvation—of elect infant children of believing parents. But this teaching also safeguards the graciousness of regeneration: the new birth is not at all the work of the sinner himself, is not at all a change dependent on the sinner's faith.

For his confession of God's sovereignty in salvation, Kuyper was accused of hyper-Calvinism.[6] Within the Reformed community, this charge is final confirmation that one is, in fact, teaching the gospel of grace (see Rom. 9:19, 20). As is always the case, the slander came not from avowed enemies of the Reformed faith but from Reformed ministers.

A third vital area of biblical truth in which the Protestant Reformed Churches have been significantly influenced by Abraham Kuyper is the doctrine of the covenant. In *De Leer der Verbonden,* Kuyper traced the covenant of grace to the triune being of God, thus suggesting that the covenant is a relationship of love and life. On the basis of Romans 5:12–21, Kuyper established that Jesus Christ is head of the covenant of grace, as Adam was head of the covenant of creation in paradise. Christ, Kuyper stated, is "Head of the covenant of grace."[7]

Christ's headship of the covenant implies that the covenant of grace is established only with the elect. This follows also from the close relationship between election and the covenant. Election and covenant are not "two (opposite) poles that exclude each other. Rather the covenant of grace is the glorious bed through which the water of life flows to us from the depths of election."[8]

Kuyper vehemently rejected the notion that the covenant differs from election by including the reprobate. The covenant of grace "aims only and exclusively at the elect. No one is a member in that covenant other than the one who receives or has been appointed to grace. The rich, glorious promises that God the Lord has included in his covenant of grace are absolutely not offered upon an uncertain chance, but are applied to the elect children of the inheritance in the light."[9]

> To say that in Baptism, according to the Form of Baptism, the promises of eternal salvation are given, personally and essentially, to every baptized child, head for head, is nothing other than a destruction (vernietigen), by Arminian poison, of the rich life that fragrantly wafts to you from this formula.[10]

This is familiar language to every Protestant Reformed Christian, though he or she may never have read a word of Kuyper.

In 1924, the CRC officially committed itself to the philosophy of Abraham Kuyper: the culture-forming, world-conforming theory of common grace. In the person of Herman Hoeksema, it banished the theology of Kuyper. This theology now finds a home in the PRC and hardly anywhere else.

Space would fail me to tell of Kuyper's defense of the antithesis and of his recovery of the autonomy of the local congregation.

What a theology!

This is our debt!

Thank God for Abraham Kuyper, the theologian and reformer of the church!

Part 4

The Reformation of 1924 in North America

23

The Reformer of 1924: "Doctor of the Covenant"

David J. Engelsma

IN THE REFORMATION OF THE CHURCH BEGUN IN 1924, the reformer was Herman Hoeksema. This is not a slighting of Henry Danhof and George Ophoff, the two ministers who were deposed with Hoeksema by the Christian Reformed Church (CRC). Danhof was influential in developing the doctrines that have come to distinguish the Protestant Reformed Churches (PRC), as his profound treatise of 1920 on the covenant, "*De Idee van het Genadeverbond*" (The Idea of the Covenant of Grace), clearly shows.[1] But Danhof soon abandoned the churches in which the reformation would be worked out in order to go his independent way. Besides, Hoeksema was the more prominent of the two in the controversy in the early 1920s.

Ophoff was Hoeksema's loyal colleague from the beginning. In the struggle in the early 1950s within the PRC to maintain the reformation, it was Ophoff who clearly saw the threat to the PRC in the covenant theology of Klaas Schilder and who insisted that this theology be rejected, whatever the cost. But originally it was Hoeksema, five years older than Ophoff, who decisively influenced the younger pastor. Even in the schism of 1953 by which the gospel of sovereign grace was preserved in the PRC, Hoeksema came to play the leading role. Ophoff was content always to work in the shadow of his towering contemporary.

Life

Hoeksema was born near the city of Groningen in the Netherlands in 1886, the year of the birth also of Karl Barth. He was the child of a broken, poverty-stricken home. His father was an unbeliever, an adulterer, and a drunkard who abandoned his wife and their four young children. Herman Hoeksema is evidence that God establishes his covenant with the children of but one believing parent (1 Cor. 7:14). He is also evidence that God delights to make something out of nothing in his church, thus "to bring to nought things that are" (1 Cor. 1:28). It is interesting that this child of a failed marriage, who saw firsthand the misery of the deserted wife and mother, later opposed the Reformed tradition by teaching that marriage is an unbreakable bond, so that even the deserted, "innocent" party is forbidden to remarry.

A godly mother had powerful influence upon her son for his own salvation and for the good of the church of Christ.

Having immigrated to the United States in 1904, Hoeksema sought the ministry in the CRC. He was trained at Calvin College (then, Calvin Preparatory School) and Calvin Seminary. In 1915, at the age of twenty-nine, he was ordained into the ministry in the CRC. When the conflict involved in the reformation reached its climax in 1924, Hoeksema was no brash novice, but a mature thirty-eight. (Luther was thirty-four in 1517.)

Although Hoeksema never engaged in graduate study or obtained an advanced degree (indeed this was impossible for him in the press of his work), he was a brilliant, well-read, and highly disciplined preacher, theologian, and author.

Hoeksema was a man of many gifts. He was physically strong and athletic, a good ice skater and a swimmer who loved to disappear over the horizon on Lake Michigan and remain there for hours. An artist, he wrote poetry, hymns, and moving devotional pieces. His meditations in the magazine of the reformation, the *Standard Bearer*, are the motions of the heart that knows the great and good God. He was a

The Reformer of 1924: "Doctor of the Covenant"

painter whose oils are lovely. As an adult, he learned the organ sufficiently to accompany his singing of the beloved Dutch psalms. More importantly, he was a faithful, loving husband and a solid family man.

Preacher/Pastor

Friend and foe alike recognized Rev. Hoeksema as a truly great preacher. His enemies tried to denigrate the reformation of 1924 as merely a matter of people mesmerized by an orator. There was stirring oratory in a deep voice from a commanding presence. There were also penetrating exegesis, excellent homiletics, and solid doctrine. There was also the mysterious unction of the Holy Spirit that alone makes the great preacher. The power and worth of his preaching are evident in the published volumes of collected sermons, for example, *When I Survey*, sermons on the suffering of Christ.[2] In fact, Hoeksema developed his theology in connection with, through, and for the sake of preaching.

Never would he surrender his pulpit, not even when the synod of the PRC offered him a full-time professorship so that he could devote more time to study and writing. As far as he himself was concerned, he was not Professor Hoeksema, but Reverend Hoeksema. All of his lifelong training of men for the ministry in the Protestant Reformed Seminary aimed solely at the production of good preachers for the churches. He had no interest in theological scholarship for its own sake. This emphasis on preaching stemmed from his conviction that the preaching of the gospel is the word of God. He took seriously the Reformed confession that preaching is the chief means of faith, grace, and salvation. When an ordained man preaches the word of truth, Christ himself speaks with his living voice to his church.

In the earlier days of the reformation, before the demands of preaching, writing, teaching, and missions took their toll on his time and energies, he was an active, effective pastor in his congregation of some five hundred families. He was a tireless worker who poured himself out for his congregation, the churches, and the truth. Gertrude Hoeksema tells of the twenty-hour days and the sleepless nights in her fine biography, *Therefore Have I Spoken*.[3] The ingratitude of many of his congregation and especially of his former students must have cut him to the quick in the cruel days of 1953, although he never said a word about it in the years of my own seminary training under him (1960–1963), a mere seven years later.

Theologian

> If you ask me what, in our time, our people need above all, in the first place, my answer is: Doctrine! If you ask me what they need in the second place, I say: Doctrine! If you ask me what they need in the third place, I say: Doctrine![4]

This was Hoeksema's published conviction already in 1921 when he was still in the CRC.

The necessary doctrine was the Reformed faith as set forth in the Reformed confessions. Central was the sovereignty of the grace of God in the salvation of elect sinners. Hoeksema drew out more clearly than had been done before the implication that grace is particular. Grace both as favor toward men and as actual power working deliverance is intended for and given to the elect alone. Hoeksema, like Paul in Ephesians 1 and like Christ in John 10, saw salvation in Christ as founded upon God's eternal predestination. G. C. Berkouwer has remarked that no one has developed theology consistently with predestination as has Herman Hoeksema.[5]

Hoeksema's main contribution, however, has been the development of the distinctively Reformed doctrine of the covenant. He explained it as a living relationship of fellowship between God and the church in Christ. Rooted in God's

The Reformer of 1924: "Doctor of the Covenant"

own triune life, it is the goal of the work of salvation, not merely a means to final bliss. Hoeksema viewed the covenant in the light of the gospel of grace, teaching that God establishes the covenant with Christ and the elect in him, and that the covenant promise is unconditional, not dependent for its realization upon man or his work.

In the turbulent time leading up to the schism of 1953, Hoeksema told the as yet united churches that "the most peculiar treasure of the Protestant Reformed Churches [is] their peculiar view of the covenant."[6] Confidently (and accurately), he stated that "he that has been captivated by this beautiful Reformed truth must have nothing of anything that smacks like Heynsian theology, nor will he ever retrogress into a traditional conditional theology."[7]

As other theologians were the "angelic doctor," or the "doctor of grace," Hoeksema was the "doctor of the covenant."

Within the framework of the confessions, Hoeksema claimed liberty to differ from the Reformed tradition. He corrected the tradition in such doctrines as the image of God in man; the covenant with Adam in paradise; and marriage, divorce, and remarriage.

Theologians express their theology in writing. Hoeksema published, among other works, *Reformed Dogmatics*, *The Triple Knowledge* (a commentary on the Heidelberg Catechism), *Believers and Their Seed*, and *Behold, He Cometh!* (commentary on Revelation). In addition, he wrote many pamphlets and brochures. A veritable treasure trove of editorials, meditations, and articles fills the first forty-one volumes of the *Standard Bearer*. Much of this remains untranslated in the Dutch language. It is now time for a Protestant Reformed man, working through this mass of material, as well as many unpublished sermons, to make the theology of Herman Hoeksema the subject of a doctoral dissertation. This would benefit the PRC and the rest of the catholic church.

Churchman

On principle, Herman Hoeksema was not a professional theologian but an ardent churchman. He loved the church. He loved her especially in the PRC, but he loved Christ's church. He worked in and for the church. He founded, guided, suffered for, and devoted himself to a denomination of churches. As a churchman—a *Reformed* churchman—he insisted on, and submitted to, the Church Order of Dordt, not only with regard to the government of the local church by elders, but also with regard to the government of the churches by the major assemblies. No independent, he! The result has been a distinctive, workable, beneficent church polity in the PRC, a fine balance of the autonomy of the local congregation and the real authority of the major assemblies.

As he had opportunity, Hoeksema manifested wider interest than only the PRC. His effort at reform in the early 1920s had the welfare of the CRC in mind. The CRC rejected its reformer. But where would the CRC be today had it hearkened to Herman Hoeksema? In the 1940s, Hoeksema enthusiastically promoted a conference with the Reformed Church in the United States. In the late 1930s and again in the late 1940s, Hoeksema extended the hand of fellowship to Klaas Schilder when other Reformed churches in the United States were at pains to distance themselves from the Dutch theologian and even to ostracize him. In the early 1950s, when some of his colleagues opposed the idea, Hoeksema urged acceptance of the invitation from the Reformed Ecumenical Synod to send observers to Edinburgh, saying that "it will be a healthful experience to rub elbows with others of the Reformed persuasion."[8]

Reformer

Against this background of preacher, theologian, and churchman must the reformer of 1924 be seen.

The Reformer of 1924: "Doctor of the Covenant"

Christ did not use him to reform a church ravaged by theological modernism, as was the case with Dr. J. Gresham Machen, although the consequences of the error of the common grace that Hoeksema fought would be sheer modernism.

Hoeksema purified the church of the destructive heresy of common grace. He did so in two main respects. He condemned the teaching that God is gracious in the preaching of the gospel to all who hear, *offering* them salvation with the wish that all will be saved. This is the introduction of the Arminian doctrine of preaching into the Reformed churches. Second, he repudiated the teaching that there is a work of grace in the unregenerated, unbelieving world that produces good culture, so that the church may cooperate with the world and allow herself to be influenced by it. Against the first error, Hoeksema asserted that the grace of God in the gospel is particular. Against the second, he posited the biblical truth of the antithesis.

As a reformer, he stood. He was a man of courage.

As a reformer, he suffered. He was hated, cursed, deposed, isolated, betrayed, and thus, killed. He paid the price.

As a reformer, he is being vindicated, not by men but by God in history. His warnings and prophecies are fulfilled. It becomes more and more difficult to oppose, or even ignore, the truths that he proclaimed.

As a reformer, he ought to be honored for the truth's sake.

This we gladly do. For, with many others, we have loved our reformer.

For the truth's sake.

24

To Win the Battle but Lose the War: Common Grace and the Janssen Controversy

Herman C. Hanko

THE CONTROVERSY OVER THE ERROR OF COMMON grace, which marks the beginning of the history of the Protestant Reformed Churches, did not begin in 1924 when Revs. Hoeksema, Ophoff, and Danhof were expelled from the Christian Reformed Church (CRC) for refusing to express agreement with this erroneous doctrine. Although common grace had been taught for some time in the history of the Dutch Reformed churches, it became an issue in connection with the controversy that swirled around Dr. Ralph Janssen, professor of Old Testament studies at Calvin Theological Seminary.[1]

Janssen was appointed to the faculty of Calvin Seminary in 1914 after he completed his studies and earned his degrees from various universities in Germany, France, and the Netherlands. Although he was a very gifted teacher, and although he had a great influence on his students, suspicions arose among other members of the faculty concerning his teachings. His colleagues asked the Theological School Committee for an investigation, and after much maneuvering, his case was presented to the Synod of the CRC in 1920. That synod exonerated him, but the suspicions continued. A study committee, of which Revs. Herman Hoeksema and Henry Dan-

Common Grace and the Janssen Controversy

hof were members, was appointed to examine his teachings and report to the Theological School Committee. Although the committee was divided in its report, the majority advised that Dr. Janssen's teachings were contrary to Scripture and the Reformed confessions. This report was submitted to the Synod of 1922, and Dr. Janssen was found guilty and deposed from his office of theological professor.

It was this controversy which brought to the attention of the churches the doctrine of common grace. Dr. Janssen himself was responsible for this. In all his writings in defense of his position, he appealed to common grace and insisted that his views would stand or fall on the one question of whether or not common grace was Reformed.

It is an interesting sidelight of history that neither the Theological School Committee, nor the study committee, nor the Synod of 1922, although they were all fully aware of Janssen's appeal to common grace in support of his position, entered into this aspect of the case. It was not so much as mentioned in all their material.

The reason for this was undoubtedly that the Theological School Committee and the study committee were divided on that question. Hoeksema and Danhof opposed common grace, while most if not all the other members of the committee held to the doctrine. All seemed to agree that to enter into the question of common grace would so badly divide the TSC and the study committee that no condemnation of Janssen would then be possible.

Hoeksema later expressed regret over this failure and said that it was a serious mistake on the part of the committee and the synod to ignore the question of common grace. In fact, because common grace was ignored, the Janssen controversy was really never settled, even though the Synod of 1922 condemned him.

Janssen was condemned for teaching higher critical views of Scripture. In the judgment of the Synod of 1922, he denied the divine inspiration of Scripture, denied the miracles, and did serious injustice to important aspects of Scripture's truth. All this was, by his own insistence, on the basis of common

Always Reforming

grace. When the Synod of 1922 condemned these views but refused to enter into the question of common grace, it left the latter issue hanging. It was this issue that arose again immediately after the Janssen controversy, in the form of objections to Rev. Hoeksema's denial of common grace; and the Synod of 1924, in adopting the three points of common grace, opened the door for Hoeksema's condemnation.

Rev. Hoeksema, after he was set outside the CRC, and when reflecting on the entire Janssen controversy, spoke prophetically when he wrote that the failure to condemn common grace would result in the views of Janssen ultimately prevailing. His prophecy proved correct, for every view that Janssen taught concerning Scripture has now been accepted in the CRC. And, strikingly, this has often happened with a specific appeal to the doctrine of common grace.

Because of the importance of this issue, we must inquire more carefully into what precisely Janssen taught and how he connected his teaching with common grace.

Janssen insisted on an organic view of inspiration rather than a mechanical view. While this was certainly proper (we also believe in the doctrine of organic inspiration and repudiate mechanical inspiration), he meant by organic inspiration a kind of inspiration that allowed room for a human element. This human element in inspiration became the launching pad for all his erroneous views.

Basically, Dr. Janssen firmly believed that much of what the Old Testament patriarchs and prophets believed and taught was borrowed from heathen sources. Abraham lived in Ur among heathens. Moses was brought up in the palace of Pharaoh. The nation of Israel and the prophets were constantly surrounded by heathen people and influenced by them. The result, according to Janssen, was that much of Israel's beliefs were received from Babylon, Egypt, and other pagan sources. The creation account came from Babylon, he said, although it may have been purged of some mythological elements by inspiration. The law and the psalms show Babylonian influences. The name *Jehovah* may have come

Common Grace and the Janssen Controversy

from heathen sources. Israel's belief in God was not a pure monotheism, but was mixed with pagan polytheistic elements. The stories of Samson were not historical, but were patterned after the heroes in the pagan world, for Israel needed its hero-myths just as the heathen did. The patriarchs' views of the resurrection from the dead and the immortality of the soul were imperfect and incomplete because they were taken from the heathen who did not understand these things perfectly. And David's desire to build a temple was nothing but an effort to imitate the temples of the heathen, all of whom worshiped in them.

Janssen also denied the supernatural character of the miracles. Here his emphasis was on scientific research. Science gave the clue to the explanation of miracles, which were to be explained in a natural way. The walls of Jericho fell because of a severe earthquake; the manna was not miraculously sent in the sense that God directly brought it, but it was rather the food found on bushes which grew in the wilderness; the water from the rock was there all the time in the rock, and Moses only happened to hit a thin piece of rock with his staff, which released the water; the sun and the moon did not stand still at Joshua's command, but reappeared after a very dark storm or an eclipse.

According to Janssen, because Scripture was not completely inspired by God, and because of a human element in Scripture, one had to approach Scripture empirically, that is, with the approach of science, to discover which parts of Scripture were actually of divine origin. Thus, parts of Scripture were not the word of God at all. Ecclesiastes contained the ponderings of a very pessimistic philosopher; the Song of Solomon was nothing but an oriental love song; Daniel was not written by the prophet whose name the book bears; and the Pentateuch was composed by many different authors, some of whom were nothing but editors.

It is evident that Janssen robbed Scripture of its divine character in most of its parts.

All of Janssen's views were connected to common grace. In

fact, Janssen used the doctrine of common grace as his sole support, and he charged his accusers with denying what to him was at the heart of the Reformed faith.

How did he do this?

The doctrine of common grace which Janssen embraced was that taught by Dr. Abraham Kuyper. One must not conclude that Kuyper would have agreed with Janssen in his views of Scripture. He would have protested them vigorously, because Kuyper held to a very strict view of Scripture. Nevertheless, imbedded in Kuyper's views of common grace were surely the conclusions to which Janssen carried them.

Kuyper believed that the common grace of God so operated in all men that sin was restrained by an internal working of the Holy Spirit, so that the heathen were able to do good works. Specifically, they were able to know God, retain knowledge of good and evil, do some degree of good, and accomplish much in the way of scientific advancement.

Taking hold of these views of Kuyper, Janssen taught that general revelation (God's manifestation of himself in creation), a product of common grace, gave to the heathen some knowledge of God which Israel borrowed in the development of its religion. Thus, although the elements of religion found in Israel's belief in God were taken from heathen sources, they nevertheless had their origin in God, because God, by his common grace, bestowed upon the heathen these crucial elements of the truth.

Janssen's denial of the miracles was also connected to common grace. Science, so Janssen taught, was the product of common grace because the heathen, full of this strange grace, could understand God through general revelation. Hence, the believer had to accept the products of science as God's work and receive it into his own faith. Applied to the miracles, this meant that to do justice to science (the fruit of God's common grace), one had to explain the miracles in scientific terms. Creation had to be explained in such a way that it did no violence to science, which discovered that the earth was very old. Science has shown that the amount of matter and energy in the creation is constant. Thus, God, having once created, could not and would not create any more matter than he created at the beginning. So the manna was already in the creation, for God could not create something not formed at the beginning. The water in the rock had been present from creation and could not have been created by God at the time of Israel's wandering, because this would make a mockery of science. And such miracles as the passage through the Red Sea, the fall of the walls of Jericho, and the standing still of the sun, could not contradict the discoveries of science, lest God's work of common grace be spurned.

So common grace became the doctrinal root of a vicious and unprincipled attack on Scripture which left God's holy word in tatters.

Janssen was rightly condemned for his teachings on Scripture; and the Christian Reformed Church, due primarily to the work of Herman Hoeksema, gained a victory in a significant battle.

But the issue of common grace was not settled and was, in fact, ignored. The result was not only that common grace continued to be taught in the church, but that three faithful ministers were ousted from the denomination for denying it. Only two short years after Janssen was condemned, the Synod of the CRC adopted the very views of common grace that Janssen used as a basis for his denial of Scripture.

Herman Hoeksema's prophecy was fulfilled. Because common grace was not repudiated but was officially adopted, while godly men were deposed and set outside the denomination, in a few decades Janssen's views of Scripture, with all their horrible consequences, were openly taught in the church and have now received official sanction within the denomination.

The battle was won, but the war was lost!

There is a lesson from history here. Let those who are troubled by the apostasy in the Christian Reformed Church learn this lesson of history. Common grace lies at the root of this apostasy. To reform the church requires that the evil be plucked out, root and all.

25

The Preaching of the Gospel: Promise and Command

Robert D. Decker

FROM THE VERY BEGINNING OF THEIR HISTORY AND continuing to the present, the Protestant Reformed Churches have been accused of teaching and defending "hyper-Calvinism." Because the Protestant Reformed Churches deny that God is gracious to all who hear the preaching of the gospel, that God sincerely desires the salvation of all who hear the gospel, and that God freely *offers* salvation to all who hear the preaching of the gospel, the Protestant Reformed Churches are dismissed by many as "hyper-Calvinist." It is charged that the Protestant Reformed preach only to the elect, regenerated sinner, that the Protestant Reformed do not believe in missions, and that they refuse to call everyone to repent and believe in the Lord Jesus Christ. My esteemed colleague, Professor David Engelsma, is precisely correct when he insists, "This is total, and usually inexcusable, misrepresentation."[1] To put it bluntly, the Protestant Reformed Churches are not guilty as charged. The Protestant Reformed Churches teach and practice missions vigorously both in North America and in foreign lands. The Protestant Reformed Churches teach and vigorously defend the truth that God calls all men everywhere to repent of their sins and to believe in the Lord Jesus.[2]

What the Protestant Reformed Churches deny most emphatically is that the preaching of the gospel is an offer in the Arminian sense, that is, an offer to all which depends on the

The Preaching of the Gospel: Promise and Command

free will of the hearers. Further, what the Protestant Reformed Churches deny is that God is gracious to all who hear the gospel preaching and that God desires the salvation of all who hear the gospel preaching.

The synod of the Christian Reformed Church in 1924 adopted three points of doctrine by which she expressed belief in the error of common grace. The first point as adopted by the CRC Synod of 1924 reads:

> Regarding the first point, touching the favorable attitude of God toward mankind in general and not only toward the elect, synod declares that according to Scripture and the Confession it is established, that besides the saving grace of God shown only to the elect unto eternal life, there is also a certain favor or grace of God which He shows to His creatures in general. This is evident from the Scripture passages that were quoted and from the Canons of Dordt, II, 5 and III, IV, 8, 9, where the general offer of the gospel is set forth; while it also is evident from the citations made from Reformed writers belonging to the most flourishing period of Reformed theology that our fathers from of old maintained this view.[3]

The latter part of this first point (sometimes called "the little point of the first point") is the CRC's official teaching of a well-meant offer of the gospel. To this teaching the PRC object on biblical and confessional grounds. We shall have to limit ourselves to a discussion of the confessional references and biblical texts cited by the 1924 synod of the CRC.

Canons of Dordt, Head 2, Article 5 reads:

> Moreover the promise of the gospel is, that whosoever believeth in Christ crucified shall not perish, but have everlasting life. This promise, together with the command to repent and believe, ought to be declared and published to all nations, and to all persons promiscuously and without distinction, to whom God out of his good pleasure sends the gospel.[4]

This article teaches that the promise of the gospel must be preached promiscuously to all nations and men without distinction. It teaches that the gospel goes where God in his good pleasure sends it. The content of the promise of the gospel, according to this article, is that whosoever believeth in Christ crucified shall not perish, but have everlasting life. Note well that the article presents the promise of the gospel as strictly particular, for it is to them that believe in Christ, that is, the elect. The gospel is not presented as a general offer which can be rejected or accepted at will, but as a command! The article certainly does not teach that the preaching of the gospel is a manifestation of the grace of God to all who hear it.

Canons of Dordt, Heads 3 and 4, Article 8 states:

> As many as are called by the gospel are unfeignedly called. For God hath most earnestly and truly shown in His Word what is pleasing to Him, namely, that those who are called should come to Him. He, moreover, seriously promises eternal life and rest to as many as shall come to Him and believe on Him.[5]

This article teaches that the calling of the gospel is unfeigned. This calling is to repent and believe. God is serious when he sends this calling to any man. No man has the right before God to remain in his sin and persevere in unbelief. God reveals in the gospel what is pleasing to him, namely, that the ones called should come to him. God seriously promises eternal life and rest not to all who hear the gospel, but to as many as believe and come to him. The promise of the gospel, therefore, is strictly particular. Certainly the article does not teach that the preaching of the gospel is grace to all the hearers.

Canons of Dordt, Heads 3 and 4, Article 9 states:

> It is not the fault of the gospel, nor of Christ offered therein, nor of God, who calls men by the gospel, and confers upon them various gifts, that those who are called by the ministry of the Word refuse to come and be converted. The fault lies in themselves; some of whom when called, regardless of their danger, reject the Word of life; others, though they receive it, suffer it not to make a lasting impression on their heart; therefore, their joy, arising only from a temporary faith, soon vanishes, and they fall away;

The Preaching of the Gospel: Promise and Command

while others choke the seed of the Word by perplexing cares, and the pleasures of this world, and produce no fruit. This our Savior teaches in the parable of the sower (Matt. 13).[6]

It should be noted that the article speaks of Christ being "offered" in the gospel. The word translated "offered" is the Latin verb *offero*, which has as its first and primary meaning "to present."[7] With this no Reformed person has a problem. Christ is presented in the preaching of the gospel to all who hear that preaching. The fault and guilt of the rejection of the gospel by the reprobate is not God's, nor Christ's, nor the gospel's, but wholly the sinner's. This article does not even come close to suggesting that the presentation or offering of Christ in the gospel is grace to all who hear.

The synod of the Christian Reformed Church in 1924 cited three passages of Scripture in support of its contention concerning the well-meant offer of the gospel. The first, Romans 2:4, reads, "Or despisest thou the riches of his goodness and forbearance and longsuffering; not knowing that the goodness of God leadeth thee to repentance?" The text does not say that it is the *intention* of God to lead to repentance, but that God's goodness, forbearance, and longsuffering actually lead to repentance. The apostle is addressing the "O man" of verses 1 and 3, and "man" here cannot be understood as an individual, for then the text would be saying of the same man that God's goodness *leads* him to repentance, while that very man does not know this, despises that goodness, and gathers to himself treasures of wrath. This is impossible. If God's goodness leads a man to repentance, that man does not despise that goodness. And if a man despises the goodness of God, surely that goodness of God does not lead him to repentance. We must, therefore, understand "man" as a class, collectively. It is true that the goodness of God leads man, that is, elect man, to repentance. It is also true that man despises the goodness of God and gathers for himself treasures of wrath, not knowing that the goodness of God leads man to repentance. This is true of the ungodly, reprobate man.

The synod also cited Ezekiel 18:23 and Ezekiel 33:11.

These texts read, "Have I any pleasure at all that the wicked should die? saith the Lord God: and not that he should return from his ways, and live?" (Ezek. 18:23). "Say unto them, As I live, saith the Lord God, I have no pleasure in the death of the wicked; but that the wicked turn from his way and live: turn ye, turn ye from your evil ways; for why will ye die, O house of Israel?" (Ezek. 33:11).

These texts do not teach that God is gracious in the preaching of the gospel to the reprobate wicked. There is no offer of grace and salvation in these texts. In both passages there is a direct statement by the God of Israel that he has no pleasure in the death of the wicked, but in that the wicked turn from his evil ways and live. In Ezekiel 33:11 this statement stands in the form of an oath, "As I live, saith the Lord God," and therefore is no offer, but a most emphatic divine assertion. Note, too, that both passages are addressed to the "house of Israel," the typical manifestation of God's church. God, because he has no pleasure in the death of the wicked, comes to his church through the prophet and calls them to turn from their evil ways and live. By the power of that word of God, the elect do indeed turn from their evil ways and live. What a rich, abiding comfort there is in these passages!

No, God is not gracious to the reprobate in the preaching of the word. God does not come with a well-meant offer in the preaching of the word. God's promise is always particular. But, most emphatically, God does "command all men everywhere to repent" (Acts 17:30). To every single one of his laboring and heavy-laden sheep Jesus comes with the command, "Come unto me... I will give you rest" (Matt. 11:28). And when those sheep hear the voice of Jesus, they do come to him and find rest (John 10:27, 28). Those who are not of Jesus' sheep also hear the voice of Jesus, but they believe not, because they are not of his sheep (John 10:25, 26).

26

1924 and the Antithesis—A Reaffirmation

Russell J. Dykstra

YOU MAY NOT KNOW EXACTLY WHAT THE ANTITHESIS is, but that is not because it is new. The antithesis is as old as the human race. In the dawn of time God placed in the middle of the garden the two well-known trees—the tree of life and the tree of the knowledge of good and evil. God set before Adam the daily obligation to serve God antithetically by eating of the fruit of the tree of life—and enjoying covenant life with God—and by rejecting the forbidden fruit of the tree of the knowledge of good and evil. That is the life of the antithesis in a nutshell—saying Yes to God and to all that he requires, and saying No to what God forbids and to all that opposes God.

The antithetical requirements became more pronounced when Satan came to tempt Eve with a lie that contradicted God's command. Clearly Adam and Eve had the responsibility to uphold God's law and to reject Satan's slander. But they failed, turning against God and joining with God's enemies. This failure of man was not a failure of God's plan, nor an unexpected turn of events to God. Rather, it was sovereignly determined by God to serve his purpose, namely, the glory of his name. For God knew that his holy majesty and glory would appear in all its radiant beauty if it were revealed against the black background of sin, death, and hell. The lines of the antithesis, between light and darkness, would be unmistakable.

By his disobedience, man brought upon himself the horrible darkness of total depravity, God's curse, and death. Yet this too was according to God's eternal purpose to establish his covenant of friendship with a people chosen and gathered out of a fallen and sinful race. Thus from Adam and Eve would come forth two seeds, as God announced in Genesis 3:15, "And I will put enmity between thee and the woman, and between thy seed and her seed; it shall bruise thy head, and thou shalt bruise his heel." God himself promised to establish the antithesis between the two seeds ("I will put enmity between...") by making the elect seed of the woman to be *his* covenant friends.

God's plan was now ready to be unfolded throughout history. His people, though from the same stock of Adam as the ungodly, and living in this world, would be called to live antithetically. They must do this, not by attempting to flee out of this world; rather, as they live in and among the ungodly seed of the serpent, the friends of God are to live for God and stand against sin and the ungodly.

Thus the people of God lived antithetically. Abraham lived in Canaan, but as a pilgrim and stranger. The Israelites lived surrounded by the nations but were enemies of the heathen, separated from them, a holy nation of priests consecrated unto God. The believer's antithetical confession is heard in Psalm 139:21: "Do not I hate them, O Lord, that hate thee?"

The antithetical calling is reinforced by the Holy Spirit in 2 Corinthians 6:14–17: "For what fellowship hath righteousness with unrighteousness? and what communion hath light with darkness? And what concord hath Christ with Belial? or what part hath he that believeth with an infidel?...Wherefore come out from among them, and be ye separate, saith the Lord."

Historically, the church understood this calling and continued to insist upon it, though not without periods of inconsistency. The early New Testament church rejected the flight from the world as advocated by the Manicheans. But she gradually slipped into both world conformity on the one hand, and world flight on the other, in the dark days before the Reformation.

1924 and the Antithesis—A Reaffirmation

God used men like Luther and Calvin to set the church back on the proper, antithetical path. On the one hand, they rejected both the monastic life of Rome and the Anabaptist world flight. On the other hand, while rebuking sin in all its forms, the reformers maintained the total depravity of fallen man. Believers were called to *spiritual* separation from the ungodly, from their entertainment, and from their corrupt living.

The Reformed churches established this teaching in the creeds by maintaining the total depravity of man, the sovereignty of God's grace, and the believer's calling to live a new and holy life, separate from sin.

Yet, in the Reformed churches in the Netherlands, the antithesis was significantly compromised by the theory of common grace—the idea that God is gracious to all men, elect and reprobate alike. This particularly affected the believer's attitude toward the ungodly, because common grace often included the thought that the unbeliever could do good. The question then arises, why must the believer be opposed to the unbeliever; why cannot they be friends? After all, *God* is gracious to the reprobate, so why cannot the believer be the same? And if the reprobate can do much good, the Christian should feel at ease to enjoy the "good" that the wicked produce and even join hands to accomplish common (good) goals.

Although these ideas were proposed and believed by many, it was not until 1924 that a church officially adopted the doctrine of common grace. In that year the Christian Reformed Church not only formulated and adopted the three points of common grace, but also deposed three ministers and their consistories for refusing to sign the same. That action was the immediate cause for the formation of the Protestant Reformed Churches in America.

In many ways, the formation of the Protestant Reformed Churches in 1924 must be considered a reformation of the church. That is emphatically true in the area of the antithesis. Early on in the controversy, the founders of the PRC recognized the destructive effect of common grace on the doctrine of the antithesis. The first issue of the *Standard Bearer* contained an article by Rev. H. Hoeksema entitled, "The Antithesis in Paradise." In this and succeeding issues Rev. Hoeksema explained the historical development of the antithesis through Adam, the fall, and the promise of Genesis 3:15. In issues numbers 3 and 4, Rev. B. J. Danhof, in a discussion of the progress of God's revelation, declared and proved that God revealed himself antithetically. Rev. G. M. Ophoff likewise stressed the importance of the antithesis over against common grace.

It is striking that from the beginning, these men explained the antithesis in light of God's eternal covenant of friendship with man—the covenant being the most significant doctrine developed within the PRC. They also continued to reaffirm the truth of the antithesis over against common grace. In a masterful article entitled "Antithesis, Synthesis, and Dualism," Rev. Hoeksema explained his opposition to common grace, and then added,

> But we are not so much concerned with the criticism and exposition of the errors of this conception as with the clear fact, that it destroys the antithesis. If it is true, that in this present life and with a view to their earthly development God is gracious to all, and has a covenant of friendship with all men, what business have we not to be friends with those to whom the Lord is gracious? Certainly, the outcry of the poet must be eliminated from Scripture: "Should I not hate them, Lord, that hate thee? I hate them with a perfect hatred!" [Ps. 139:22]. God is the friend of all, be it only for the present and with a view to the affairs of the present time. We have no business to be enemies of those that are in this life the friends of God. Besides, do we not live from a common principle of life in this world? The world does good. Not saving good, it is true, but good in the sight of God. It does so from the grace of God wrought in their hearts by the Holy Spirit of God. Shall we then separate ourselves and condemn the good and lovely works of the world? No, but we shall rather unite with them, and do things in common. Together we can labor for the building up of the home, of society, of the state, of commerce and industry, of science and art... The calling of God's people to live from a

different principle than the world is denied. The antithesis is absolutely destroyed! We may be in the world and of the world both, for together we live of the power of common grace![1]

Hoeksema remained equally opposed to world flight. In the same article he wrote, "But this is not the only way in which the principle of the antithesis is destroyed. It is denied just as well by all those movements that would separate themselves from the world in the sense that they would go out of the world."

But, sad to say, the theory of common grace continued to bear its fruit in the mother church of the PRC. The first noticeable problem had to do with the entertainment, or the "amusement problem." In response to various overtures, the CRC Synod of 1927 appointed a committee to report the next year on movies, dancing, and card playing. Rev. Hoeksema was pointed in his criticisms, not only because part of the report was based on common grace, but also because he believed the report gave legalistic rules that failed to set forth the antithetical life required of the believer. In 1928, Rev. Hoeksema predicted that "presently you may see consistories investigating whether or not a play or movie is good or bad, in order to determine whether or not anyone becomes subject to the discipline of the Church by attending it." And he added that "within a short time we will see the day, that the whole matter of the theatre... is dropped, or their frequenting is sanctioned by some Synod."[2] Thirty-eight years later it happened, and at least part of the reason why a believer could view movies was that "sin is being restrained by God's common grace."[3]

Eleven years later the CRC approved of dancing on the same basis as movies had been. The point of mentioning this is not simply to criticize the CRC. Rather it is to show that the denial of the antithesis, by adopting common grace, has produced these disastrous, un-Reformed fruits.

The list goes on. In other areas, the "good" of unbelievers can be used by the church to interpret the Bible. Sociologists can be cited to allow for homosexual tendencies, despite the condemnation of the Bible. They can also be used to deny the headship of the man in the home and church. The conclusions of ungodly scientists on the origin of the earth can be used to interpret Genesis 1 and make room for evolutionism. The destruction of the antithesis by common grace bore bitter fruits.

Again, the purpose is not simply to be critical, nor is it to say to the mother church, "We told you so," a wicked response indeed. Rather the point is that the formation of the PRC in 1924 was a *needed reforming* of the church of Christ in this area, among others. The truth of the antithesis was reaffirmed in 1924, and developed in the years after. But most importantly, it could be, and is yet *preached* in the PRC! The antithesis preached means that the people of God are called to a life of obedience, loving and serving God, over against the sins of every age. The entertainment of the world, the friendship with the world, dancing, movies, and worldly music are condemned in the preaching and writing. Participation in them still results in personal admonitions from the pastor and elders. The members of the PRC do not claim to be better than other Christians. But the rejection of common grace by the PRC means that sins can still be exposed, rebuked, and disciplined in her midst. Since the doctrine of the antithesis is inseparably interwoven with the glorious doctrine of the covenant, the result is that the preaching continues to call all believers to live antithetically as covenant friends of the holy God.

In 1928 Rev. Hoeksema wrote,

> Hence, we must maintain the antithetic view of life and the world. God establishes His covenant with us antithetically. We cannot serve Him without rejecting and fighting mammon. In the world and not of the world, living in all the domains of life, but from the principle of light, condemning the darkness, such is the purpose of God with His people and our calling, till the victory is won![4]

That is the privilege of the Protestant Reformed Churches. May God keep her faithful.

27

The Development of the Covenant of Grace: A Rich, Consistent Reformed View

Charles J. Terpstra

But, I ask, what is the heritage of the Protestant Reformed Churches? Is there any part of the truth which they have emphasized and further developed in distinction from other Reformed Churches?

If you ask me what is the most peculiar treasure of the Protestant Reformed Churches, I answer without any hesitation: their peculiar view of the covenant.

And what is their peculiar conception?

It stands closely connected with their denial of common grace, and with their emphasis on the doctrine of election and reprobation.

Moreover, it emphasizes and carries out the organic idea. Briefly stated it teaches that God realizes His eternal covenant of friendship, in Christ, the Firstborn of every creature and the First-begotten of the dead, organically, and antithetically along the lines of election and reprobation, and in connection with the organic development of all things.

That is, in a nutshell, the peculiar Protestant Reformed heritage.[1]

So wrote Herman Hoeksema in 1950 on the occasion of the twenty-fifth anniversary of the Protestant Reformed Churches (PRC), revealing what he believed to be the distinctive contribution of the PRC to the Reformed faith, as well as their distinctive stand in the Reformed church world. And he would have known, not only because he had served as a pastor in these churches for all of those twenty-five years and preached this truth, but also because he was personally responsible for the development of the covenant of grace in the denomination as her leading theologian. The heart of this development was the application of the Reformed doctrine of God's sovereign, particular grace to the doctrine of the covenant. The result was a doctrine of the covenant that was profoundly rich in, and thoroughly consistent with, all the doctrines of the Reformed faith.

The Reasons for this Development

The development of this distinctive view of the covenant of grace in the Protestant Reformed Churches did not take place in a theological or ecclesiastical vacuum. There were specific, contemporary factors that contributed directly to this development, factors that made this development a true continuation of the Reformation of the church and her doctrines.

First, there was the prevailing view of the covenant in the Reformed church world. The Reformed faith had always been covenantal over against the dispensational, Baptist views of the radical right of the Reformation. But the view of the covenant that held sway in the Reformed churches was not thoroughly biblical nor consistent with the whole of Reformed doctrine. Basing their view on contracts between men and treaties between kings and subjects, Reformed theologians defined God's covenant of grace with his people in terms of a mutual agreement, in which God and man as co-parties agreed to certain terms and conditions.[2] The establishment and realization of the covenant, then, depended on God's meeting the demands of his conditions, but equally on man's fulfilling his conditions. They were careful to teach that these conditions were fulfilled on behalf of elect sinners by the work of Christ, and in them by the work of the Spirit in

The Development of the Covenant of Grace

the heart, and therefore by God's grace alone. Yet, the ideas of mutual agreement and conditions were seen as essential to the covenant. With this Hoeksema and others in the PRC took issue.

Second, and more specifically, there was an errant view of the covenant in the PRC's mother church that contributed to this development. In connection especially with the Reformed doctrine concerning God's covenant with the children of believers, Prof. William Heyns, a professor of theology in the Christian Reformed Church, taught that the covenant of grace is essentially a promise that God offers to all the children of believing parents on condition that they repent and believe. God offers to all these children that he will be their God if they turn to him and believe on him.[3] Hoeksema saw in this view not only the same errors of agreement and conditionality, but also the added error of the well-meant offer of salvation, which he had condemned as part of the first point of common grace in the controversy of 1924 within the CRC.

Third, the development of a distinctive view of the covenant of grace was prompted by a specific controversy in the PRC over the nature of the covenant. This was still to come in the late 1940s and early 1950s, and was related to developments in the Netherlands. Dr. Klaas Schilder, a prominent minister and professor in the Reformed Churches in the Netherlands (Gereformeerde Kerken in Nederland, GKN), was deposed from these churches and formed the "Liberated" churches because he objected to the GKN's position that infants of believers are to be baptized on the basis of their presupposed regeneration (the view of Dr. Abraham Kuyper). Schilder stressed that God's promises to these children are *promises,* not *suppositions.* But he went on to teach that these promises of God are also conditional, dependent for their fulfillment on the faith of the child.[4] Hoeksema initially had sympathized with Schilder and his struggles, but when Schilder took this position, Hoeksema was deeply disappointed and strongly opposed it, calling it "Heynsianism." The truly sad thing, however, was that Schilder's view of the covenant found ready acceptance among many ministers in the PRC. Without seeing the plain contradictions to the faith they professed, they openly embraced and publicly taught a conditional covenant with its general promise. The outcome was a split in the PRC in the early 1950s over the doctrine of the covenant. As sad as this controversy was, it was necessary for the development of the doctrine of God's covenant of grace with his people along truly biblical and Reformed lines.

The Main Lines of this Development

The development of this view was along the following main lines. First, the very *essence* of the covenant was redefined. Instead of the traditional idea of the covenant as an agreement or as a promise, Hoeksema found the essence of the covenant to be that of a *relationship*, the bond of friendship and fellowship between God and his people in Christ. This is how he described it:

> The idea of the covenant is neither that of a pact or agreement, nor that of the promise, nor that of a way of salvation; but it is the eternal and living fellowship of friendship between God and His people in Christ, according to which He is their Sovereign-friend, and they are His friend-servants.
>
> By friendship we mean a bond of most intimate fellowship, based on the highest possible likeness of nature by personal distinction.[5]

This rich, warm, and personal concept he saw in the Scriptures themselves in such places as Exodus 29:42–46, Psalm 25:14, Matthew 1:23, John 1:14, James 2:23, and Revelation 21:3.

Second, the fundamental *nature* of the covenant was thus also redefined. Rejecting the idea of the covenant as a bilateral agreement, Hoeksema spoke of it as a unilateral relationship. According to this view, there are not two parties in the covenant, but only one: God himself, who takes his people into his own party (side). This does not deny that God's

The Development of the Covenant of Grace

people have a part in the covenant, as the Form for the Administration of Baptism speaks of it (to love and obey God), but it rejects the Pelagian synergism inherent in the agreement idea and preserves the biblical truth that God alone establishes his covenant with his people (Gen. 6:18, Gen. 15:8–18, and Gen. 17:2–8).

Closely related to this, Hoeksema condemned the idea that the covenant is *conditional* and maintained that the covenant is *unconditional.* Repentance and faith are not conditions that man fulfills in order for the covenant to be established and realized, but the divinely-bestowed *means* by which the bond of the covenant is applied to the sinner and is received and enjoyed by him. The Protestant Reformed Churches see in this notion of conditionality the insidious error of Arminianism, since it was the Arminians who talked so proudly of conditions the sinner must fulfill by his free will in order to be saved. With the Canons of Dordt the they condemn this idea out of hand as contrary to Reformed teaching.[6]

The PRC do not deny that there are conditional clauses in Scripture, but they do deny that these "if" clauses mean that God is dependent on the willing and working of us or any sinner. As Calvin stated in his response to those who wanted to use these conditional sentences to advance free will, God speaks with "ifs" to "prick the consciences" of unbelievers and make them understand that because of their sins they are "justly excluded from those blessings due the true worshipers of God." And contrariwise, God uses them for believers to "apprize us of our misery and how wholeheartedly we disagree with his will," and then to "prompt us to call upon his Spirit to direct us into the right path."[7]

Third, the development of the doctrine of the covenant in the Protestant Reformed Churches also involved the application of God's *particular* grace to the covenant. Rejecting the theory of common grace, Hoeksema understood that the idea of a general, covenantal promise offered to all children of believing parents, or offered to all sinners in general in the gospel, is contrary to the Reformed truth of double predestination. He rightly believed that the doctrine of election and reprobation meant that God's saving grace revealed in his covenant and promises is not for all men or for all children of believers who are baptized, but only for the elect. God's covenantal grace is particular in its intention, in its objects, and in its effect. Hoeksema stated it in summary form in this way:

> Historically this covenant is realized in the line of the continued generations of believers. These generations receive the sign of the covenant, circumcision in the old, baptism in the new dispensation, and, in general, are addressed and treated as the real covenant people of God; yet, God's election and reprobation cut right through these generations, and "God is merciful to whom He will be merciful, and whom He will He hardens."[8]

It was in the way of this development that the Protestant Reformed Churches defended, preserved, and advanced the *absolute sovereignty* of God in the salvation of his people. According to this doctrine of the covenant, it is the triune God, as the *sovereign* God of salvation, who alone establishes, preserves, and realizes his covenant with his people. It is this fact which makes the covenant a work of true and pure *grace*. All the other conceptions ultimately make the covenant one of *works*—*man's* works. Precisely at this point the great Reformation fought its fundamental battle. Precisely at this point the Protestant Reformed Churches have carried on this battle with regard to the doctrine of the covenant.[9]

The Ongoing Relevance of this Development

And still the reformation continues; still the battle on the front of the covenant goes on. This is evident from the fact that many in the Reformed community still view the covenant of grace as a conditional agreement or as a general promise. In the August 1995 issue of *Tabletalk*, for example, editor R. C. Sproul, Jr. compares God's covenant with his people to the game "Let's Make a Deal": "When we make a deal with

The Development of the Covenant of Grace

Him, when we choose the covenant of grace, we do so because He first chose us. We sign the deal because He sends His Spirit to change our hearts, because He predestined that we would sign."[10] Such an attempt to give a Reformed slant to a wrong idea of the covenant fails miserably.

In the same issue Mark Seeley states that it is time for Reformed Christians to "slay the sacred cow" of defining the covenant in terms of God's relationship to man, as the Westminster Confession does, and rather define it as "a commitment confirmed by an oath." This idea, he claims, is supported by Scripture and "Near Eastern suzerain-vassal treaties."[11] But according to this conception, the covenant again becomes a bilateral agreement, since it depends on the commitment of both God and man. This the Reformed faith must emphatically not have; this is the "sacred cow" we must slay. So the battle goes on in defending the truly biblical and Reformed conception of the covenant of grace.

But defending this truth is not sufficient. It is also our calling to battle for the continued *development* of this truth of the covenant. The truth of God is never stagnant or static; it marches forward. So those who hold to the truth of God's sovereign covenant of grace must never be satisfied with the development of the past; they must go on to develop it according to the truth of Scripture and the Reformed confessions. Hoeksema himself stated this at the time of the twenty-fifth anniversary of the Protestant Reformed Churches:

> But rather than go backward, he [the Reformed Christian who loves this truth] will go forward and continue to develop the pure Protestant Reformed truth of God's eternal covenant. To do this is the specific calling of the Protestant Reformed Churches. Failure to do this is our death. It is the end of our distinctive existence.[12]

May the Lord give us grace to rise up and face this challenge in the years ahead.

Recommended books on the covenant of grace:

Hanko, Herman. *God's Everlasting Covenant of Grace.* Grand Rapids, MI: Reformed Free Publishing Association, 1988.
Hoeksema, Gertrude. *A Watered Garden: A Brief History of the Protestant Reformed Churches in America.* Grand Rapids, MI: Reformed Free Publishing Association, 1992.
Hoeksema, Herman. *Believers and Their Seed.* rev. ed. Grandville, MI: Reformed Free Publishing Association, 1997.

28

Reformation of Church Government

Barrett L. Gritters

THE MINISTER IS A HERETIC. OR SCHISMATIC. OR WALKing in disobedience to one of the other commandments. What shall be done? Shall the next meeting of classis proceed to his suspension, and then deposition? Shall the synod exercise this discipline? May the classis and synod exercise this authority? If the synod advises the minister's consistory to discipline the minister, but the consistory ignores that advice, may the synod proceed to depose the whole consistory? These questions bring out the issues of church government involved in the separation of 1924.

The reformation of 1924 was a return to the historical and biblical roots in the church's *government*. When gatherings of classis of the mother church of the Protestant Reformed Churches (PRC) deposed ministers and consistories, they were guilty of hierarchy—taking to themselves authority and power that belong to the local congregation alone. For anyone today to think that government is not an important aspect of Christ's church, let him only observe the current hierarchy of some Reformed synods as well as the understandable overreaction to this abuse of power.

The PRC hold to the autonomy (self-rule) of each local congregation. While the Protestant Reformed Churches, faithful to the Reformed tradition, vehemently oppose *independentism* (witness their strong denominational ties and their stand regarding the *real* authority of the broader assemblies), they just as strongly oppose *hierarchy*—both the misuse of the authority that the broader assemblies rightly possess and the taking to themselves of authority that belongs only to the local congregation. The error of the churches early in this century was that of hierarchy. The error to avoid in reaction to this sin is that of independentism.

What was that early error of hierarchy? When the teaching of common grace was made official denominational dogma by the CRC Synod of Kalamazoo in 1924, the ministers of the churches were called by the synod to conform their teaching to that dogma. When the fathers of the PRC refused, Classis Grand Rapids East, in November, 1924, began the process of discipline of the Rev. Herman Hoeksema, suspending him from his office of minister of the gospel, and declared his consistory at Eastern Avenue CRC outside of the federation of churches. On January 24, 1925, Classis Grand Rapids West deposed the ministers and consistories of Hope CRC (the Rev. George M. Ophoff), and First CRC in Kalamazoo (the Rev. Henry Danhof).[1]

The stand of the PRC is that no classis and no synod has the right from Jesus Christ to exercise the keys of the kingdom. Only the local congregation and consistory may exercise discipline.[2]

The wrongful taking of power by broader assemblies in 1924 was only a continuation of a long history of departure from the right way of synodical behavior. As in all reformation, there is a long process of deformation and misbehavior that must finally be corrected.

The history of the church in the Netherlands is also the history of the PRC. As early as 1816 the decrees of King William I gave the synod of the Reformed churches there the power to discipline office bearers.[3] In 1834, Rev. Hendrik de Cock of Ulrum was suspended by the classical board of Middelstum and then deposed by the provincial board at Groningen. Fifty-two years later, five ministers, forty-two elders, and thirty-three deacons in the Dutch Reformed Church in Amsterdam were deposed by the 1886 synod. In the CRC in the United States, Classis Muskegon deposed the consistory of Muskegon CRC in connection with the Bultema heresy in 1918. Dr. Geelkerken, who denied the historicity of the first chapters of Genesis, was deposed by the Synod of Assen in the Netherlands in 1926. Because this practice continued in the Netherlands, Dr. Klaas Schilder was deposed by these same churches in 1944.

Neither "surprising" nor "justified" should be the words that describe the discipline of the PRC's spiritual fathers in 1924 and 1925. The actions were violations of Reformed church polity, not without opposition in the churches.

All along God's people in the churches cried out at the injustice of broader assemblies exercising discipline. Committed to the truth of the autonomy of the local congregations, these voices called the church back to the historic Dutch Reformed practice, which allowed no "broader assemblies" but only consistories to exercise discipline.

Be clear on the issues here. In 1924 there was disagreement on the question of the rights of classis. But already then the disagreement was not over the essential issue. Although one party opposed a classis deposing a *consistory,* they defended the position that a classis may depose a *minister* or an *elder.* We maintain the issue to be this: May a classis (or synod) exercise the keys of the kingdom at all?

In defense of classis and synod exercising discipline, appeal was always made to Articles 36 and 79 of the Church Order. The decision of Classis Grand Rapids West in 1925 read, "Classis Grand Rapids West deposes the aforesaid Consistory by virtue of its jurisdiction over the Consistory as expressed in Art. 36 of our Church Order—'The Classis has the same jurisdiction over the Consistory as the Particular Synod has over the Classis and the General Synod over the Particular.'"[4] The logic is clear: since the classis has *jurisdiction* over the consistory, classis must be able to *discipline* and *depose* consistory members. In addition, because Article 79 requires the *sentence* of a neighboring consistory and the *judgment* of classis for deposition of a minister, the conclusion is reached that these other bodies *discipline* a minister.

The logic is clear. It is also mistaken.

Article 36 of the Church Order gives to the classis jurisdiction (authority) over the consistory, the same jurisdiction as the synod has over the classis. What often fails to be noticed is that the article does not give classis and synod the same *kind* of authority that the consistory has over the congregation—the authority to exercise the keys of heaven's kingdom. The classis has authority, but not to discipline the office bearers in the member churches.

That also becomes plain from Article 79. Unquestionably, the consistory may not act *alone* in discipline. The beauty of Reformed church government is the safety of the multitude of counselors and the mutual supervision of the churches. (We grieve that independent churches do not have this.) Without the concurrence of the neighboring consistory, no consistory member may be suspended or expelled, and without the judgment of the classis, no minister may finally be deposed. Nevertheless, the consistory suspends and the consistory deposes, not the classis or synod.

Defense of synod's authority to exercise discipline, in spite of the fact that Article 79 does not give this authority, on the reasoning that the Church Order does not address itself to all the possible situations that might arise, is weak. The authority to depose an office bearer is no small, nor rare, matter. Besides, the Church Order does speak of the involvement of classis and synod in discipline, and it *limits* their power to the approval of a consistory's decision to depose. Nor is it possible to claim that the deposition of ministers was a matter that Reformed churches considered to be a detail, a matter too infrequently occurring, to address; and that, had they addressed the issue, they would have written into the Church Order permission to depose. The churches did face the question early in their history, resulting already in 1581, in a change in the Church Order, requiring the concurring judgment of a neighboring classis when an officebearer was deposed.[5] *Deliberately,* the early Dutch Reformed synods did not codify for themselves the right to exercise discipline. This interpretation of Reformed church polity has staunch defenders in Reformed church history.

Gijsbertus Voetius (1588–1676), one of the young Dutch delegates to the Synod of Dordt, staunch defender of Reformed Calvinism and champion of Reformed church government, supported the right of the synod to excommunicate a consistory, but meant by excommunication not their formal discipline and deposition, but the setting of them outside of the fellowship of the churches.

Since then, the general Reformed stand has disallowed the right of discipline to the broader assemblies. Shortly after the hierarchical actions in 1924 and 1925, a Rev. G. Hoeksema (not to be confused with the Rev. Herman Hoeksema) wrote a pamphlet defending the right of a classis to depose a minister and consistory. In it, he does our cause service by admitting that "Formerly it was considered fundamentally unreformed to depose a consistory, through classical or synodical action." Referring to the deposition of the heretic Dr. Geelkerken, Rev. G. Hoeksema said, "The synod of Assen has done what the authorities in the Netherlands had, since the time of the Doleantie, condemned as hierarchy."[6]

Although Abraham Kuyper's son, Prof. H. H. Kuyper, defended synod's right to discipline, Abraham Kuyper himself believed it wrong. So did the recognized church order authorities H. Bouwman and F. L. Rutgers. In a published, personal letter to a Rev. Van Lonkhuyzen, who also opposed synod's right to discipline, Dr. H. Bouwman wrote,

> Your question whether I have ever in my lectures said that a classis can depose a consistory, surprises me somewhat. I do not remember ever having taught this and I would say that this is impossible. The Classis can help the consistory in the position of an elder. The Classis can also, when a consistory is completely in error or acts contrary to the right of the Church and her confessions, help the congregation in the election of another consistory, but the Classis may not act without the congregation... The churches in general must not do what belongs to the consistory.

According to Reformed Church Right, if the whole consistory is corrupt and there is no normal way to rectify it, the power of the church reverts back to the congregation, and the denomination can and must then offer help so that another consistory is chosen in the place of the unfaithful one.[7]

The best known English language authority on Reformed church order, Van Dellen and Monsma's *Church Order Commentary*, takes the strong view that, to be true to Reformed principles, no synod and no classis may ever exercise discipline over office bearers.[8]

Standing with the Protestant Reformed Churches in this are also the American and Canadian Reformed Churches ("liberated," or *vrijgemaakt*) and the Free Reformed Churches of Australia (also "liberated"). Their W. Meijer, in his *Young People's History of the Church*, repeatedly teaches the children of his churches the danger of hierarchy of synods that take to themselves the power to depose ministers.[9]

Presbyterian students of Reformed church government recognize this stance as the Reformed view, which they see to be the significant difference between Presbyterian and Reformed church government. Edmund P. Clowney puts his finger directly on the difference when he says, "Some aspects of Reformed order, as distinct from Presbyterian polity, reflect the place of primacy given to the local church and its consistory. Ministers of the gospel are members of the local church and are *subject to the discipline of the consistory*."[10] The Presbyterian brother recognizes this to be Reformed, in distinction from Presbyterian, where ministers are subject to *the discipline of the presbytery*. He is correct in his analysis of what is *properly* Reformed.

Related is the question whether the local congregation is the church or whether the broader assembly is the church. Note the PRC's repeated reminder that we are Protestant Reformed *Churches* and not Protestant Reformed *Church*. If the gatherings of the local congregations have the right to discipline, they also have the right to baptize, administer the Lord's supper, and preach. We believe the Lord gave these

Reformation of Church Government

rights to the local congregation alone. Our Presbyterian brothers would disagree. Presbyterian church polity has the credentials and membership of a minister in the presbytery (classis), with ordination by the presbytery. Thus, rather than discipline by the congregation, discipline is exercised by the presbytery, which is also considered the church.

As the Church Order gives authority to discipline to the local consistory alone, so does the Scripture. To no one else is this authority given.

Acts 15, the basis for all appeals to the authority of broader assemblies, indeed gives authority to broader assemblies. We thank the Presbyterian brothers for reminding us of that and emphasizing that. But Acts 15 does not give authority to the assembly of churches to discipline.

In 1 Corinthians 5 the authority to discipline is given to the local congregation at Corinth. In a worship service of the church ("when ye are gathered together") the local congregation exercises discipline over her members.

The Reformed Form for Ordination of Elders and Deacons has it straight. In Jesus' instruction to the apostles as to how discipline must be exercised over any member of the congregation, the "church" that must be told is the body of elders in the local congregation.

In reformation, the churches must never overreact. Needing attention was the un-Reformed practice of hierarchy. But we must not reject all the authority of, and blessings from, the broader assemblies.

May God save us from abusive, hierarchical synods and classes. May God also save us from neglecting to show the unity of the body of Jesus Christ.

Part 5

The Reformation of 1953 in the Protestant Reformed Churches

29

1953: Continuing Reformation

David J. Engelsma

1953 STANDS FOR THE DOCTRINAL CONTROVERSY THAT convulsed the Protestant Reformed Churches in the late 1940s and early 1950s. The controversy concluded with the schism in 1953 in which a majority of churches, members, and ministers left the PRC, soon to return to the Christian Reformed Church.

The issue was the doctrine of the covenant—no minor matter, especially for Reformed churches.

The issue came to a head in two statements in two different sermons by one of the ministers. A classis judged the statements heretical. But the real issue was the introduction into the PRC of a doctrine of the covenant that held that God makes his covenant with all the physical children of believing parents alike. God makes his covenant with all alike by promising every one of them salvation at his or her baptism. This promise depends, however, on the child's performing the condition of believing when he or she grows up.

Implied is a grace of God—a covenant grace of God—for all the children of believers, those who perish as well as those who are saved, and a desire of God to save them all. Expressed is the failure of the promise of God in many cases and the dependence of salvation, in the final analysis, on the will and act of the child. One of the patriarchs of the PRC, who also played a leading role in the struggle, the Rev. Gerrit Vos, impressed upon me that the issue was this doctrine of the covenant. During my seminary days, which began only seven years after the schism, Vos told me, "People argue about the two statements. They were bad statements. But they were not the issue. The issue was the conditional covenant with all the children. We all knew that this was the issue."

The struggle was fierce, as only a church struggle over doctrine between former brothers and sisters can be. Although I was only fourteen in 1953, I remember vividly the church services that were tense, depending on who was preaching; the loud, heated arguments on the church grounds after the services; and, especially painfully, the rage and shouting that broke up family gatherings of long standing and reduced bewildered children to tears.

Close friends separated; families divided; schools and churches emptied.

One needs only to read the issues of the *Standard Bearer* of that period to sense the intensity of the conflict.

Not all the fire was holy—not on the side of the PRC either.

The struggle spilled over the borders of the little PRC. The Reformed churches in the Netherlands followed the controversy. One of the Dutch denominations was indirectly involved since it was their covenant view that occasioned the struggle. A prominent Baptist preacher in Grand Rapids advertised his Sunday evening sermon topic in the *Grand Rapids Press*, "Who is right: Hoeksema or De Wolf?" There is disquieting reason to suspect that conservative Christian Reformed ministers, then in power in the CRC, were secretly involved with the Protestant Reformed ministers responsible for the conflict already before the break took place in 1953.

The outcome of the doctrinal controversy was the declaration by the PRC in a synodical decision that the covenant promise of God, particularly at baptism, is made to the elect children alone. The faith of the child is not a condition upon which the promise and its salvation depend, but is itself part of the blessing given by the promise. The covenant grace of God is particular, not general. It is for the elect alone. In its bestowal and reception, this grace is sovereign, neither de-

1953: Continuing Reformation

pendent on the sinful child, nor effectual, even in part, by virtue of the child's will and deed.

By grace the children are saved in the covenant through faith, and that faith is not of themselves, but is the gift of God (Eph. 2:8). As is the case with all others who are saved, the origin of the salvation of the covenant children is God's eternal election in Christ (Eph. 1:4).

This official declaration on the covenant is called "The Declaration of Principles of the Protestant Reformed Churches." As the appropriate and necessary response to controversy, it expresses the faith of the PRC as to the teaching of Scripture and the Reformed confessions on the covenant.

The controversy over the covenant ended with the churches' official condemnation of a conditional covenant (in the classis' judgment that the two statements were heretical) and in the churches' official adoption of the doctrine of an unconditional covenant of grace (in the Declaration).

This was continuing reformation of the church.

It was also continuing reformation of the PRC. The PRC carried through consistently in the doctrine of the covenant the truth of sovereign, particular grace that they had confessed from the beginning of their existence as churches.

Make no mistake, the churches had always taught, and been taught, the doctrine of an *unconditional* covenant. Those ministers who in the late 1940s and early 1950s became enamored of a conditional covenant and were determined to introduce it into the PRC knew full well that they were overthrowing what the PRC had always stood for.

As early as 1927, in a series of articles in the *Standard Bearer* that were soon published as the booklet *Geloovigen en Hun Zaad* (Believers and Their Seed), Herman Hoeksema had set forth in detail the covenant conception that he insisted was fundamental to the very existence of the PRC. At the same time he sketched the conditional theory of the covenant with which the doctrine that threatened in 1953 is essentially identical and damned it as "the old Pelagian error applied to the doctrine of the covenant."[1]

This was in 1927!

The schismatic preachers in the PRC were dishonest when they told the people that Hoeksema himself had earlier advocated a conditional covenant and that the PRC had no definite covenant doctrine.

But before 1951-1953, the PRC had not officially adopted the doctrine of the covenant that they had always believed and confessed. Men could, therefore, contend that the prevailing covenant doctrine was merely that of Professors Hoeksema and Ophoff. So also, I suppose, prior to the adoption of the Lutheran creeds men could say that justification by faith only was merely the view of Luther, and prior to the Synod of Dordt men could say that double predestination was merely the view of Calvin.

In 1951-1953, the doctrine of a particular, unconditional covenant, in Christ the head of the covenant, with believers and their elect children became the official doctrine of the PRC. In formulating and adopting the doctrine, the PRC simply applied to the covenant the truth of sovereign, particular grace for which they contended in their controversy with the CRC over the well-meant offer of the gospel.

Thus, the teaching of universal, ineffectual grace in the covenant was purged from the PRC.

There was consistency.

There was development of the truth.

There was rejection of the opposing false doctrine.

There was continuing reformation of the PRC.

1953 represented also the continuation of the great Reformation of the sixteenth century. Churches and theologians will dismiss this claim as ridiculous, but the fact remains.

The Reformation of the sixteenth century restored to the church Augustine's gospel of particular salvation by sovereign grace alone, while developing this truth in the doctrine of justification by faith alone.

The Synod of Dordt defended the Reformation's gospel of salvation by grace alone through (not on account of) faith alone against the universal, conditional grace of Arminian free-willism. It did so in such a way as to make the prevailing

1953: Continuing Reformation

doctrines of the Reformation the official teachings of the Reformed churches worldwide.

But Dordt did not explicitly address the issue of grace in the covenant, that is, in the family of believers.

After Dordt, two opposite teachings appeared in the Reformed and Presbyterian churches. Often, they contended with each other in sharp conflict, as in the churches of the Secession in the Netherlands in the nineteenth century. The one holds, in one form or another, that God makes his covenant with every physical child of believers by conditional promise to each of them. The other holds that God's covenant is with Christ and, in him, with elect believers and their elect children, by unconditional promise.[2]

The former is, in reality, the teaching of universal grace in the covenant, grace wider than Christ and his elect church, grace dependent upon man's will and work (faith as a condition).

The latter is, in reality, the gospel of particular grace in the covenant, grace as wide as, but no wider than, Christ and his elect church, grace dependent only upon the promising God and inclusive of the gift of faith.

This latter, the PRC, through the fire of white-hot, fierce, painful church struggle, have been guided to believe and confess.

This is genuine continuation and development of the Reformation of the sixteenth century.

Here we stand!

30

Through Warfare to Victory

Herman C. Hanko

T**HE CHURCH OF OUR LORD JESUS CHRIST ON EARTH IS** sometimes called the church militant. The name is apt, for Christ calls his church to warfare as long as she is in the world. God himself has put enmity between the seed of the woman and the seed of Satan, and that enmity can only result in open and perpetual hostilities.

The church is called to fight, however, with spiritual weapons, for the battle is spiritual. The enemy is Satan and his allies—the world of wicked men. Their weapons are worldliness and false doctrine.

Sometimes the enemy is outside the walls of the city of God; sometimes the enemy appears within the walls. False doctrine can be defended by wicked men outside the church; more often, though, false doctrine is taught by men within the church. The latter is what happened in the late 1940s and early 1950s.

The Enemy and His Weapons

The enemy was men within the Protestant Reformed Churches (PRC) who introduced into the teachings and doctrine of the churches ideas and views that were directly contrary to what the churches had always taught and contrary as well to the truth of Scripture and the Reformed confessions.

The men who were responsible for this were ministers of the gospel who occupied pulpits throughout the denomination, elders and deacons who supported these erroneous teachings, and people in the pew, many of whom were men of influence and stature who openly encouraged such teaching.

The weapons they used were in general the doctrines of a conditional salvation, and in particular, the doctrines of a general and conditional promise in the covenant.

When the Protestant Reformed Churches were founded in 1925, they were established because the truth of God's sovereign, unconditional, and particular grace had to be defended over against common grace. The errors introduced in the 1940s and 50s were the heresies of conditional salvation, that is, that man had to fulfill the condition of faith before he could be saved.

The Battlefields

While no single congregation, and indeed no single home was left unaffected, the battle raged particularly in three areas: in the church papers, in First Protestant Reformed Church in Grand Rapids, Michigan, and in the ecclesiastical assemblies of the churches—classes and synods.

The battle was fought particularly in First PRC because one of the three pastors there, Rev. Hubert De Wolf, openly taught heresy from the pulpit in the course of his preaching. It was fought in the broader assemblies because the Declaration of Principles was hated for its clear statement of the truth. It was fought in the church papers because supporters of De Wolf needed a place to air their views outside of the *Standard Bearer*, and so they started their own magazine, called *Concordia*.

The Course of the Battle in the Church Papers

It was really in the church papers that the long and difficult battle began. When some of the ministers in the PRC began to defend conditional theology, they made use of *Concordia* to do it. The magazine had appeared already in 1944, and ironically, in defiance of its name, which means "harmony," it sowed discord and division in the church. Because it entered nearly every home in the denomination, it sought to introduce false doctrine into every home. And because PR homes were, above all, covenantal homes, an open defense of a conditional covenant was a direct attack on the spiritual structure of the home.

It was no wonder, then, that Rev. Herman Hoeksema, editor-in-chief of the *Standard Bearer,* engaged in a defense of a sovereign and unconditional covenant in the columns of the paper for which he was responsible.

The polemics continued throughout the controversy. Perhaps no other aspect of the battle involved the membership of the churches more than the conflict in the church papers.

The Course of the Battle in First Church

When Rev. Hoeksema, pastor of Eastern Avenue Christian Reformed Church, Grand Rapids, Michigan, was suspended from office by a CR classis for refusing to agree to the three points of common grace, many in his congregation followed him out of the denomination, which became known as the Protestant Reformed Churches. First Protestant Reformed Church, Grand Rapids, was built for this group of people and their minister. In those days it could have been called the flagship of the denomination. It was the largest congregation in the fledgling PRC, numbering some 560 families. It became the "mother church."

Because of its size, it had three pastors: Rev. Herman Hoeksema, Rev. Hubert De Wolf, and my father, Rev. Cornelius Hanko. While both Revs. Hoeksema and Hanko were strong defenders of unconditional salvation, Rev. De Wolf was not of that mind at all. He was intent on promoting a conditional theology in the congregation.

While De Wolf promoted his theology in catechism classes and personal contacts, he finally brought it to the pulpit on April 15, 1951, when he made this bold statement in a sermon on the parable of the rich man and Lazarus: "God promises every one of you that if you believe, you will be saved."[1] Here was the clearest possible defense of a general and conditional promise in the covenant.

The statement brought protests from members of the congregation and put the controversy squarely into the hands of the elders. The consistory of First Church found it difficult to deal with the problem, chiefly because the elders reflected in their own ranks the divisions in the congregation. With the passing of the months, the battle grew in intensity.

The congregation was affected by it, of course. Although discussions over the issues and heated debates over the doctrines involved took place at every occasion, the worst, from my viewpoint, was the difficulty in worshiping. My father often spoke of the difficulty in preaching because the absence of the Holy Spirit from the congregation was palpable, but the worship of the congregation was also noticeably affected.

Our home life was also affected. While we did not know what was taking place in the consistory meetings, we could tell the toll the battle was taking on my father, and we were constantly worried about his well-being.

After almost a year and a half, the struggle in the consistory had somewhat faded into the background, and some expressed hope that the whole difficulty could be solved in such a way that the congregation would remain intact. But then, on September 14, 1952, De Wolf, throwing caution to the winds, openly reaffirmed in the most emphatic way his commitment to conditional theology. In a preparatory service, held with a view to the administration of the Lord's supper, he preached on Matthew 18:3 and defended this proposition: "Our act of conversion is a prerequisite to enter the kingdom."[2]

The congregation nearly exploded, and once again the elders took up the issues. In February of 1953, De Wolf was subjected to an examination of his orthodoxy. Because of a majority in the consistory, his examination was approved and he was cleared of all heresy charges. Some elders protested this decision exonerating De Wolf and appealed to Classis East of the Protestant Reformed Churches.

And so the matter came to Classis.

The committee appointed to study the matter was composed of three ministers and two elders. The ministers prepared a report defending De Wolf's statements as not necessarily heretical. The two elders, in a minority report, recommended the condemnation of the statements by Classis. After De Wolf himself repudiated the majority report, Classis decided that the statements of De Wolf were literally heretical and that De Wolf had to apologize for them or be subject to the discipline of his consistory.

A committee was appointed to bring the decision to the consistory of First Church, which it did in June of 1953. By a majority vote the advice of Classis was accepted. Shortly afterward De Wolf made a statement to the congregation in which he apologized for offending some in the congregation, but he did not apologize for his heresy. A meeting of the consistory on June 21 ended in chaos. But on June 22, the faithful elders, along with Revs. Hoeksema and Hanko, met with the consistory of Southeast PRC and proceeded to De Wolf's suspension and the deposition of the office bearers supporting him. De Wolf's supporters took over the church property, changed the locks, and proceeded to make use of the premises. The faithful remnant, less than half of the congregation, worshiped in the chapel of Grand Rapids Christian High School.

The Course of the Battle in the Assemblies

The battles in the assemblies concentrated in the Declaration of Principles. Because the PRC were working among Dutch immigrants in Canada who were for the most part from Liberated churches in the Netherlands, where conditional theology was maintained and defended, the missionary Rev. Andrew Cammenga asked the Mission Committee of the PRC for a statement concerning the doctrinal position of the PRC to be used on the mission field. This request came to the Synod of 1950, and a document called the Declaration of Principles was drawn up, provisionally approved, and sent to the churches for examination and discussion with a view to final approval at the Synod of 1951.

The document set forth the biblical and confessional teachings over against such doctrines as common grace, the well-meant offer, and conditional salvation. Although adopted nearly unanimously by the Synod of 1950, it stirred up bitter debate throughout the churches when the supporters of conditional salvation began to understand what was implied in it.

Although the Synod of 1951 officially adopted the "Declaration of Principles of the Protestant Reformed Churches" by a vote of 9–7 (reflecting the split in the churches), the controversy continued unabated.

Classis East, as we noticed, became a battlefield when it considered protests against De Wolf from First Church. It became a battlefield at the next classis when delegates from De Wolf's consistory and delegates from First Church both appeared and requested to be seated. When Classis decided to seat the delegates from First Church (after lengthy debate that lasted days), De Wolf and his supporters, also from other congregations, walked out of the classis. The split then took place in the member churches.

Classis West was the scene of struggle when the announcements of De Wolf's suspension were sent to the churches. Classis West, most of which favored De Wolf, repudiated the decisions of First Church. That was the occasion for the rift to spread through the congregations beyond the Mississippi. And so the battle resulted in a schism which rolled through the denomination like a deep chasm in the ground brought about by an earthquake. All the congregations were affected, and some congregations were lost completely to the Protestant Reformed Churches.

The Aftermath

When the dust of battle had settled, it became obvious that the results of the split were, from an earthly point of view, disastrous.

The membership of the denomination was sharply reduced. The yearbook of 1952 lists 24 churches, 28 ministers, and 5449 individuals. The yearbook of 1954 lists 16 churches, 14 ministers, and 2353 individuals. Families and friends had been separated, and the bitterness that all controversy engenders remained for years.

The work of the churches was made much more difficult. Mission work ceased. The seminary continued, though with a sharply reduced enrollment. The energy of the churches was in a measure devoted to legal battles rather than the work assigned to her by Christ. The Christian schools, supported by the parents of the denomination, were hard hit and had a more difficult struggle to continue. A great battle-weariness settled over the saints. Though victorious, the troops were wounded and bleeding.

Was it worth it?

In a sense the question is inappropriate. In the final analysis it does not matter at all what happens to us or the churches of which we are a part when the truth of God is the issue. Whatever has to be done must be done when God's glory, revealed in the truth of his sovereign and particular grace, is threatened by false doctrine. What the cost may be is immaterial and of no account. To ask whether the price was too high to pay is to ask the wrong question.

Nevertheless, God gave the PRC the victory even though at times it seemed as if the denomination was to be reduced to rubble. The victory was, so to speak, by the skin of our teeth; but this is the way God often works. From the controversy emerged, through the work of the Spirit, a denomination stronger, more deeply devoted to her own distinctives, more determined than ever to get on with the work of the Lord, purged from those who troubled her, and ready to move forward when once she had caught her collective breath.

God has blessed the PRC. He rescued us when our cause seemed to be defeated. He has been with us since that time and has given us countless tokens of his favor and love. Above all, he has preserved us in the heritage of the Reformed faith for which our fathers fought so valiantly.

31

The Declaration of Principles: What? When? Why?

Dale H. Kuiper

THE CLOSING YEARS OF THE 1940s WERE YEARS OF UNrest and change. The United States was welcoming home her servicemen from active duty in the European and Pacific theaters of operations. Many thousands of her soldiers, sailors, marines, and airmen did not return, or returned only to be buried in home soil. Huge factories that had been turning out tanks, planes, trucks, ships, and munitions were being retooled for domestic production. There were many shortages: cars, appliances, apartments. Of course, all these things affected the members of the Protestant Reformed Churches (PRC) as well.

But there were also winds of unrest and change of a more important, doctrinal nature rustling in the churches around the time that Rev. Herman Hoeksema suffered a severe stroke in 1947. Dr. Klaas Schilder had visited the United States in 1939 and again in 1947. Canada, with its open immigration policy, was welcoming many immigrants from Europe, especially from the Netherlands. Among these were many from the Liberated churches of which Dr. Schilder was the leader. After a visit to the Netherlands by Protestant Reformed ministers Revs. J. DeJong and B. Kok, during which visit they assured the Liberated brethren that there was no official view of the covenant held by the PRC, the immigrants to Canada were advised to join these churches and that there was room

The Declaration of Principles: What? When? Why?

for them there. Missionary work was carried out by the PRC in the province of Ontario, and two congregations were organized there: Hamilton (1949) and Chatham (1950). By 1952 these congregations had left the denomination. This short history was not harmonious nor the relationship smooth.

With one dissenting vote, the 1951 Synod of the PRC adopted a rather lengthy document entitled "A Brief Declaration of Principles of the Protestant Reformed Churches." This document became the focal point of much discussion for several years throughout the churches and her assemblies, and revealed basic differences in doctrinal positions not only between the Liberated and the Protestant Reformed, but also among the members and clergy of the PRC. When the smoke cleared in 1953, the denomination remained intact with the same precious doctrines they had always maintained, but it had lost approximately half of the membership and clergy.

Before we analyze the contents of the Declaration we want to note two things. First, the contention of some that the PRC never had an officially adopted view of the covenant had some truth to it. No classis or synod had ever spoken to this issue from 1924–1951. There was no need for such a decision. Since no protest or appeal had ever been brought for adjudication, it was assumed that all held the same view. However, it must be remembered that the view of the covenant embodied in the Declaration and defended successfully by the churches in 1951–1953 against all other views was inherent in the history and positions since the PRC began. Particular grace, not common grace, applied to the area of the covenant certainly means a particular, unconditional covenant that God establishes only with his particular people, the elect. Second, the charge was made repeatedly against the adoption of the Declaration that it was a new confession, which was not needed. We hope to show this charge to be false, and that the Declaration was a wise, masterful, and necessary compilation of articles from the existing three forms of unity under certain points or principles "as these have always been maintained in the Protestant Reformed Churches."[1]

The Contents of the Declaration

A brief outline of the Declaration will show the truth of the last statement above. There are four main points.

First, the PRC repudiate the errors of the three points of common grace adopted by the synod of the CRC in 1924, and over against them maintain "that the grace of God is always particular, i.e., only for the elect, never for the reprobate;" "that the preaching of the gospel is not a gracious offer of salvation on the part of God to all men, [and now notice] nor a conditional offer to all that are born in the historical dispensation of the covenant, that is, to all that are baptized, but an oath of God that He will infallibly lead all the elect unto salvation and eternal glory through faith;" and "that the unregenerate man is totally incapable of doing any good, wholly depraved, and therefore can only sin."[2]

The second main point sets forth the confessional stance that election is "the unconditional and unchangeable decree of God to redeem in Christ a certain number of persons, [and this election] is the sole cause and fountain of all our salvation." Further, "Christ died only for the elect and... the saving efficacy of the death of Christ extends to them only."[3] After quoting Article 8 of the second head of the Canons for proof, the Declaration states:

> 1. That all the covenant blessings are for the elect alone.
> 2. That God's promise is unconditionally for them only: for God cannot promise what was not objectively merited by Christ.
> 3. That the promise of God bestows the objective right of salvation not upon all the children that are born under the historical dispensation of the covenant, that is, not upon all that are baptized, but only upon the spiritual seed.[4]

When the Heidelberg Catechism is quoted in proof (Questions and Answers 65, 66, and 74 concerning the means of grace), the Declaration makes the points that "the promise of the gospel which is sealed by the sacraments concerns only the believers, that is, the elect;" and only the spiritual children

The Declaration of Principles: What? When? Why?

of believers are meant, for "little infants surely cannot fulfill any conditions. And if the promise of God is for them, the promise is infallible and unconditional, and therefore only for the elect."[5] The final point made under the second section is "that faith is not a prerequisite or condition unto salvation, but a gift of God, and a God-given instrument whereby we appropriate the salvation in Christ."[6]

The third main section repudiates the teachings "that the promise of the covenant is conditional and for all that are baptized" and "that we may presuppose that all the children that are baptized are regenerated." Contrariwise, the Declaration maintains

1. That God surely and infallibly fulfills His promise to the elect.
2. The sure promise of God which He realizes in us as rational and moral creatures not only makes it impossible that we should not bring forth fruits of thankfulness but also confronts us with the obligation of love, to walk in a new and holy life, and constantly to watch unto prayer.
3. That the ground of infant baptism is the command of God and the fact that according to Scripture He established His covenant in the line of continued generations.[7]

The last brief point states that the Protestant Reformed Churches "believe and maintain the autonomy of the local church."[8]

This brief survey shows that the original, historical position of the PRC that the grace of God is sovereign and particular can only lead to the conclusion that the covenant of God with us and our children is a covenant that is sovereignly established and maintained, that it is unconditional and without human prerequisites, and that it is indeed a covenant that is dominated, defined, delineated, and controlled by God's eternal election of his people! We plead guilty to this charge, if indeed that be a charge.

This brief summary also shows that the Declaration, though officially adopted by Synod, is not the full expression of the covenant view of the PRC. It sufficed to safeguard the truth in the conditional covenant dispute with the Liberated brethren, but it does not reflect the development of covenant doctrine that had already taken place among the PRC at that time, and that continues to be developed. The word *friendship*, which denotes the heart and essence of the covenant, is not found in the Declaration. The relation of friendship between God and his people in Christ is not described in terms of the covenant life of the triune God, the most basic consideration in our covenant view. How the Father-Son relationship within the Trinity is manifest in God's saving of believers and their seed is not entered into at all. We repeat, the Declaration sufficed for the task at hand, but it is not the final, complete word on the Protestant Reformed covenant position.

The Nature of the Declaration

That the Declaration is not a fourth confession is clear from two considerations. First, approximately ninety percent of its contents is made up of quotations from the three forms of unity, the liturgical forms, and the Church Order. Really, the Declaration breaks no new ground, but brings the Reformed confessions to bear upon the vital subjects of the promise of God, the covenant of grace, and infant baptism. Second, that this is no fourth confession is brought out by the preamble to the Declaration, which sharply limits its use. A church's confession is not limited in its use; the Declaration is. "Declaration of Principles [is] to be used only by the Mission Committee and the missionaries for the organization of prospective churches on the basis of Scripture and the confessions."[9]

Note that word "only." If a member of a congregation is not satisfied with the preaching of his minister, complaining that it is not Reformed, he has no right to use the Declaration to show that his minister's preaching is not Reformed. He must use the confessions in an attempt to show that. Office bearers, when ordained into office, are not required to sign the

The Declaration of Principles: What? When? Why?

Declaration of Principles; they are required to sign the Formula of Subscription, which signifies their agreement with the confessions and the Church Order.

When a missionary is laboring with a group of people with a view to organizing a Protestant Reformed congregation, he not only may, but he also must include the contents of the Declaration in his teaching. The calling consistory of the missionary, as well as the Mission Committee that oversees the work for the churches in common, must judge the progress of the work, the spiritual growth of the people, and their readiness for organization for one thing on the readiness of the group to embrace, confess, and rejoice in the contents of the Declaration.

We may not allow the Declaration to lie at the back of our church order book as a dead document of little historical significance. It was adopted because the very basis of the PRC was at stake! It was adopted only after a long and bitter struggle for the truth of God's sovereign particular grace. It was adopted after hard toil, through broken friendships, and with a split denomination as the result. To refuse to use the Declaration as it was intended would be a betrayal of our fathers of 1951–1953 and a lack of appreciation for the reformation that the Spirit of truth worked in the PRC just after the war.

What Authority?

Does the Declaration of Principles have authority in the PRC? If so, what or what kind? Even though the Declaration is not a creed, and even though its use is limited to the mission field so that groups of believers who wish to be organized as Protestant Reformed congregations may know that we do have an official view of the covenant, the Declaration does have authority over every member of the denomination. Synod has taken a decision. And the decisions of Synod are settled and binding throughout the churches. Do you want to sharpen your understanding of the Reformed doctrine of the covenant? You may study the Declaration. Do you have opportunity to speak with others about the most important distinctive we have as churches? You may say to them, "Here, this is what we believe about the promise of God, the covenant of grace, and holy baptism."

As we reflect on the necessity for ongoing reformation in the church of Jesus Christ, and as we understand that controversy and struggle in the church always lead to a deeper understanding of and appreciation for the truth, let us not fail to appreciate what was safeguarded and gained in the early 1950s, especially for the work in preaching the Reformed faith to the nations.

32

God's Unconditional Covenant

Robert D. Decker

IN APRIL OF 1951 THE REV. HUBERT DE WOLF, ONE OF the three pastors of First Protestant Reformed Church in Grand Rapids, made the statement in his sermon, "God promises every one of you that if you believe, you will be saved." About a year and a half later Rev. De Wolf made another statement in a sermon: "Our act of conversion is a prerequisite to enter into the kingdom."[1] Protests were lodged with First's consistory against both of these statements. When Rev. De Wolf refused to apologize for and retract the two statements, a split occurred in First Church in June 1953. The split soon spread throughout the entire denomination with some two-thirds of the clergy and membership leaving the Protestant Reformed Churches (PRC).

While the two statements of Rev. De Wolf certainly became the immediate cause of the split, the deeper cause was the fact that a good number of the ministers were enamored of Dr. Schilder's view of the covenant. This was the doctrinal issue that made the split in the Protestant Reformed Churches inevitable.

To present an accurate summary of Dr. Schilder's view of the covenant is no easy undertaking. "It should therefore be stated immediately that nowhere in any of his numerous writings did he offer a detailed and systematic exposition of his views on the covenant. The situation is rather that the covenant constantly crops up in his theological writings, sometimes unexpectedly."[2]

Schilder was concerned with two matters. In opposition to those (Rev. Herman Hoeksema among them) who insisted that one's point of departure in understanding the biblical teaching concerning God's covenant should be the eternal decrees of God, Schilder preferred to make his point of departure the historical deeds of God. In this connection Schilder was determined to do full justice to the responsibility of man.

While Schilder taught that the covenant is unilateral in its origin, he emphasized that the covenant is bilateral in its existence. The covenant originates in God. God establishes the covenant. What Schilder meant was that God unilaterally establishes a bilateral relationship between himself and us. The covenant, according to Schilder, is a mutual agreement between two parties, God and man: two immeasurably unequal parties, but two parties nonetheless. In the covenant, God treats man as an actual and responsible partner. The covenant, according to Schilder, is a legal arrangement that confers legal status upon the members of the covenant people. In the covenant, God's gifts of love come to us in a legal relationship and with legal guarantees.

Further, the covenant that is a bilateral relationship with a legal character contains two parts, namely, the promise and the demand. With the promise, Schilder said, comes the assurance of reward (salvation) in the way of faith, and with the demand comes the threat of punishment in the case of unbelief and disobedience.

In answer to the question whether such an emphasis on the responsibility of man does not undermine the certainty of the covenant, Schilder stressed that the promise of the covenant can never be separated from the demand of the covenant. If one would separate the promise from the demand, he would change the promise into a mere prediction. If one would separate the demand from the promise of the covenant, he would introduce a new law. Promise and demand are inseparable.

God's Unconditional Covenant

It was in this connection that Schilder introduced what he called a "Reformed doctrine of conditions." Baptism seals in a sacramental way the promise of the gospel. But this promise demands from us that we in faith appropriate for ourselves what is promised and so make it our own. Faith, which Schilder insisted is God's gift to us, is the condition of the covenant. God has decreed that salvation can never be realized without faith. One's baptism, therefore, does not imply a dogmatic proclamation that God confers salvation on the elect. But in baptism, Schilder taught, one receives a concrete address from God, a message that God proclaims to everyone who is baptized, personally: If you believe you will be saved.

The Protestant Reformed Churches, following the leadership of Herman Hoeksema, reacted strongly to Schilder's covenant views. The view of Schilder regards the covenant as a means to an end, the end being salvation. The PRC regard the covenant as the highest end in itself. As to its idea, the covenant is the bond of friendship that God unilaterally establishes, maintains, and realizes with his elect in Christ.

That the covenant is a bond of friendship between God and his people in Christ is clearly taught in Scripture. In paradise God revealed himself to Adam and spoke with him as a Friend with his friend, and Adam knew God in the cool of the day. Enoch and Noah walked with God, implying friendship and fellowship (Gen. 5:22; 6:8–9). Abraham is called the friend of God (Isa. 41:8; James 2:23). To Moses, God spoke as a man speaks with his friend (Ex. 33:11). In the tabernacle and temple God dwelt with his people. In Psalm 25:14, Scripture declares that "the secret [familiar acquaintance] of the Lord is with them that fear him; and he will shew them his covenant." The Lord promises to dwell with the church, walk with her, and be her God (2 Cor. 6:16). God's covenant of friendship will be realized in heavenly perfection in the new creation. "Behold, the tabernacle of God is with men, and he will dwell with them, and they shall be his people, and God himself shall be with them, and be their God" (Rev. 21:3). In the new Jerusalem God's people shall walk in the light of the glory of God, and they shall see his face (Rev. 21:23, 24; 22:4).

Scripture makes unmistakably clear as well that God establishes and maintains and realizes his covenant unilaterally. God said to Noah, for example, "And I, behold, I establish my covenant with you, and with your seed after you; And with every living creature that is with you, of the fowl, of the cattle, and of every beast of the earth with you; from all that go out of the ark, to every beast of the earth" (Gen. 9:9, 10). And to Abraham God said, "And I will establish my covenant between me and thee and thy seed after thee in their generations for an everlasting covenant, to be a God unto thee, and to thy seed after thee" (Gen. 17:7).

With whom does God establish his covenant of friendship? With the elect in Christ, believers and their children. The Lord Jesus Christ is

> the image of the invisible God, the firstborn of every creature: For by him were all things created, that are in heaven, and that are in earth, visible and invisible, whether they be thrones, or dominions, or principalities, or powers: all things were created by him, and for him: And he is before all things, and by him all things consist. And he is the head of the body, the church: who is the beginning, the firstborn from the dead; that in all things he might have the preeminence. For it pleased the Father that in him should all fulness dwell (Col. 1:15–19).

To Christ are given the elect, conformed by God's choosing to his image (Eph. 1). For these sheep the Good Shepherd lays down his life at the cross and takes it again in the resurrection (John 10).

Are all the children of believers elect, friends of God in Christ? We know better. There are Esaus born of believing parents as well as Jacobs. In the Old Testament era these Esaus were circumcised, and in the new they are baptized. Does this mean that God promises them salvation if they believe? Never! The sacrament, like the preaching of the word, is to the reprobate a "savour of death unto death" (2 Cor. 2:16).

Does this biblical view of the covenant deny the responsibility of man? Again, never! The fact that God establishes his

God's Unconditional Covenant

covenant of friendship with the elect in Christ obligates them to new obedience. To use the language of the Form for the Administration of Baptism, they must cleave to their God, forsake the world, crucify their old natures, and walk in a new and holy life![3] This life of sanctification is not to be conceived of as a fulfilling of conditions in order that the covenant may be realized. This is the fruit of God's marvelous grace and love at work in the hearts of his covenant people.

For further study of this important subject, the reader may consult Herman Hanko, *God's Everlasting Covenant of Grace;* Herman Hoeksema, *The Triple Knowledge: An Exposition of the Heidelberg Catechism,* vol. 2 (Grand Rapids, MI: Reformed Free Publishing Association), 495–527; and for a presentation of the Liberated view, see J. Kamphuis, *An Everlasting Covenant* (Launceston, Tasmania, Australia: Publication Organization of the Free Reformed Churches of Australia, 1985).

33

How We View the Children of the Covenant

Arie J. den Hartog

THE DOCTRINAL CONTROVERSY OF 1953 HAS PRACTIcal importance. It did not involve theological issues that are so abstract that they lack real spiritual value for the daily lives of God's people. The two great doctrines that were especially involved in that controversy in the Protestant Reformed Churches (PRC) were the doctrines of God's sovereign elective grace in the saving of his people and the doctrine of the covenant of God with his people. These two doctrines are absolutely central to the Scriptures. No truly Reformed believer would dispute that. It must also be said that the two sides that were engaged in the controversy of 1953 desired to maintain these doctrines. Which side actually has remained most faithful to these great doctrines must be judged in the light of the word of God. Through the stormy history that always accompanies doctrinal controversy, the church is led by God's grace and Holy Spirit into a deeper and richer understanding of the word of God. We humbly believe that God has so led our Protestant Reformed Churches.

We shall focus especially on the significance of the doctrinal controversy of 1953 for how we view our children in God's covenant. This is a subject very dear to the hearts of Reformed believers because we love our children as covenant children of God. May the Lord keep us from carnality in that

How We View the Children of the Covenant

love for our children, from a love merely for our own flesh and blood, and from the proud imagination that our children are better than those of the world simply because they are ours. We confess with our baptism form that we conceive and bring forth our children in sin. By nature, there is no more hope for the children of believers than there is for the poor, wretched, miserable sinners that are the parents of these children. Our only hope is in the grace of God.

More specifically, this hope is in the sovereign, gracious covenant of God with believers and their children. We bring forth our children as our covenant calling before God. Our faith in regard to them is antithetical to the world's philosophy of birth control. There are still many large families in the PRC for this reason. We take confidence in God's covenant purpose in our calling. Without this confidence we would despair at bringing children into the ungodly, wicked world in which we live. We bring our children to church to be baptized as infants because we believe that God in his gracious purpose has very really included the children of believers in his covenant.

How we view our children in the covenant is of vital importance for how we raise our children. It is the basis for our hope for their salvation. We lay hold by faith on the promise of God to Abraham that he will be our God and the God of our children after us. We find our hope in the promise announced at Pentecost: "For the promise is unto you, and to your children, and to all that are afar off, even as many as the Lord our God shall call" (Acts 2:39). We plead on the basis of the promise of the covenant when we pray for our children.

We admonish our children daily to turn from their sins in repentance to God. With a proper understanding of the truth of God's covenant, we exhort them to crucify their old sinful nature and to live a new and godly life. We are convinced that we are right in bringing our little ones to Jesus, because to such belongs the kingdom of heaven. Based on the truth of the covenant, we comfort our children with the promises of God's word. We assure them that the promises of the gospel belong to them as well as to us as adults. We also admonish even those who are of our own flesh and blood that if they lead a wicked and carnal life, they have no part in the covenant and kingdom of God, and that they stand exposed to the wrath of God unless they repent and turn from their wicked ways.

An excellent confessional expression of the truth of the covenant with regard to our children is found in Question and Answer 74 of the Heidelberg Catechism:

> Are infants also to be baptized? Yes; for since they, as well as their parents, belong to the covenant and people of God, and both redemption from sin and the Holy Ghost, who works faith, are through the blood of Christ promised to them no less than to their parents, they are also by Baptism, as a sign of the covenant, to be ingrafted into the Christian Church, and distinguished from the children of unbelievers, as was done in the Old Testament by Circumcision, in place of which in the New Testament Baptism is appointed.[1]

This beautiful confessional expression of the biblical truth of the covenant of God as it applies to children cannot be read to mean that God makes only an objective promise to covenant children conditioned on their own personal acceptance later in life. The children of the covenant are as much in the covenant from birth as their covenant parents are.

The promise of which the Heidelberg Catechism speaks includes the promise of redemption from sin by the blood of Christ and by the Holy Spirit, the author of faith. God does not promise these things to covenant children merely objectively or externally. He promises to apply the blessings of salvation to the hearts of the children of the covenant by the working of his Holy Spirit. The faith of covenant children is a gift of God to his elect. It is not the condition that covenant children fulfill later in life. This God-given faith is not dependent for its fulfillment on the action of man, but on God alone. God gives faith to covenant children by his sovereign, effectual operation of the Spirit in their hearts. This truth cannot find any other basis than God's election. Without such a sovereign, effectual working of the Spirit of God, none of

How We View the Children of the Covenant

our covenant children would ever have faith and none would ever be saved. This is all very practical. We have these things in our minds and hearts when we bring our children with us to church. The Protestant Reformed Churches do not go along with the modern-day fad of "children's church," which separates children from families before the beginning of the sermon. We believe that our children very really belong to the church of Jesus Christ already as infants. We believe that the preaching that takes place in the congregation is addressed to children as well as to adults. For this reason also the inspired apostles of the Lord addressed children as well as adults in the letters they sent to the churches. God gives spiritual receptivity to children in the covenant. Though their understanding of the preaching is no doubt less than that of adults, covenant children can and do receive spiritual blessing in the worship service when the word of God is faithfully preached and properly applied.

We believe that the church must maintain a solid and thorough program of catechism instruction for covenant youth. Such programs are a rarity today in Presbyterian and Reformed churches. If there is still any significant measure of instruction of children in many churches, it is done in superficial Sunday school classes, many of which are at best very shallow and some of which are simply Arminian in their approach to covenant children. The purpose of catechism instruction is to bring covenant children to maturity in the faith. This would not be possible if the Spirit of God had not been given to them in their hearts.

Our covenant convictions constrain us to establish our own covenant Christian day schools wherever possible. We do all in our power by the grace of God to keep the covenant perspective of these schools. We do not consider these schools little missionary institutions to bring people from the outside world into the church. Mission work is the calling of the church through the preaching of the gospel and the testimony of her members, but not of the school. We do not throw open the doors of our schools to anyone in the community

Always Reforming

who might be attracted to the excellent academic character and discipline that characterizes our schools. We believe that these schools are for covenant children. They are not in existence to convert the children of the world, if that were possible. All of this we say with thankfulness to God to illustrate of what great practical importance the doctrine of the covenant is and how important it is to maintain this doctrine in all purity for the glory of God and not the praise of men.

There are two errors which the Protestant Reformed Churches have sought steadfastly to avoid in the covenant perspective from which we strive to raise our children. We repudiate the error of presupposed regeneration. This view holds that all children born of covenant parents are presupposed to be children of God unless in later life they reveal themselves by a wicked life-style as not being part of that covenant. It is simply not true to the word of God to say that all children born of covenant parents are God's elect; nor may we simply assume that they are. The PRC have always rejected this error, even though some have falsely accused us of holding to it. The error of presupposed regeneration has had evil consequences in many Reformed churches. It has given the carnal seed in these churches the idea that in spite of an ungodly life-style, they may assume that they are children of God. Because of this false teaching, wicked, ungodly young people who grow up in the church are not warned and admonished as God's word requires. This false doctrine has over the years filled many Reformed churches with carnal members and tolerated the grossest iniquity among the youth of the church.

The Protestant Reformed Churches also reject the idea that the covenant of God in the church is conditional. This idea is that God really makes his covenant with all the children of covenant parents. In spite of the fact that God's covenant is with them, some of these covenant children are still lost through their own unbelief and rejection of the covenant promises offered to them. According to this scheme the covenant promise is conditioned on the faith confessed in later life by covenant children. The reason why we reject this

How We View the Children of the Covenant

perspective of the covenant is that the conclusion of this teaching is that God's covenant is based ultimately on the work of man and not completely on God. Though the proponents of this theory have often denied this, the conclusion is inescapable. God is then not sovereign in realizing his covenant promise in the hearts of covenant children. For some covenant children the promise of God is made of no effect. God, from their birth, promised to be their God, but in the end failed to save them.

We believe that the covenant of God with the children of believers is limited by God's purpose of election. This is not a truth that we have come to by some sort of evil rationalism independent from a study of and meditation on the word of God. The Bible teaches that in the sphere of the covenant there are born Esaus and Jacobs. In the Old Testament, both of these were circumcised according to the command of God. Both of these were given the same instruction in the sphere of the covenant home and in the nation or church in which they were raised. It was revealed later in life that Esau was a carnal and profane reprobate. Jacob was, by God's grace, in spite of his sinfulness, an elect child of God with whom God by sovereign grace continued his covenant.

The inspired apostle Paul answers the question in Romans 9 to 11 whether the word of God was made of no effect by the unbelief of the majority of the Jews. The answer of the word of God is that "they are not all Israel, which are of Israel" (Rom. 9:6). In Romans 11 Paul answers the question whether the unbelief of many in Israel means that God has cast away his people, with the strong statement, "God forbid!" The purpose of election shall stand. The promise of God is sure to all of God's elect. "Even so then at this present time also there is a remnant according to the election of grace" (Rom. 11:5). These and other passages of Scripture clearly teach that God's covenant purpose is controlled by his purpose of sovereign, eternal election. The limiting clause of Acts 2:39, "as many as the Lord our God shall call," is a reference to the realization of God's purpose of election in the generations of God's people.

We acknowledge that we bring forth a twofold seed, a carnal and a spiritual. This is a very difficult truth about the way of God's working. It is nevertheless the way of his sovereign purpose. Sometimes the carnal seed in the church are clearly revealed in connection with carelessness on the part of parents to fulfill their covenant obligation in nurturing their children in the fear of the Lord, although this is not always the case. It is very difficult to live with the possibility that one of your own children may be carnal and reprobate. Paul said that he could wish that he were accursed from Christ for his brethren's sake. We pray for our children until the day that we die. Only God knows those who are truly his. But even when it seems that we have carnal children, our final comfort and assurance is in God's sovereign purpose, which we know is always good and will serve for the glory of his name. Believing this truth takes great faith, but that faith alone comforts us in the deep sorrow of impenitent, rebellious children in the covenant home. Almost every pastor has been called upon to advise and to comfort godly parents in situations such as these. It is not an easy task, but one that can only be performed with sound teaching of the word of God (sound doctrine).

When we sit around our tables with our covenant children, we address them from the perspective of the covenant of God, even though we do not know that every one of them is definitely an elect child of God. Only God knows that. Scripture gives us the direction to address our children from this perspective. The minister in church addresses his congregation from this same perspective. This is not the same as presupposed regeneration. In our dealing with our children we admonish them about sin. We call them to daily repentance and conversion. We warn our carnal children with grief and sorrow of heart that if they live an ungodly life they have no right to be called the children of God. We warn them about the severe judgments of God that shall come upon those who were taught the way of the Lord and then forsook that way when they came to years of responsibility. We leave the effect of such warning up to the Lord. For some this warning will be unto repentance; for others, to hardening and judgment.

The mighty incentive to godly living for the children of the covenant is not the admonition that if only they will fulfill the condition of faith, the covenant promises of God will really and spiritually become theirs. Such admonitions will only leave these children with the fear that at some point in life they might fail to fulfill the necessary condition and still be lost. The mighty incentive to godly living for covenant children is the wonderful, blessed, sure covenant promise of God in Christ Jesus realized from beginning to end only by the sovereign grace of God. We have the solemn obligation to live godly lives because we are, by the grace of God, members of his covenant. We are moved to do so in humble gratitude to God for all that he has done for us through his Son Jesus Christ. We do not become God's covenant people by our own action of faith. Our faith is a chief part of the blessings of the covenant that he bestows upon us and our children. We teach our children that because of our sinful nature, even as children of God we are daily prone to sin. Our love and thankfulness to God must cause us to abhor that sin and flee to the cross daily for forgiveness.

It is such teaching that God uses and applies to the hearts of the true children of the covenant as he realizes his sovereign, gracious covenant purpose with them. When we and our children sometimes fall into sin—and we do all too often—we must not despair of God's mercy or continue in sin, knowing that God has established an eternal covenant of grace with us.[2] The teaching of God's sovereign grace does not lead to carelessness in the lives of God's people, no matter how often it has been falsely charged. This teaching will do that only if it is wrested by evil men unto their own destruction. Teaching God's sovereign, elective grace in his covenant to our children will, by the grace and Spirit of God, be the mighty incentive to them to live godly lives. This is the calling of God to his covenant people.

34

Authority of Major Assemblies: Advice or Jurisdiction?

Gise J. Van Baren

IN THE CONTROVERSY OF 1924, THE QUESTION WAS raised concerning the authority of the classis or synod over the local consistory. The 1924 Synod of the Christian Reformed Church (CRC), meeting at Kalamazoo, Michigan, adopted what was known as the three points of common grace.[1] The decision was taken in answer to protests that were made against the teaching of the Rev. Herman Hoeksema of the Eastern Avenue Christian Reformed Church. That same synod declared that Rev. Hoeksema was Reformed, howbeit somewhat one-sided, and it also refused to adopt a motion demanding that this pastor submit to the decisions concerning common grace or be suspended or deposed from office.[2]

Later, when additional appeals were made by members of Eastern Avenue to Classis Grand Rapids East, that classis finally suspended Rev. Hoeksema and deposed his elders from office. The small minority of members of that congregation who opposed Rev. H. Hoeksema managed, through court action, to strip the majority of their property and name.

The Protestant Reformed Churches (PRC) expressed their disagreement with the above actions for two principal reasons. The synod had declared Rev. Hoeksema to be Reformed though "one-sided," but had refused to demand his submission to the adopted three points of common grace or face suspension and deposition. Classis Grand Rapids East had no legal authority to suspend or depose office bearers of a local church, a right that belongs only with the consistory of the church.

The Protestant Reformed Churches adopted this name ("churches"—in the plural) to express the truth that the local church is autonomous. It is not the denomination that is the "church," but the local church is the manifestation of the body of Christ. That is in distinction from the Christian Reformed Church—the name implying that the denomination is itself the "church." A large number of those who have been leaving the Christian Reformed Church in recent years have come to understand this distinction—and some have now repudiated this position of the CRC.

This question surfaced again in the split of 1953 in the Protestant Reformed Churches. There was a question of the binding nature of decisions of a classis or synod (Article 31 of the Church Order).[3] There were questions concerning the idea and significance of the autonomy of the local congregation. While both sides claimed to adhere to the principles maintained at the time of the 1924 controversy, there were obvious differences of opinion how this applied in the situation of 1953.

It is beyond our scope here to consider all of the questions raised and issues presented. By the nature of the case, it was a very unusual situation within the churches. Schism of this sort affects decisions taken. A careful analysis of all the events of that time might be profitable but would involve a very lengthy article, or even a book.

The court case of the First Protestant Reformed Church of Grand Rapids, Michigan, before Judge Thaddeus B. Taylor reveals some of the diversity of opinion. Both sides agreed on the autonomy of the local congregation. But the two sides obviously disagreed on the relationship of the local church to the classis or synod and how Article 31 applied.

The Rev. Bernard Kok expressed what seemed to be the

general view of the dissidents. His statements under oath show strikingly the driving force behind many of the decisions made by the De Wolf group.

Q. [by attorney Jay W. Linsey] Well, let us assume, as in this case, that Classis advised the suspension or deposition of De Wolf if he did not apologize, would it be up to—would the Consistory have to follow that advice?
A. No, sir.
Q. If they refused to follow that advice, would that have any effect upon the local property or congregation?
A. No.
Q. Here, as this has been interpreted, this law has been interpreted in your church, the church is autonomous churches?
A. Autonomous churches, yes.
Q. Is there any penalty if you should refuse, if the Consistory should refuse to follow the advice of Classis or Synod?
A. No penalty whatsoever.
Q. Now, then, if the Classis in this case said call in a neighboring Consistory and suspend De Wolf if he doesn't apologize, do I understand the Consistory would not have to follow that advice?
A. May I hear that question again? (Question thereupon read by the reporter.).
Q. Consistory of the First Church, do they have to follow that advice?
A. No, sir, and Classis has no business giving that. In the question of suspension, Classis has nothing to say whatsoever; in the suspension and deposition of elders and deacons, Classis has nothing to say. In the suspension of the minister, Classis has nothing to say. The only stipulation in the Church Order is that the minister may not be deposed without the advice of Classis, but in the suspension, the Classis has no voice at all.
Q. Well, how about the deposition?
A. The deposition is to be done by the Consistory, but according to the Church Order, may not be done without the advice of Classis. They may suspend a minister without the advice of Classis, by the preceding sentence of the consistory and the neighboring consistory, but they may not depose the minister without first having obtained the advice of Classis and the approval of the synodical delegates.
Q. Now, in this case, it appears that Rev. Hoeksema—strike that

Authority of Major Assemblies: Advice or Jurisdiction?

out—it appears that the consistory of the First Church approved the doctrine of Rev. De Wolf as explained by him, and it appears that Rev. Hoeksema took an appeal from that decision to Classis upon the question of doctrine. Did that give classis any authority, under the law as it is interpreted by your church, to depose or suspend the minister?
A. No, sir.
Q. Or even advise it?
A. Not even advise it.[4]

Under cross-examination by attorney Robert S. Tubbs, Rev. Kok provided further explanation of his views:

Q. The Church Order, itself, however, is the constitution of your church, is it not?
A. And the Church Order, Article 31, allows, when it states that all decisions by majority vote shall be binding unless—that means unless in my conscience it is contrary to the Word of God or the Church Order, then it is not binding.
Q. Is the word "conscience" in Article 31?
A. That is our interpretation of Article 31.
Q. Whose interpretation?
A. Rev. Ophoff.
Q. What is your interpretation?
A. The same as Professor Ophoff.
Q. What is the interpretation of the synod of your church?
A. I don't think we have any, do we—let me look up Article 31. (Referring to Church Order) Doesn't say anything about it.
Q. Now, the use of the word "proved" in that article has meaning, does it not?
A. Yes, do you want me to read from Professor Ophoff what it means?
Q. No, I want you to answer my question.
A. Yes, it has meaning.
Q. To whom is the proof given?
A. How?
Q. To whom is that proof given under Article 31?
A. You must attempt to give that proof to either classis or synod.
Q. You must not only attempt, you must actually furnish the proof, must you not?
A. Not necessarily. If I do not actually furnish the proof that is sat-

isfactory to the synod or classis, I still have the right of my opinion.
Q. Under Article 31?
A. Under Article 31.
Q. You reserve the right to have your own opinion?
A. That is right.
Q. But action of synod or classis is binding on you?
A. It is not.
Q. You mean you can flaunt a decision of classis?
A. Yes, guaranteed me by contract.
Q. And still remain a minister of the gospel of the Protestant Reformed Church?
A. Of the Protestant Reformed Church, of a Protestant Reformed congregation, yes. Whether they want to put me out of the association, that is their privilege. They have a right to deny me the fellowship, but they have no right to touch my office as minister in the Protestant Reformed Church of the congregation I represent.[5]

The above quotations give an idea of the erroneous view presented of Article 31 of the Church Order. It appears, according to this presentation, that anyone may ignore the decisions of a classis (or synod) if he proves to his own conscience that he is right and classis is wrong. The only thing a classis can do, if the matter is of sufficiently serious a nature, is to sever relationships with the congregation which refuses to follow its advice. The statements of Rev. Kok go a long way to explain what occurred both in Classis West and some of the churches of Classis East. These would not be bound by Article 31 of the Church Order.

The Protestant Reformed Churches do maintain the autonomy of the local church and its consistory. These churches do make a distinction between "broader" (correct) and "higher" (incorrect) bodies when speaking of a classis or synod. These churches have insisted that only the consistory can suspend, depose, or otherwise discipline its office bearers or members. But surely they have not taught that Article 31 means one need merely to prove to one's own conscience from Scripture and the Church Order that a decision of a classis or synod is

Authority of Major Assemblies: Advice or Jurisdiction?

wrong in order then to ignore or violate that decision. Such action would result in anarchy in the churches (as was seen also in 1953). According to Article 31 of the Church Order, the decisions of the broader bodies are binding. Those who disagree with the decisions of the broader gatherings must prove from Scripture and the Church Order, to the satisfaction of those bodies, that the decision is wrong. If that is not thus proved, and if the church or individual refuses to abide by the decisions of the broader gatherings, they put themselves outside of the pale of the churches—and these gatherings must declare them to be out. If one can do as he pleases despite the decisions of the broader gathering, then protests, appeals, and overtures would mean nothing.

If the PRC learned one important lesson in 1953, it was surely this: We must abide by the Church Order adopted by the churches and not have each do what is "right in his own eyes" (Judges 17:6). Decisions taken by the broader gatherings must be binding in the churches, or there would be anarchy and surely no denominational unity.

35

The Split of 1953: Reflections

Cornelius Hanko

Forty-three years later it is still painful for me to think back upon and write about the split of 1953. This is because I was personally involved in all that took place, sat through many difficult meetings of consistory, classis, and synod; and experienced that there were those, among whom were my most intimate friends ever since the student days in the seminary, who now were out to destroy our churches by opposing the truth that we held most precious. I recall the nights after consistory meetings when Rev. George Ophoff and I would walk the streets of Grand Rapids in utter weariness, how I would receive unpleasant phone calls just before going to the pulpit, and how difficult it often was to preach, knowing that there was so much opposition in the congregation.

In times like that, the devil seems to work overtime. He knows how to create dissension, arouse suspicions, gossip, backbiting, and slander, and stir up bitterness, wrath, and even hatred. These were also times of much prayer, fervent prayer, pleading with God.

> With steadfast courage I design
> No wrong to speak or do;
> Thy path of life I choose for mine
> And walk with purpose true.

The Split of 1953: Reflections

For help, O God, I cry to Thee,
Assured that Thou wilt answer me.[1]

The question often arises, was this split unavoidable? The answer is that under the circumstances it was inevitable.

In 1945, when I was in Oaklawn, Illinois, I accepted a call from Manhattan, Montana, which brought me out of Classis East and into Classis West. Soon after attending classis meetings a few times, I noticed a spirit of discontent.

Some of the ministers were unhappy that their congregations failed to grow. They had looked forward to a more or less rapid growth, and yet there seemed to be so little outside interest.

Contact had been made with the German Reformed churches in South Dakota, and conferences were held between both groups. But Rev. Hoeksema and Rev. Ophoff discovered that some of the German churches were far from Reformed, judging from the remarks made at the conferences and from the literature they distributed. These two ministers discouraged any effort to join with them, which was likely a contributing factor that brought an end to these conferences. It was also quite obvious that particularly in the west the ministers resented the leadership of Rev. Hoeksema, even accusing him of being domineering.

There was also an effort toward independentism; that is, members of Classis West were unwilling to cooperate in the work that was being carried on in Classis East. A radio broadcast had been started in Grand Rapids over radio station WFUR, called "The Reformed Witness Hour," which was also aired over other stations. But men of Classis West began their "Sovereign Grace Hour." In Grand Rapids a weekly paper was published known as *The Church News*. Our churches in the midwest began to publish *Concordia*. Still worse, the synod had adopted catechism books to be used in our churches, but in the midwest the ministers prepared their own catechism books.

In 1948 I received a call from First Protestant Reformed Church in Grand Rapids, Michigan. Since Rev. Hoeksema had suffered a stroke in June of 1947, the consistory decided to call a third minister. While I was considering the call, I received a letter from Rev. Hoeksema, explaining the need for another minister, adding that there were serious problems in the congregation that he hoped I would not ignore in considering the call.

After I accepted the call and came to Grand Rapids, I soon discovered that the problems referred to by Rev. Hoeksema were far more serious than I had realized.

From the very beginning of our existence as Protestant Reformed churches, some individuals had joined us not for the sake of principle or out of conviction, but for various other reasons. Since First Church was a large congregation, it demanded no sacrifice to join us, so that various outsiders, some of whom had married members of the church, joined without actually desiring the truth that was preached. In fact, these outsiders, and possibly others, complained that the preaching was too doctrinal, the society life too formal and lifeless. They wanted skits and other forms of entertainment. A spirit of worldly-mindedness was creeping into the church.

On family visitation I discovered that there were people who showed no interest in the church or in spiritual matters. There was not only a lethargy, but also a cold indifference. They objected to solid Reformed preaching, and they especially shied away from the idea of being distinctly Reformed. Many objected to having our own school. In fact, there were a few who were members of a labor union, but had managed to remain undetected.

All of this came to a head when Dr. Klaas Schilder of the Liberated churches in the Netherlands visited the United States. He sought contact with the PRC, was heartily received, and spoke in our various churches. Many of our ministers and members of the congregations found him to be a very congenial person, whose visit and interest in us was greatly appreciated.

In the effort to be more practical in their preaching, to lay more emphasis on man's responsibility, many of the ministers began to preach the conditional theology of the Liberated churches. Articles appeared in *Concordia* not only defending the idea of conditions unto salvation, something that man must do, emphasizing the "must," but also defending the idea that faith is a condition unto salvation. No matter how they tried to defend that, it had the Arminian connotation of man's part in the work of salvation.

What brought matters to a head was the fact that immigrants began coming into our country and into Canada, many of them from the Liberated churches and seeking to join with us. These Liberated had just gone through a doctrinal struggle in the Netherlands, which had resulted in the birth of the Liberated churches in distinction from the Gereformeerde Kerken in Nederland (Reformed Churches in the Netherlands). These individuals were determined to cling to their conception of the covenant and conditions in the covenant even when they joined us. This was evident, for example, from a protest that was sent to our consistory from two young men who had come from the Liberated churches and now were protesting against the sermons of Rev. Hoeksema and me as not being Reformed.

All this forced the Mission Committee to propose to synod to adopt a Declaration of Principles in which would be clearly expressed the specific truths maintained by the PRC in regard to common grace, the general offer of salvation, and the covenant. Especially the truth of God's covenant, following out of our stand for God's sovereignty, as developed by Rev. Hoeksema, we considered to be our peculiar mark of distinction among the churches.

This Declaration was adopted by the synod of 1950 with but one dissenting vote. It was only later that serious opposition arose among our ministers and members.

In Canada two churches were organized under the pretense of agreeing with us doctrinally. I was personally told by more than one of the immigrants that the people in Hamilton, Ontario, had deliberately deceived us. When they felt strong enough numerically and financially to be on their own, they left us and organized their own churches.

Obviously the split of 1953 was inevitable.

We may also ask: Was the split necessary for the welfare of our churches?

This question could also be formulated to read: Did God have a divine purpose with this split for our good? The answer is: We would have lost the very truth of God's sovereign grace for which we have always striven. Today we can plainly see that, had the split not happened, we either would no longer exist or we would have no right of existence as defending the truth of God's sovereign grace.

It is indeed true that the Protestant Reformed Churches were greatly reduced at the time. In fact, we lost more than half of our ministers, churches, and membership. Yet the Lord has turned that to our good. The Lord has plainly sent a purifying trial as by fire, through which our churches not only survived, but also were spiritually blessed. Our view of God's covenant friendship established with his people in Christ has not only been preserved, but also delivered from any taint of conditions that might have been found in it before the conflict.

Still more, that truth has been more fully developed. We see more clearly than ever that this covenant view is entrusted to us to cherish and to find our comfort in it. The very idea is worth giving our lives for, because we are sons and daughters of the living God, having a rightful place in God's house as part of that blessed family that will be completely united in heavenly perfection before the throne, forever reflecting the glory of God and living in intimate communion of life with him to the praise of the glory of his grace.

Are there lessons to be learned, danger signs that must be heeded as a result of this experience?

Having lived through the reformation that took place in 1924 and the split in the Protestant Reformed Churches in 1953, I cannot avoid comparing the events that led up to both.

In both instances there was a strong opposition to sound doctrine. Before 1924 there were those in the churches who emphasized a general, well-meant offer of salvation. The Arminian theory of the free will, so strongly condemned at the Synod of Dordt (1618–1619), was again lifting its vile head in

The Split of 1953: Reflections

the church. In the 1953 controversy the truth of God's sovereignty was challenged by the ambition to introduce conditions unto salvation that man must fulfill.

In 1924 there was the evil of worldly-mindedness. There was the common grace theory holding that natural man can do much that is good in the sight of God. A bridge was being spanned between the church and the world toward a certain synergism, or working together. In 1953 there were many in our churches who showed no desire at all to be distinctively Reformed and to manifest that in a truly sincere Christian life and walk.

Along with this, there was a cold lethargy preceding both the reformation of 1924 and the split of 1953. Church attendance was for many a mere formality, something that was expected of them. Societies for Bible study in many cases languished. There was no longer a keen interest in the study of God's word. Few prepared for a lively Bible discussion. Instead, in order to retain interest in the church, there was a clamor for entertainment in the church activities. Church papers that emphasized the truth, such as the *Standard Bearer*, were either not desired or laid aside unread. Along with all this, there were those who felt that they were spiritually benefited by some outside meetings or activities that they could not obtain in the home church.

As a result, the preaching and teaching became less doctrinal. God did not receive the emphasis but man did. There was in both instances an emphasis on man's responsibility, man's part in the work of salvation, man's activity of faith. People did not know, nor were they interested in, sound doctrine. Religion became a mere formality for many, setting themselves wide open for heresy.

Is there among us today a lack of interest in sound, doctrinal preaching? Do we clamor for less emphasis on doctrine and more emphasis on daily living?

Is there a trend among us toward worldly-mindedness, even though we may not be aware of it?

Have we become lethargic?

A bit of self-examination may be beneficial to all of us.

Endnotes

Part I

[1] Thomas Scott, *The Articles of the Synod of Dordt* (1856, reprint, Harrisonburg, PA: Sprinkle Publications, 1993), 27.

Chapter 1

[1] "Historical Foreword to the Acts of the Synod of Dordt," Appendix A in Homer C. Hoeksema, *The Voice of Our Fathers* (Grand Rapids, MI: Reformed Free Publishing Association, 1980), 48. At least two translations of the "Historical Foreword Addressed to the Reformed Churches of Christ" are readily available. One is found in Homer C. Hoeksema's excellent and thorough exposition of the Canons of Dordt cited above. It is also included in Thomas Scott's translation, *The Articles of the Synod of Dordt* (1856, reprint, Harrisonburg, PA: Sprinkle Publications, 1993), 94–240.
[2] Ibid., 49.
[3] Ibid., 49.

Chapter 2

[1] The Five Arminian Articles, Art. 1, *The Creeds of Christendom*, ed. Philip Schaff, vol. 3 (1931, reprint, Grand Rapids, MI: Baker Book House, 1998), 545, 546. The Five Arminian Articles are also known as the Five Articles of the Remonstrants.
[2] Five Articles, Art. 2, in Schaff, *Creeds of Christendom*, 3:546.
[3] Five Articles, Art. 3, in Schaff, *Creeds of Christendom*, 3:546, 547. Homer C. Hoeksema insisted that the English translation of Article 3 should be, "That man has not saving faith..."

[4] Canons of Dordt, *The Confessions and the Church Order of the Protestant Reformed Churches* (Grandville, MI: Protestant Reformed Churches in America, 2005), 171–173.
[5] Five Articles, Art. 4, in Schaff, *Creeds of Christendom*, 3:547.
[6] Five Articles, Art. 5, in Schaff, *Creeds of Christendom*, 3:548, 549.

Chapter 3

[1] Homer C. Hoeksema, *The Voice of Our Fathers*, 27.
[2] Ibid., 27.

Chapter 4

[1] Canons of Dordt, 1, Art. 6, 7, in Schaff, *Creeds of Christendom*, 3:582.
[2] Canons of Dordt, 1, Art. 17, in Schaff, *Creeds of Christendom*, 3:585.
[3] Canons of Dordt, 3 & 4, Art. 16, in Schaff, *Creeds of Christendom*, 3:591.
[4] Canons of Dordt, 3 & 4, Art. 11, in Schaff, *Creeds of Christendom*, 3:590.
[5] Ibid.
[6] Canons of Dordt, 3 & 4, Art. 12, in Schaff, *Creeds of Christendom*, 3:590.
[7] Canons of Dordt, 3 & 4, Art. 16, in Schaff, *Creeds of Christendom*, 3:591.
[8] Canons of Dordt, 3 & 4, Art. 12, in Schaff, *Creeds of Christendom*, 3:590.
[9] Canons of Dordt, 3 & 4, Art. 11, in Schaff, *Creeds of Christendom*, 3:590.
[10] Canons of Dordt, 5, Art. 14, in Schaff, *Creeds of Christendom*, 3:595.

Chapter 5

[1] The interested reader is referred to Marten H. Woudstra's excellent chapter entitled "The Synod and Bible Translation," in *Crisis in the Reformed Churches: Essays in Commemoration of the Great Synod of Dordt, 1618–1619,* Peter Y. DeJong, ed. (Grand Rapids, MI: Reformed Fellowship, 1968).

Endnotes

[2] P. Biesterveld and H. H. Kuyper, *Ecclesiastical Manual Including the Decision of the Netherlands Synods and Other Significant Matters Relating to the Government of the Churches*, trans. Richard R. De Ridder (Grand Rapids, MI: Calvin Theological Seminary, 1982), 200.
[3] Ibid., 186.
[4] Ibid., 187.

Chapter 6

[1] Belgic Confession of Faith, Art. 14, in Schaff, *Creeds of Christendom*, 3:399.
[2] *Christelijke Encyclopaedie voor het Nederlandsche Volk*, ed. F. W. Grosheide et al., vol. 1 (Kampen: Kok, 1925), 634–636.
[3] Thomas Scott, *The Articles of the Synod of Dordt*, 166.

Chapter 7

[1] This translation by Homer C. Hoeksema appeared originally in the February 15, 1984, issue of the *Standard Bearer*.

Chapter 8

[1] "Seceders dominated in the first immigrant wave; some 13,000 emigrated between 1845 and 1880, and they comprised 65 percent of all emigrants in the peak years 1846–1849. In 1847, the founding year of the major colonies in Michigan, Iowa, and Wisconsin, 79 percent of all emigrants were Seceders. This was at a time when barely one percent of the Dutch populace were Seceders... Of the 114 clerics ordained in the CRCNA from 1857 to 1900, *every one* had been affiliated with the Afscheiding" (Robert P. Swierenga, "True Brothers: The Netherlandic Origins of the Christian Reformed Church in North America, 1857–1880," http://www.swierenga.com/Kampen_pap.html).
[2] No. 213, third stanza, *The Psalter* (Grand Rapids, MI: Eerdmans, 1995). See the first eight verses of Psalm 78.
[3] Henry S. Lucas, ed., *Dutch Immigrant Memoirs and Related Writings*, rev. ed. (Grand Rapids, MI: Eerdmans, 1997), 1:15.
[4] Maurice G. Hansen, *The Reformed Church in the Netherlands* (New York: Board of Publication of the 4eformed Church in America, 1884), 290.

5 Lucas, *Dutch Immigrant Memoirs*, 2:368.
6 D. H. Kromminga, *The Christian Reformed Tradition* (Grand Rapids: Eerdmans, 1943), 80.
7 Henry S. Lucas, *Netherlanders in America: Dutch Immigration to the United States and Canada, 1789–1950* (Ann Arbor, MI: University of Michigan Press, 1955), 43.
8 Jacob Van Hinte, *Netherlanders in America*, ed. Robert Swierenga, trans. Adriaan de Wit (Grand Rapids, MI: Baker Book House, 1985), 362.
9 Scholte's charges were probably correct, since Brummelkamp was the one who introduced the theology of the well-meant offer into the Secession churches.
10 Disinterest in Christian education, the use of hymns and choirs in worship, doctrinal laxity and Arminianism in the RCA, lodge membership, ecumenism, open communion, a lack of catechetical instruction, and neglect of catechism preaching were all issues in the dispute that led to the formation of the CRC in North America.
11 H. Algra, *Het Wonder van de 19e Eeuw: Van Vrije Kerken en Kleine Luyden* (Franeker: T. Wever, 1966), 107.
12 De Cock later published the Canons, another act for which he was vilified by his enemies.
13 The Form for the Administration of Baptism asks parents whether they "acknowledge the doctrine which is contained in the Old and New Testament, and in the articles of the Christian faith, and which is taught here in this Christian church to be the true and perfect doctrine of salvation?" Protestant Reformed Churches in America, *The Confessions and Church Order of the Protestant Reformed Churches* (Grandville, MI: PRC in America, 2005), 260.
14 Peter Y. De Jong, "The Dawn of a New Day," in *The Reformation of 1834* (Orange City, IA: Pluim Publishing, 1984), 33.
15 Lucas, *Dutch Immigrant Memoirs*, 2:510.
16 Herman Hanko, *Portraits of Faithful Saints* (Grandville, MI: Reformed Free Publishing Association, 1999), 357.
17 It was through this weaker southern branch that the doctrines of a well-meant offer and a conditional covenant found their way into the Secession churches. Brummelkamp especially was responsible for introducing the theology of the well-meant offer of the gospel into the churches.

Endnotes

[18] Albert Hyma, *Albertus C. Van Raalte and His Dutch Settlements in the United States* (Grand Rapids, MI: Eerdmans, 1947), 39.
[19] Kromminga, *The Christian Reformed Tradition*, 87, 88.
[20] Lubbertus Oostendorp, *H. P. Scholte: Leader of the Secession of 1834 and Founder of Pella* (Franeker: T. Wever, 1964), 73.
[21] Ibid.
[22] Van Hinte, *Netherlanders in America*, 92.
[23] Homer C. Hoeksema, "The Sesquicentennial of the Afscheiding," *Standard Bearer* 60, no. 9 (Feb. 1, 1984): 197.
[24] Quoted in Nelson D. Kloosterman, "The Doctrinal Significance of the Secession of 1834," in *The Reformation of 1834* (Orange City, IA: Pluim Publishing, 1984), 37.
[25] No. 427, second stanza, *The Psalter.*
[26] The Belgic Confession of Faith states, "As for the false Church, she ascribes more power and authority to herself and her ordinances than to the Word of God, and will not submit herself to the yoke of Christ. Neither does she administer the Sacraments as appointed by Christ in his Word, but adds to and takes from them as she thinks proper; she relieth more upon men than upon Christ; and persecutes those who live holily according to the Word of God, and rebuke her for her errors, covetousness, and idolatry." Belgic Confession, Art. 29, in Schaff, *Creeds of Christendom*, 3:420, 421.
[27] Homer C. Hoeksema, "Act of Secession or Return," *Standard Bearer* 60, no. 10 (Feb. 15, 1984): 222.
[28] Heidelberg Catechism, Q & A 54, in Schaff, *Creeds of Christendom*, 3:324, 325.

Chapter 9

[1] This is a translation of the first part of the sermon *De spijs van Jezus* preached by Van Velzen, a father of the secession, in December 1886, when he was seventy-seven years old. The sermon is found in *Avondstemmen: Opstellen van Wijlen Prof. S. Van Velzen* (Leiden: D. Donner, 1897). We include it in this volume as a sample of Secession preaching.
[2] Biblical references in brackets are supplied by the translator. Van Velzen did not give the references.

Chapter 11

[1] J. A. Wanliss and W. L. Bredenhof, ed. and trans., *According to the Command of the Lord: Rev. H. DeCock's Case Against Hymns* (n.p., 1998), 4.
[2] James D. Bratt, *Dutch Calvinism in Modern America: A History of a Conservative Subculture* (Grand Rapids, MI: Eerdmans, 1984), 6.
[3] D. H. Kromminga, *The Christian Reformed Tradition*, 82.
[4] Ibid.
[5] J. J. Van Oosterzee, *Practical Theology* (London: Hodder and Stoughton, 1889), 397.
[6] Ibid., 397, 398.
[7] Wanliss and Bredenhof, *DeCock's Case Against Hymns*, 2, 3, 6.
[8] Ibid., 6.
[9] Ibid., 3.
[10] Ibid.
[11] *Classis Holland Minutes 1848–1858* (n.p., 1943), 241, 242.
[12] Quoted in Michael Bushell, *Songs of Zion* (Pittsburgh, PA: Crown and Covenant Publications, 1980), 169, 170.

Chapter 12

[1] H. Bouwman, *Gereformeerd Kerkrecht* (Kampen: J. H. Kok, 1928), 1:517–521.
[2] Elton J. Bruins and Robert P. Swierenga, *Family Quarrels in the Dutch Reformed Churches of the 19th Century* (Grand Rapids, MI: Eerdmans, 1999), 10.
[3] Ibid.
[4] Gerrit J. ten Zythoff, *Sources of Secession: The Netherlands Hervormde Kerk on the Eve of the Dutch Immigration to the Midwest* (Grand Rapids, MI: Eerdmans, 1987), 25–26.
[5] Bruins and Swierenga, *Family Quarrels*, 10.
[6] ten Zythoff, *Sources of Secession*, 27, 28.
[7] "To this group belonged such men as Simon Van Velzen, George Frans Gezelle Meerburg, Albertus C. Van Raalte, and Louis Bahler. All except the last became with de Cock the first pastors of Secession congregations." Peter Y. DeJong and Nelson Kloosterman, ed., *The Reformation of 1834, Essays in Commemoration of the Act of Secession and Return* (Orange City, IA, Pluim Publishing, 1984), 20.

Endnotes

[8] Ibid., 62.
[9] Janet Sjaarda Sheeres, *Son of Secession: Douwe J. Vander Werp* (Grand Rapids, MI: Eerdmans, 2006), 40–41.
[10] D. H. Kromminga, *The Christian Reformed Tradition*, 98.
[11] *Classis Holland Minutes 1848–1858* (Grand Rapids, MI, 1943), 26.
[12] The reference here is to the Dutch Reformed Church in America, which would become known in 1867 as the Reformed Church in America.
[13] *Classis Holland Minutes 1848–1858*, 52.
[14] Van Hinte, *Netherlanders in America*, 256.
[15] Ibid., 257.
[16] Ibid., 258.
[17] Marian B. Schoolland, *The Story of Van Raalte* (Grand Rapids, MI: Eerdmans, 1951), 89.
[18] Ibid.
[19] Van Hinte, *Netherlanders in America*, 870.

Chapter 13

[1] See pages 45–47 for a translation of the "Act of Secession or Return."
[2] Belgic Confession of Faith, Art. 30, 32, in Schaff, *Creeds of Christendom*, 3:421, 423.

Chapter 14

[1] C. Veenhof, *Prediking en Uitverkiezing* (Kampen: Kok, 1959), 77. [This and the other quotations of the Dutch in this article are my translations—DJE.]
[2] H. Algra, *Het Wonder van de 19e Eeuw: Van Vrije Kerken en Kleine Luyden* (Franeker: T. Wever, 1966), 107.
[3] Ibid.
[4] Helenius de Cock, quoted in B. Wielenga, *De Reformatie van '34* (Kampen: Kok, 1933), 41. The emphasis is de Cock's.
[5] Ibid., 80. The Dutch is irresistibly forceful: *Ik laat mij liever den hals afsnijden, dan dat ik de Dordtsche leerregels zou onderteekenen.*
[6] Hendrik de Cock, "Korte Verklaring van den Kinderdoop," in *Vragen en Antwoorden, in Verzamelde Geschriften* (Houten: Den-Hertog, 1986), 494. I express my thanks to Mr. Marvin Kamps

for obtaining for me this and some of the other Dutch writings I have read for this article.

[7] Jelle Faber, *American Secession Theologians on Covenant and Baptism* (Neerlandia, Alberta, Can.: Inheritance Publications, 1996), 26, 27.

[8] Simon Van Velzen, "Brief over de Heiliging van de Kinderen der Geloovigen in Christus," *De Bazuin* (Aug. 14, 1857). *De Bazuin* was the magazine of the Secession churches. The magazine is not paginated.

[9] Simon Van Velzen, *De Bazuin* (Jan. 20, 1865). The article by Pieters, which editor Van Velzen freely footnoted in order to add his running rejoinders, is titled, "Eenige Opmerkingen over de 69e vr. en Antw.van den Katechismus."

[10] Anthony Brummelkamp, quoted in H[elenius] de Cock, Hendrik de Cock, *Eerste Afgescheiden Predikant in Nederland Beschouwd in Leven en Werkzaamheid* (Delfzijl: Jan Haan, 1886), 569, 570. The emphasis is Brummelkamp's.

[11] Quoted in Hendrik de Cock, *Verzamelde Geschriften*, 530.

[12] Quoted in Veenhof, *Prediking en Uitverkiezing*, 59.

[13] E. Smilde, *Een Eeuw van Strijd over Verbond en Doop* (Kampen: Kok, 1946), 27.

[14] The full Dutch title is *De Kinderdoop volgens de Beginselen der Gereformeerde Kerk in Hare Gronden, Toedieningen en Praktijk. Op Nieuw Onderzocht, Beoordeeld en van Vele Schijnbare Zwarigheden Ontheven* (Franeker: T. Telenga, 1861). The book has not been translated.

[15] The Dutch is Christelijke Afgescheidene Gereformeerde Kerk.

[16] Pieters and Kreulen, *De Kinderdoop*, 6.

[17] Ibid., 28, 30.

[18] Ibid., 48.

[19] Ibid., 56.

[20] Ibid., 58, 59.

[21] Form for the Administration of Baptism, *Confessions and Church Order of the Protestant Reformed Churches*, 260.

[22] Pieters and Kreulen, *De Kinderdoop*, 67, 68 (the emphasis is theirs).

[23] Ibid., 31.

[24] Ibid., 48 (the emphasis is theirs).

[25] Ibid.

Endnotes

[26] Ibid., 28 (the emphasis is theirs). They added, confusing the issue, "even though it were the case that they [Abraham's descendants] possessed neither faith nor godliness." What Reformed theologian ever taught that the "absolute" (that is, unconditional) promise to Abraham would be fulfilled in Abraham's seed "even if it were the case that they possessed neither faith nor godliness"? Orthodox Reformed theology teaches that God fulfilled the "absolute" (that is, unconditional) promise to Abraham by giving faith and godliness to the seed of Abraham. Besides, Pieters and Kreulen ignored that, according to Galatians 3:16, the "seed" of Abraham is Christ. Was also the covenant promise to Abraham concerning Christ conditional?

[27] K. J. Pieters, "Eenige Opmerkingen over de 69e vr. En antw. Van den Katechismus," *De Bazuin* (May 12, 1865). Emphasis is mine—DJE.

[28] Pieters and Kreulen, *De Kinderdoop*, 55 (the emphasis is theirs).

[29] Melis te Velde, *Anthony Brummelkamp* (Barneveld: De Vuurbaak, 1988), 285.

[30] Veenhof, *Prediking en Uitverkiezing*, 66.

[31] H. Joffers, *De Kinderdoop, met zijn Grond en Vrucht* (Kampen: S. Van Velzen Jr., 1865), 3. The emphasis is his.

[32] Simon Van Velzen, quoted in Smilde, *Een Eeuw van Strijd over Verbond en Doop*, 45.

[33] Simon Van Velzen, "Het Verbond der Verlossing," *De Bazuin* (January 20, 1865).

[34] Ibid. Van Velzen mistakenly gave the reference as Jer. 33:3.

[35] Van Velzen, commenting on K. J. Pieters' article, "Eenige Opmerkingen over de 69e vr. en antw. van den Katechismus, *De Bazuin* (January 20, 1865).

[36] Ibid.

[37] Ibid.

[38] Van Velzen, commenting on Pieters' article, "Eenige Opmerkingen over de 69e vr. en antw. van den Katechismus," *De Bazuin* (May 12, 1865). "*Eene algemeene en krachtelooze genade*" were the words Van Velzen used.

[39] Van Velzen, commenting on Pieters' article, "Eenige Opmerkingen over de 69e vr. en antw. van den Katechismus," *De Bazuin* (May 19, 1865).

[40] H. Joffers, *De Kinderdoop, met zijn Grond en Vrucht*, 7.

[41] Ibid., 6.

[42] Ibid., 4.
[43] Ibid., 18.
[44] Ibid., 29.
[45] Ibid., 30.
[46] Ibid., 20, 21. The Dutch original of "has more support in the history of the church" is: "*meer kerkelijkheid in de geschiedenis bezit.*"
[47] Ibid., 36.
[48] Ibid., 6.
[49] Ibid., 19.
[50] Ibid., 7.
[51] Ibid.
[52] Ibid., 30.
[53] Ibid., 3.
[54] Ibid., 4.
[55] Ibid.
[56] Herman Bavinck, *Reformed Dogmatics,* vol. 3, ed. John Bolt, tr. John Vriend (Baker: 2006), 193–232. See also my review article, "Herman Bavinck's Reformed Dogmatics, Volume Three: Covenant and Election," *Protestant Reformed Theological Journal* 40, no. 1 (April 2007): 83–95.
[57] G. Vos, quoted in Veenhof, *Prediking en Uitverkiezing,* 173.
[58] Ibid., 80.
[59] Smilde, *Een Eeuw van Strijd over Verbond en Doop,* 49.
[60] Veenhof, *Prediking en Uitverkiezing,* 81.
[61] Ibid., 81, 82. Having noted Joffers' protest against the synodical decision approving the doctrine of a conditional covenant, Veenhof commits the illicit, but effective, logical fallacy of "poisoning the well." In a footnote that goes on for three and a half pages in small print, the "liberated" theologian demonstrates that Joffers was "harsh," "brutal," "rude," and "fanatical." The student of church history recognizes these qualities as the attributes of virtually all those men whom the Spirit of Christ has used to preserve the truth of the gospel in time of departure. One can easily imagine the Galatian errorists describing the apostle Paul by these epithets. See Veenhof, *Prediking en Uitverkiezing,* 174–177.
[62] Ibid., 83.
[63] Ibid., 85–87.
[64] H. Joffers, *De Kinderdoop, met zijn Grond en Vrucht,* 4.

Endnotes

[65] "Declaration of Principles of the Protestant Reformed Churches," in *Confessions and Church Order of the Protestant Reformed Churches*, 418.
[66] Ibid., 424.
[67] Veenhof, *Prediking en Uitverkiezing*, 299.
[68] Ibid. The emphasis is Veenhof's.
[69] Ibid.
[70] See David J. Engelsma, *The Covenant of God and the Children of Believers: Sovereign Grace in the Covenant* (Jenison, MI: Reformed Free Publishing Association, 2005).
[71] "One of the first publications that Hendrik de Cock provided for was the republication of the Canons of Dordt. With this the '*Credo*' of the Secession as a reformation movement had been expressed" W. van't Spijker, "*De Synode en de Remonstranten*," in W. van't Spijker and others, *De Synode van Dordrecht in 1618 en 1619* (Houten: Den Hertog, 1987), 120.

Chapter 15

[1] James D. Bratt, ed., *Abraham Kuyper: A Centennial Reader* (Grand Rapids, MI: Eerdmans, 1998), 54.

Chapter 16

[1] Abraham Kuyper, "Confidentially," in Bratt, *Abraham Kuyper: A Centennial Reader*, 114.
[2] Kuyper, "Modernism: A *Fata Morgana* in the Christian Domain," in Bratt, *Abraham Kuyper: A Centennial Reader*, 98.
[3] Ibid., 103, 104.
[4] Ibid., 116.
[5] Kuyper, "It Shall Not Be So Among You," in Bratt, *Abraham Kuyper: A Centennial Reader*, 130, 131.
[6] Ibid., 134.
[7] Ibid., 137.

Chapter 17

[1] Louis Praamsma, *Let Christ Be King: Reflections on the Life and Times of Abraham Kuyper* (Jordan Station, Ontario, Canada: Paideia Press, 1985), 92, 93.

² Hendrik Bouma, *Secession, Doleantie, and Union: 1834–1892*, trans. Theodore Plantinga (Neerlandia, Alberta, Canada: Inheritance Publications, 1995), 64.
³ Ibid., 31.
⁴ Ibid., 34.
⁵ Ibid., 35.
⁶ Ibid., 35, 36.
⁷ Ibid., 41.
⁸ Not all the churches of the CGK agreed to join the new denomination. The "dissenters" held a synod in 1893 and maintained the name of the Secession churches—the Christelijke Gereformeerde Kerken. These churches exist to the present day. Eventually they established their own seminary in Apeldoorn. They hold to a conditional covenant, but have some differences with the Liberated. Their sister churches in North America are the Free Reformed Churches.

Chapter 18

¹ Editor's note: The Dutch title of this book is *Dat de Genade Particulier Is*. Mr. Kamps has translated the book into English. All quotations are from the English translation.
² Abraham Kuyper, *Particular Grace: A Defense of God's Sovereignty in Salvation*, trans. Marvin Kamps (Grandville, MI: Reformed Free Publishing Association, 2001), 3.
³ Ibid., 21.
⁴ Ibid., 21, 22.
⁵ Ibid., 63.
⁶ Ibid., 5.
⁷ Ibid., 54.
⁸ Ibid., 57.
⁹ Ibid., 73.
¹⁰ Ibid., 75, 76.
¹¹ Ibid., 77.
¹² Ibid., 80.
¹³ Ibid., 82–84.
¹⁴ Ibid., 85.
¹⁵ Ibid., 85, 86.
¹⁶ Ibid., 86.
¹⁷ Ibid., 86, 87.

Endnotes

[18] Ibid., 89.
[19] Ibid., 90.

Chapter 19

[1] Excerpts from this work have recently been translated into English and published in the fine volume *Abraham Kuyper: A Centennial Reader*, edited by James D. Bratt.
[2] Herman Hoeksema, *The Protestant Reformed Churches in America*, 2nd ed. (Grand Rapids, MI: n.p., 1947), 85.
[3] Ibid., 377.
[4] See David J. Engelsma, "The Reformed Worldview" and "The Failure of Common Grace," *Standard Bearer*, vol. 74 (May 15, 1998; Aug. 1, 1998; Sept. 1, 1998; Sept. 15, 1998).

Chapter 20

[1] The Dutch here is *de mogelijkheid onderstelt*. [The translations of the Dutch are my own—JAL.]
[2] Abraham Kuyper, *E Voto Dordraceno: Toelichting op den Heidelbergschen Catechismus* (Amsterdam: Hoveker & Wormser, 1905), 3:21. This is Kuyper's commentary on the Heidelberg Catechism.
[3] Canons of Dordt, 1, Art. 17, in Schaff, *Creeds of Christendom*, 3:585.
[4] Form for the Administration of Baptism, *Confessions and Church Order of the Protestant Reformed Churches*, 260.

Chapter 21

[1] Frank VandenBerg, *Abraham Kuyper* (St. Catherines, Ontario, Canada: Paideia Press, 1978), 147–149.
[2] Praamsma, *Let Christ Be King*, 135.
[3] VandenBerg, *Abraham Kuyper*, 251.

Chapter 22

[1] Henry Danhof and Herman Hoeksema, *Van Zonde en Genade* (n.p., 1923), 9. This and all other quotations from Dutch titles in this chapter are my translation. *Van Zonde en Genade* has been

translated by Rev. Cornelius Hanko and published as *Sin and Grace* (Grandville, MI: Reformed Free Publishing Association, 2003).
[2] Herman Hoeksema, "Sketches on the Theory of Doctrine: Dr. Abraham Kuyper and Common Grace," *Standard Bearer* 6, no. 13 (April 1, 1930): 304.
[3] Praamsma, *Let Christ be King*, 114, 115.
[4] Dr. A. Kuyper, *Dat de Genade Particulier Is*, vol.1 of *Uit het Woord* (Amsterdam: J. H. Kruyt, 1884). This work has been translated by Marvin Kamps and published as *Particular Grace: A Defense of God's Sovereignty in Salvation*.
[5] Dr. A. Kuyper, *De Leer der Verbonden*, vol. 2 of *Uit het Woord* (Amsterdam: J. H. Kruyt, 1885), 320.
[6] Praamsma, *Let Christ be King*, 91.
[7] Ibid., 197.
[8] Kuyper, *De Leer der Verbonden*, 319.
[9] Ibid., 325.
[10] Ibid., 326.

Chapter 23

[1] Henry Danhof, "The Idea of the Covenant of Grace," trans. David J. Engelsma, *Protestant Reformed Theological Journal* 29, no. 2 (April, 1996):51–61; 31, no. 1 (November, 1997):10–19; 31, no. 2 (April, 1998):13–23; 32, no. 1 (November, 1998):2–19.
[2] Herman Hoeksema, *When I Survey... : A Lenten Anthology* (Grand Rapids, MI: Reformed Free Publishing Association, 1977).
[3] Gertrude Hoeksema, *Therefore Have I Spoken: A Biography of Herman Hoeksema* (Grand Rapids, MI: Reformed Free Publishing Association, 1969).
[4] Ibid., 123.
[5] G. C. Berkouwer, *A Half Century of Theology*, trans. and ed. Lewis B. Smedes (Grand Rapids, MI: Eerdmans, 1977), 98, 99.
[6] Herman Hoeksema, "Protestant Reformed," *Standard Bearer* 26, no. 12 (March 15, 1950): 269.
[7] Ibid.
[8] Protestant Reformed Churches in America, *Acts of Synod* (1952), 83.

Endnotes

Chapter 24

[1] See Herman Hanko, thesis, *A Study of the Relation Between the Views of Ralph Janssen and Common Grace* (Grand Rapids, MI: Calvin Theological Seminary, 1988), reproduced as a syllabus for seminarians at the Theological School of the Protestant Reformed Churches; Herman Hoeksema, "Of Love and Hatred," *Standard Bearer* 30, no. 15 (May 1, 1954): 340–341; and Herman Hoeksema, *The Protestant Reformed Churches in America*, 17–26.

Chapter 25

[1] David J. Engelsma, *Hyper-Calvinism and the Call of the Gospel: An Examination of the "Well-Meant Offer" of the Gospel*, rev. ed. (Grand Rapids, MI: Reformed Free Publishing Association, 1994), 29.

[2] Anyone who is sincerely interested in what the Protestant Reformed teach and what they deny relative to the points under discussion ought to read Engelsma's book *Hyper-Calvinism and the Call of the Gospel* and the doctrinal part of Herman Hoeksema's *The Protestant Reformed Churches in America*.

[3] Herman Hoeksema, *The Protestant Reformed Churches in America*, 85.

[4] Canons of Dordt, 2, Art. 5, in Schaff, *Creeds of Christendom*, 3:586.

[5] Canons of Dordt, 3 & 4, Art. 8, in *Psalter*, 68. The clause translated "that those who are called should come to him" is incorrectly translated as "should comply with the invitation" in some English editions of the Canons. The Latin original is "*ut vocati ad se veniant.*" (See Philip Schaff's *Creeds of Christendom*, 3: 565, 566.)

[6] Canons of Dordt, 3 & 4, Art. 9, in Schaff, *Creeds of Christendom*, 3:589.

[7] *Cassell's New Latin Dictionary*, D. P. Simpson (New York: Funk & Wagnalls, 1959), 410.

Chapter 26

[1] Herman Hoeksema, "Antithesis, Synthesis, and Dualism," *Standard Bearer* 4, no. 15 (May 1, 1928): 356, 357.

[2] Herman Hoeksema, "Dr. Martin Luther on the Stage," *Standard Bearer*, 4, no. 9 (February 1, 1928): 198.
[3] H. C. Hoeksema, "Prediction Fulfilled," *Standard Bearer*, 43, no. 8 (January 15, 1967): 173. Hoeksema quotes pages 33 ff. of the CRC *Acts of Synod, 1966*.
[4] Herman Hoeksema, "Antithesis, Synthesis, and Dualism," 357.

Chapter 27

[1] Herman Hoeksema, "Protestant Reformed," *Standard Bearer* 26, no. 12 (March 15, 1950): 269.
[2] See John Calvin's commentary on Genesis 17:2, 4, 7.
[3] See Herman Hoeksema's treatment of Heyns' view in the first two chapters of *Believers and Their Seed*, rev. ed. (Grandville, MI: Reformed Free Publishing Association, 1997), 1–28.
[4] See the pamphlet "The Main Points of the Doctrine of the Covenant," which is a speech given by Dr. Schilder in 1944 (translated by T. van Laar, 1992, and available from Inheritance Publications, Neerlandia, Alberta, Canada).
[5] Herman Hoeksema, "The Liberated Churches in the Netherlands," *Standard Bearer* 22, no. 12 (March 15, 1946): 269.
[6] See the Canons of Dordt, Head 1, Rejection of Errors 4, 5, 7; Head 2, Rejection of Errors 3; Head 5, Rejection of Errors 1, in *Confessions and Church Order of the Protestant Reformed Churches*, 155–178.
[7] John Calvin, *Institutes of the Christian Religion*, ed. John T. McNeill, trans. Ford Lewis Battles (Philadelphia: Westminster Press, 1975), 2.5.10.
[8] Herman Hoeksema, "The Liberated Churches in the Netherlands," 269.
[9] These main points of the covenant of grace received official standing in the PRC with the adoption of the Declaration of Principles at the Synod of 1951. See "Declaration of Principles of the Protestant Reformed Churches," in *Confessions and Church Order of the Protestant Reformed Churches*, 410–431.
[10] R. C. Sproul, Jr., *Tabletalk* (August 1995), 2.
[11] Ibid., 22.
[12] Herman Hoeksema, "Protestant Reformed," *Standard Bearer* 26, no. 12 (March 15, 1950): 269.

Endnotes

Chapter 28

[1] For this history, see Herman Hoeksema's *The Protestant Reformed Churches in America*.

[2] The question may be raised here, but not answered because it is beyond the scope of this article, whether these ministers were bound by Article 31 of the Church Order of Dordt to consider settled and binding the synodical decisions of 1924, and therefore not to agitate against them. On the one hand, dogmas were declared, and the ministers called to conform their teaching to them. On the other hand, Synod of 1924 also decided to "urge the leaders of our people, both ministers and professors, to make further study of the doctrine of Common Grace; that they give themselves account carefully [*sic*] of the problems that present themselves in connection with this matter, in sermons, lectures, and publications" (Herman Hoeksema, *Protestant Reformed Churches in America*, 95). Even if the judgment is made that the public opposition to these synodical decrees was unjustified and sinful, the contention here is that the classis had no right to exercise the power of discipline to depose ministers and consistories.

[3] This is a long, complicated history that is worth pursuing. For a beginning and a good bibliography, see Richard DeRidder, "A Survey of the Sources of Reformed Church Polity and the Form of Government of the Christian Reformed Church in America," Calvin Theological Seminary syllabus (1983), 83–91. The development of church government in the Reformed Churches of the Netherlands cannot be understood apart from the church's relationship to the civil government, just as Presbyterian distinctives must be understood in the light of the civil government in England and Scotland.

[4] Herman Hoeksema, *Protestant Reformed Churches in America*, 250, 251.

[5] Idzerd Van Dellen and Martin Monsma, *The Church Order Commentary* (Grand Rapids, MI: Zondervan Publishing, 1941), 327–329.

[6] Find reference to G. Hoeksema's brochure, "Can a Classis Depose a Consistory," chapter 1, translated into English in part by Rev. G. M. Ophoff, in a long series of articles in the *Standard Bearer*, beginning in volume 4, no. 8 (Jan. 15, 1928), 179.

[7] Quoted in the minority committee report to the CRC Synod of 1926 regarding the question at issue.
[8] Van Dellen and Monsma, *Church Order Commentary* (Grand Rapids, MI: Zondervan Publishing House, 1941), 327–329.
[9] W. Meijer, *Young People's History of the Church* (Launceston, Tasmania, Australia: Publication Organization of the Free Reformed Churches of Australia, 1973), 3:16, 63, 93–95, 108, 118. The Free Reformed Churches of Australia are not to be confused with the Free Reformed Churches in America.
[10] Edmund P. Clowney, "Distinctive Emphases in Presbyterian Church Polity," in *Pressing Toward the Mark: Essays Commemorating Fifty Years of the Orthodox Presbyterian Church*, ed. Charles G. Dennison and Richard C. Gamble (Philadelphia: Committee for the Historian of the Orthodox Presbyterian Church, 1986), 108. [Emphasis mine—BLG.]

Chapter 29

[1] Herman Hoeksema, *Believers and Their Seed*, 14.
[2] See the chapter earlier in this book, "The Covenant Doctrine of the Fathers of the Secession."

Chapter 30

[1] Gertrude Hoeksema, *A Watered Garden*, 176.
[2] Ibid., 177.

Chapter 31

[1] "Declaration of Principles of the Protestant Reformed Churches," in *Confessions and Church Order of the Protestant Reformed Churches*, 412.
[2] Ibid., 412 (I, D, 1); 413 (I, D, 2 and I, D, 3).
[3] Ibid., 416–417 (II, A; II, B).
[4] Ibid., 417, 418 (II, B, 1–3).
[5] Ibid., 418, 419 (II, B, 3; II, B, 3, a).
[6] Ibid., 423 (II, c).
[7] Ibid., 424 (III, A, 1, a & b); 426 (III, B, 1, 2); 430 (III, B, 3).
[8] Ibid., 430 (IV).
[9] Ibid., 412.

Endnotes

Chapter 32

[1] Gertrude Hoeksema, *A Watered Garden*, 176, 177.
[2] S. A. Strauss, "Schilder on the Covenant," in *Always Obedient: Essays on the Teachings of Dr. Klaas Schilder*, J. Geertsema, ed. (Neerlandia, Alberta, Canada: Inheritance Publications), 19.
[3] Form for the Administration of Baptism, *Confessions and Church Order of the Protestant Reformed Churches*, 258.

Chapter 33

[1] Heidelberg Catechism, Q & A 74, in Schaff, *Creeds of Christendom*, 3:331.
[2] Form for the Administration of Baptism, *Confessions and Church Order of the Protestant Reformed Churches*, 258.

Chapter 34

[1] Herman Hoeksema, *Protestant Reformed Churches in America*, 85.
[2] Ibid., 79, 80, 86.
[3] Article 31 states: "If anyone complain that he has been wronged by the decision of a minor assembly, he shall have the right to appeal to a major ecclesiastical assembly, and whatever may be agreed upon by a majority vote shall be considered settled and binding, unless it be proved to conflict with the Word of God or with the articles of the Church Order, as long as they are not changed by the general synod."
[4] "The First Protestant Reformed Church of Grand Rapids, Michigan, a Michigan Corporation, Plantiff, vs. Hubert De Wolf, et al.," *State of Michigan in the Superior Court of Grand Rapids, in Chancery*, vol. 1, 124.
[5] Ibid., 138.

Chapter 35

[1] No. 32, second stanza, *The Psalter*. See the first six verses of Psalm 17.

Contributors

RONALD CAMMENGA is a professor of theology at the Theological School of the Protestant Reformed Churches.

ROBERT DECKER is a professor emeritus of the Theological School of the Protestant Reformed Churches.

ARIE DEN HARTOG is a minister in the Protestant Reformed Churches.

RUSSELL DYKSTRA is a professor of theology at the Theological School of the Protestant Reformed Churches.

DAVID ENGELSMA is a professor emeritus of the Theological School of the Protestant Reformed Churches.

BARRY GRITTERS is a professor of theology at the Theological School of the Protestant Reformed Churches.

CORNELIUS HANKO (1907–2005) was a minister in the Protestant Reformed Churches.

HERMAN HANKO is a professor emeritus of the Theological School of the Protestant Reformed Churches.

RONALD HANKO is a minister in the Protestant Reformed Churches.

HOMER C. HOEKSEMA (1923–1989) was a minister and professor in the Protestant Reformed Churches.

MARVIN KAMPS is a member of the Protestant Reformed Churches.

Contributors

STEVEN KEY is a minister in the Protestant Reformed Churches.

KENNETH KOOLE is a minister in the Protestant Reformed Churches.

DALE KUIPER is a minister emeritus of the Protestant Reformed Churches.

JAMES LANING is a minister in the Protestant Reformed Churches.

CHARLES TERPSTRA is a member of the Protestant Reformed Churches.

GISE VAN BAREN is a minister emeritus of the Protestant Reformed Churches.

SIMON VAN VELZEN (1809–1896) was one of the leading ministers in the reformation of the Reformed churches in the Netherlands known as the Secession of 1834. Van Velzen is recognized as the outstanding theologian of the Secession. He served for many years as professor in the theological seminary of the Secession churches in Kampen.